RIGHT OR WRONG

Right or Wrong

The Memoirs of Lord Bell

Tim Bell

Edited by Charles Vallance and David Hopper

BLOOMSBURY

LONDON • NEW DELHI • NEW YORK • SYDNEY

First published in Great Britain 2014

Copyright © Tim Bell, Charles Vallance and David Hopper, 2014

The moral right of the authors has been asserted

A Continuum book

Bloomsbury Publishing Plc
50 Bedford Square
London WC1B 3DP

www.bloomsbury.com

Bloomsbury is a trademark of Bloomsbury Publishing Plc

Bloomsbury Publishing, London, New Delhi, New York and Sydney

A CIP record for this book is available from the British Library.

ISBN 9781472909350

10 9 8 7 6 5 4 3 2 1

Typeset by Fakenham Prepress Solutions, Fakenham, Norfolk NR21 8NN

Printed and bound in Great Britain by CPI Group (UK) Ltd, Croydon CR0 4YY

To Daisy and Harry

There are two sides to every issue: one side is right and the other is wrong, but the middle is always evil.

Ayn Rand (For the New Intellectual)

Contents

Prologue
In the Cathedral

I was born under the star sign of Libra, which means that I'm always searching for some harmony in my life. Some people might not see this as one of my more recognisable traits and, indeed, I suspect that half of the material in this book may call into question its very first sentence. It also needs to be said that, on far too many occasions for my liking, disharmony finds me and I trip up and it hurts. But I know me and I know what I strive for.

It was the same with Margaret – another Libran – who also wanted harmony. She will never be remembered like that, because she would stand up and fight for what she believed in. She didn't believe, any more than I do, in 'balance' when it came to the economy, or a balance between the Right and the Left, or between right and wrong. She did not believe in woolly compromises, and she would have regarded coalition government as no government at all. She simply believed that conviction was the best route to the harmony she sought.

On Wednesday 17 April 2013 – 34 years after I first met her – I sat in the second row at St Paul's and watched her coffin being carried in. Below Wren's great dome, I remember thinking that it was not a time to be maudlin. Most of the thankfully few histrionic tears came from people with no right or reason to be shedding them. What goes after death – the funeral, the memorial service, and all the conversations about the past – can provide reason for optimism and hope by making you remember the good things rather than mope over what can't be brought back.

I have to begin this story with Margaret because she changed me completely. I've never made any secret of the effect that she had on me. She made me 100 per cent politically aware. She was a colossus in our island's history, and I was incalculably lucky to have been in the right place at the right time to meet her, work with her, and be influenced by her.

Like me, she was an outsider, and I think there was an unspoken awareness between us that we were both trying to make our way through a scowling establishment that did not really recognise either of us as one of its own. There were many lonely times for her – as there would be for me. We would both feel the isolation when vilified by people from all sides of an argument.

Much of her vision of harmony came from her family environment, in Grantham, which had been a calm and ordered one. And it's why, when she was about to enter Downing Street in 1979 for the first time, she quoted St Francis of Assisi: 'Where there is discord, may we bring harmony ...' It was a quote from her heart. Of course, she got pilloried for it, because some people hated her voice and thought she was just being pompous quoting a saint. But she meant every word. And the disharmony, when it inevitably came – and for which she always took personal responsibility – often really hurt her. Few people had actually witnessed this. But I had.

There in St Paul's, several decades later, I felt that those of us who had worked on the funeral arrangements had more or less managed to get the balance right. I think it had the appropriate tone, respect and affection, and the address by the Bishop of London, Richard Chartres, was pitch-perfect. Much public comment was good, or at least respectful, and the number of people who were vile was not excessive. When the coffin was carried out and the doors opened, you heard the ascending sound of clapping from outside like birds fluttering away. It was a beautiful and moving occasion – there was a harmony.

Much less so when we got to the crematorium. Then my mood changed. With Metropolitan Police outriders flanking us, the journey to Mortlake only took 20 minutes, where occurred a perfectly nice ceremony with a nice choir, some nice hymns and people there whom you would expect. There were only about five of us who weren't actually members of the family: Julian Seymour, the director of her private office; Cynthia 'Crawfie' Crawford, her personal assistant; Mark Worthington; Barry Strevens, her long-standing police bodyguard; and then me – a very intimate little group. But after the uplift of St Paul's, it was the most terrible coda – a really awful, black, bleak finality. Even the name of the place has death in it. I didn't like it at all. I went to my own mother's cremation, and I'm haunted by the sense in these places of getting rid of the absolute last vestige of the person – by burning it. At the end of a cremation ceremony, there is nothing. Just an empty silence, an empty feeling, and some dead ash.

I'm an ambivalent soul, and I can suffer considerable mood-swings – up one minute and down the next. It can feel physiological, and, at various stages of my life, I've been on medication to deal with it. I was all right at the Cathedral, but at the crematorium the black clouds started coming down, and I had to struggle not to allow in the despair. You have to block it. You have to fill the void with something that will be a positive force, not wait for the negative to take you down. You need the birds, not the silence.

That's partly why I decided to write a memoir. To fill that silence. I once had a journalist friend, who had known me well enough to want to help with it, and had persuaded me to do it, but then sadly he died and that felt like a sign. The pessimist in me questioned whether anyone would want to read it, and then in that instance, the superstitious part of me finally killed the idea. I'm not always good with death – especially the prospect of my own! And I didn't want to tempt fate with what might quickly become an epitaph. But these days, I'm trying to let my optimism win the battles, and that part of me says that the past is only meaningful if it can give a voice to the present. I felt that in the Cathedral.

In their book, *The Branded Gentry*, Charles Vallance and David Hopper wrote a chapter about me. Then, around the same time as the funeral, they put it to me that I should tell the wider story – and that they would be keen to help me with it. It seemed to be another indication that the right moment had arrived: like the funeral, a moment for beginning, not ending. In that spirit, then, let me begin this narrative. I set out ever hopeful that I can avoid too much doleful nostalgia and regret: because there's plenty of stuff too depressing for me to even want to remember anyway; and because there are ample things happening in the present to occupy our disdain. Especially in politics.

My opinions, for the most part, place me into a diminishing tribe of what might be termed Real Conservatives – as opposed to, shall we say, many of the current crop. I am a very straightforward person and I have a very clear life philosophy and very clear political views, and actually nothing has ever shaken those basic views. I probably didn't articulate them as clearly as I now can until I met Margaret. And then she articulated them and that made it easier for me.

There is an e-book by Kurt Schlichter, an American writer, called *I am a Conservative*, which happens to be quite funny, but sums up so much of where I sit, politically speaking. My starting point is the principle that people should live freely, in a civil society, there being three elements needed for that civil society: first, that people should act with restraint; second, that they should act with honour; and third, that they should act according to their own moral code – and I can't think of any greater encapsulation of Conservatism than these three.

But it's going the other way. Wherever you look – in politics, in media, in the world – the forces of subterfuge and evil and the soggy, wet, progressive faux compassion in which they camouflage their hypocrisy are slowly but surely reducing everything to a low, homogeneous, common mess. Intolerance disguised as political correctness; fundamentalism disguised as liberation; repression disguised as emancipation; censorship as freedom of expression – I think the world is getting like a giant pulp machine, taking any upstanding trees it finds in its way and pulping them into the horrible grey swamp of modern thinking.

When I first worked for Thatcher, I could never make up my mind whether it was the last throw of the Right, or the first throw of its newest incarnation. But Conservatism in the truest sense of the word was completely emasculated, to everyone's detriment, as a function of Tony Blair's 'New' Labour Party and of the absurd idea that you *have* to occupy the centre ground of politics to win a working majority. The tendency of a significant proportion of Conservative thinking (or Coalition thinking, latterly) is to seek sanctuary in the centre ground, trying to please everyone, by telling them anything they want to hear and doing nothing about it (which was very much Blair's *modus operandi*). It is, I believe, one of the tragedies of the modern political landscape. The Centre is not halfway between Right and Left, but halfway between right and wrong. The Centre is nowhere at all.

Twice recently, I've been on BBC's *Newsnight* and, in both instances, I've come away thoroughly disenchanted. Not because of anything I did or didn't say, but because of the sloppy, soggy journalism on display. *Newsnight* was not always like this. I like Jeremy Paxman. I know him well, and he is a staggeringly clever bloke, worth having proper arguments with – which I have done in the past. He is usually on top of his brief, but when he interviewed me, either he hadn't bothered or the researchers hadn't done a very good job. Either way, he wasn't up to scratch with his facts and I got annoyed with him – in a polite kind of way, of course. It meant that the interview just tailed off into a sort of old pals' act, with him finally talking like he couldn't be arsed with the subject any more. I'm not surprised that he's now had enough of it all, and resigned. Good luck to him.

The second time was different. I was on a panel opposite the MP Sarah Wollaston, with Emily Maitlis doing the interviewing. And within seconds, I just knew it was a waste of time, because neither of them was honestly interested in the subject in question. I had a lot of things I wanted to say about the partial register of lobbyists, but I couldn't get any of them out because the pair of them started having a conversation about plain cigarette packaging and speculating whether Lynton Crosby (the Conservative Election adviser but also an adviser to a cigarette company) had put pressure on the Prime Minister. I hate that sort of childishness where you just smear an absent target, without any evidence one way or another. On the subject of lobbying and the subject of tobacco I am not fearful of anything. I have smoked all my life, I have done anti-smoking campaigns and I've done smoking campaigns, sometimes in the same 12 months. I have debated the subject and discussed it probably for 50 years and I know it inside out, so I am not in the least bothered by being questioned on it. But they were like kids in the playground saying, 'I bet he did this; I bet he did that!' It was all mock outrage. That's what *Newsnight* has become, I fear – a BBC playground for the half-briefed or badly briefed saying, 'Ya, boo, ain't it awful' to each other. So much of the media has now become an establishment that feigns indignation at the very entitlement from which it feeds; so many now bolster their self-worth by joining in with the chatter of envy.

It is, however, no use me getting irascible about not having the chance to say my piece. Time to speak up, I fear. Time for this book, perhaps. Leaving legacies – whether it be in word or spirit – is not my thing. My desire for children was never in order to continue my bloodline, and I never wanted to create a memoir to secure an undeserved place in history. I have none of those feelings. So this book is not a stab at immortality. It's just that I've probably reached the point – or maybe the age – where I really ought to try to make some use of my life experience, whether it's to put it to work against the wooliness of the present-day progressive liberal group-think, or just to provide an engaging diversion with it. Or, ideally, both.

Being in a reasonable position to chronicle a life with some semblance of hindsight is possibly the only thing to be said for being old. The rest of it is horrible. Illness, pain, loss ... I'm minded of Mick Jagger in Hyde Park asking if anyone in the audience was older than he was, and only about three of us put up our hands. He was once the *enfant terrible* of anarchical youth: how did he become old? If you could avoid senescence other than by premature pop-star death, then you should avoid it. But you can't. And finding yourself in that position, as the living all must one day, you really ought to do something to justify your place amongst the remaining.

It's the prerogative of the old, of course, to hark back to when things seemed better; or when people seemed bigger. I well remember people like Duncan Sandys, Harold Macmillan, Peter Thorneycroft, Selwyn Lloyd: big, grown-up, wise, experienced politicians, who were worth listening to because they talked with such depth and could draw on such compelling experiences of their own, in support of what they were saying – and which you could look at and understand. I remember how big Ronald Reagan seemed when I first met him: big in sheer physical presence in the room but also big in what he represented and the authority he commanded; plus big enough to be a really nice guy when you met him. One of the reasons that I was so attracted to Thatcher was that she read all the time, and would quote from history or from previous political masters, Left and Right.

I wonder if such people can exist any more – in a world populated by those terrified of straying away from the centre ground or saying anything meaningful at all, in case anyone doesn't understand them or doesn't like something that looks like a proper idea. Instead we are thrown slivers of glibness that mean nothing and require neither effort nor investment from people or politicians. Over the years, I have watched the politicians get younger, get smaller, and get less interesting, with ever less substance to what they say.

Now, all they do is work out if they should say they listen to the Arctic Monkeys or eat Jammy Dodgers. And do you know what the saddest thing about that is? It's not that some of them lie about it. It's that some of them actually *do* spend half their time listening to their iPods. Which is worse: the lying that you like some kind of wannabe pop band, or *actually* liking them? This stuff is what preoccupies them now. The Prime Minister going on Twitter is the end of Grown Up as far as I am concerned. Reagan, Thatcher, Mandela, de Klerk – they were just completely different; they were giants. Do you seriously think they would feel the need to tell the public what kind of biscuits they ate? I also think the same thing about commentators and about journalists and editors. People like Harold Evans and David English. You went into the room hoping that they would not think you a waste of their time. Nowadays, I can think of many a secretary of state, president or prime minister in whose presence I would feel it was *my* time that was being wasted.

I consider myself very fortunate to have been brought up in an era of respect for great people, which, in turn, created an environment for great people. By the time I was in my teens, I knew Mountbatten (through my grandfather), who used to send me a Christmas card and a birthday card, and I'd even momentarily once met Churchill. They were huge figures. Now there is no one to respect any more (or the word 'respect', like so many others, has been appropriated for some ghastly alternative meaning), because society doesn't want to accept that some people know better than others and thus deserve respect and attention on that basis. There are celebrities instead, who attract attention – but rarely deserve much respect – through some grotesque party-trick that has allowed them to get sensationalised on global media. The sadness is that many politicians mistake this for the only game in town and try to follow it – with gruesome results.

These days, the heroes are certainly not the people who are positioned as such. (In fact, 'hero' is another word that has been neutered; too un-PC to stay in common currency.) Perhaps there are some 'heroes' in the old sense of the word lurking about the place who haven't been spotted or who would have become heroes if the tabloids hadn't caught them with their trousers off and annihilated their entire reputation in one headline. Indeed, the demonstration that the great and the good actually have feet of clay is now a lifetime job for the media and the hate-bloggers and everybody else. Meanwhile, every other Tom, Dick or Harry is filling the space with their own self-styled internet-supported personal trivia. So the environment for a reflection of true heroism shrinks and shrinks until it is no more.

I think the news media is as confused about this as anybody, but they hang on to the belief that they have a duty to tell the public something that they otherwise wouldn't know – often whether it's right or wrong. They're actually goaded into this by the politicians, who have suddenly discovered the word *transparency* and go around the place talking as though they have the faintest idea what that might mean in principle. I don't know if you have ever met anybody who is transparent, but it means that you can see through them. And the modern politician is very easy to see through, not least because there is often not very much there.

When I was younger, politicians bothered about their words being accurate, and they actually meant what they were saying and their words meant something to the people listening. No more. Now politicians seem less concerned about leading, and more about being like the 'normal' man or woman in the street (the one not always being compatible with the other, of course), and all that does is make them seem insubstantial. Like jellyfish. So we lose yet more of the respect needed to engender inspirational figures, and the media feel ever more inclined to be ever less respectful and respecting. Thatcher, Reagan, Gorbachev, Mandela – they probably could not operate today. I'm not sure you can have heroes any more – or giants in politics.

Margaret was without doubt the biggest influence in my life; the work that I did with her was what made me achieve a reputation as an adviser, and the political work that I did was what enabled me to have a reputation for being good at both the strategy of politics and its execution. The Saatchis had a huge impact on me as well, as did Jeremy Sinclair and Gordon Reece. I was extremely fortunate to be able to learn from these great figures. But it was Margaret who gave me the opportunity to meet with other great figures, such as Ronald Reagan and F. W. de Klerk.

F. W. was a truly sublime figure and a remarkable man. The impressive thing – and he is a very impressive person indeed – was how he was such a restrained, private individual: strong in his views, yet never prone to lecturing people. In common with Margaret, he was not one for small talk (I'm not sure South Africans are), but he was a very good listener, which is a very powerful – and all too rare – quality in a politician.

Being a good listener was *not* one of Margaret's strongest qualities. She got into a mess in her third term when – contrary to some popular myths – she probably listened too much to the wrong people and not enough to the right ones. But what I don't think anybody understands about her is that, despite all this, she wasn't just interested in the nation and in political ideology; she was actually interested in people. She couldn't be interested in everybody, and a lot of things outside of politics well and truly bored her. She hadn't a clue about sport or comedy, for example, so there could be no meaningful conversation around these subjects. She never wanted the small talk or any flattery, so if you ever complimented her on her looks or clothing, she would not react. But she would be interested in the people who were close to her, and she guided me in all sorts of things that were nothing to do with politics, but were everything to do with the ups and downs in my life.

Like my mother, Margaret had been a person to whom I could and would go with a problem, and, in due course, as with my mother, I watched her deteriorate. It was like watching a great cricketer who once scored centuries and then couldn't even hold a bat any more. It reminds you of the ineluctable frailty of the human condition – ahead of us all, the same dismal process. It will happen to you and me, to the young nurse who tends to us, and to the younger nurse who will in time tend to her. That's the cycle. That's how it works. I have seen so many people who have been important to me and in my life suffer a sad and cruel decline. After we'd divorced, my first wife died of cancer. Witnessing other people's suffering has, in many ways, been far more difficult to bear than all the illnesses and medical conditions that have afflicted me directly. There have been times when it has hit me badly.

The irony was that, for years, I was rude about people who had a professional therapist – I thought they were wet and weak and insipid and stupid. But when I was about 45, I met a fantastic guy called Robert Lefever – he's quite well known now as an addiction specialist – who became a very close friend and who actually saw doctoring as dealing with mind as well as body. (I collect physicians with names that are highly appropriate: my doctor is called Professor Gazzard and my urologist was called Dr Castro.) When my second wife Virginia and I separated recently, he was shocked by what had happened, because he had known both of us for a long time, and now he saw the trauma. He'd been through a lot himself – he'd lost his wife, gone bankrupt, all sorts of bad stuff – and he told me I needed to talk to a professional; someone other than him because we were too close for that.

I told this to my secretary, Wendy Ridley, who has been with me for nearly 40 years and knows exactly what I'm like. She recommended a therapist called Charrisse Cooke – for whom she'd once worked, and who she thought would be just the right kind of person. So I took the plunge and rang her. In fact, for about three weeks, I would just talk with Charrisse on the phone and that seemed to really help, and then, when she was in London, I went to see her. She's a very striking South African lady, incredibly clever and wise, and has become the therapist that I once thought no one should ever need.

I am a work in progress, but then life is a work in progress and I don't feel like a wimp because I have a therapist. Instead, I think I am lucky that I can afford it, and I know somebody who has found a way to enable me to deal with the ups and downs of life in a more balanced and more harmonious way than I had been doing. You only have to know me to know that when the sun shines, I am in a good mood – but there is also a very large black dog in my character. I am very affected by my emotions and I am very affected by the environment. I had the three most traumatic experiences of life in a short space of time: a marital separation, moving home (prompted by the separation), and Margaret Thatcher's death. I got the three over a period of a couple of years, so actually, I am bloody glad that I did have a therapist to help me cope.

I think I have a very high sense of personal responsibility. That doesn't mean I'm a saint; it means I take responsibility for all my actions, both good and bad; and it means taking responsibility for what you do to yourself, which in my case includes the chain-smoking. It is something that a good therapist teaches you: that you can't expect other people to look after you; nor can you influence other people's behaviour. You have to deal with your own behaviour – physically, financially, emotionally. Only you can do it and you can't keep looking round and asking somebody else to do it for you.

One of the differences between the Right and Left, is that, at its purest, the former is committed to the individual – to personal responsibility, to aspiration, and even competitiveness. The Left, meanwhile, sees people as a collective – or at least a series of collectives – to be manipulated and manoeuvred in the interests of power and the status quo. There is no better example of this than the vast client-state created under Blair and Brown, which has a vested interest in keeping people dependent, and thus maintaining a huge population of public sector bureaucrats and bureaucracies serving that dependency. When the Left defends welfare, it has no interest in the betterment or safeguarding of the individual – rather, it is simply defending a huge self-perpetuating industry of its own making.

The time when I am worst is when people have disagreed with me or condemned something I have done or not understood what I am trying to do. That is when I am at my most irritated and depressed. That is why marriage break-up is such a killer – because it is impossible to find a satisfactory resolution to it. And oddly, I keep meeting people in similar situations. The awful thing about divorce or separation after a long marriage is that it is so much of your life. You have this feeling that you should write it all off, forget about it, kick it back into the past. But to do that is to annihilate all those years of your own existence – not just any bad, but all of the good as well. It might make you temporarily feel better if you could say it was someone else's fault. But that is ultimately as unsatisfying as hating yourself for breaking what you had.

My day job goes on, of course, as Chairman of Bell Pottinger, which we reformed as part of a management buy-out last year, and which is another good reason for me to put into print what I think – in this case about the public relations business.

So this is where we find ourselves, you and I. At a late beginning. If I think about it, there is a lot to talk about – and, I can assure you, a fair amount not to. This is what we might call a 'working memoir', rather than anything approaching a full autobiographical account or a detailed analysis of my entire life. I've been unashamedly selective about the stories that I thought might be of interest (and my frustratingly inconsistent memory has no doubt made sure that many more will remain untold), which makes this a more arbitrary than comprehensive history, but one that I hope will be the more readable for being so.

Looking back, I shudder over some of the things that have happened to me, and know how lucky I've been over very many other things. I have met countless important people and I have hung on to their coat-tails, and bathed in their charismatic glow. And I have supped with many who do not glow so brightly too. I have been through the highest of highs and the lowest of lows. Many of these things are still with me – some in reality, others as memories. That's life; that's my life. It's time to talk about it. And let's see where we get to when we do.

Early Starter

I remember no more of my first day on earth than I know about my last, but I ought to begin my story by putting the former date into some kind of context – whilst hoping that the latter date keeps its distance for a while yet. I was born on a Saturday, in the middle of the Second World War – 18 October 1941. Fortunately, the worst of the Blitz was over, as was the immediate threat of invasion.

The Nazis had nearly succeeded in subjugating the population of the world to their ideology and behaviour, destroying in the process many of those who wouldn't or couldn't conform to that. In Britain, we had lived to tell the tale – at least, the lucky ones had – and, for some time after the fighting had ended, that weighty thought hung over people, along with the smoke from the smouldering ruin that was London. People's families had been destroyed; parents had lost children and children had lost parents; spouses found themselves single again. So if you had lived through the war and come out the other side, you probably felt that you now deserved something.

We were a middle-class family in a decent North London suburb called Southgate, in a detached house – but I was starting life as the child of the *real* austerity generation. An awful lot of things were in very short supply, and rationing would continue until the 1950s. Most people took buses, trams and trains – and most certainly had little conception of car ownership. The mood was of relief and acceptance, yet the immediate post-war Brits were looking for something back for their suffering. Thus it was that, in 1946, the electorate took the view that they were more likely to get this from Clem Attlee, who they duly elected as the new Prime Minister. His opponent, Winston Churchill, had got them to where they were, but he was a memory of something that they wanted to forget. Attlee's promises of implementation of the Beveridge Report and a welfare state soothed a bruised, battered and burned people and felt like the future. And so began my childhood, under a man who – mistakenly in my view – shares with Margaret Thatcher the accolade of being Britain's greatest post-war Prime Minister.

I was educated in the state system, at Osidge Junior School where I passed my 11+, which then took me to the Queen Elizabeth Grammar School in Barnet. It was a traditional, well-run and disciplined place, but I enjoyed it: there was camaraderie, it was good fun, and I don't have any tales about being bullied or riddled with angst. I was good at English, good at sport, and liked smoking. That's really the essence of my school-life. My parents would give me an allowance (which was, I concede, a bit unusual in that environment), so I had more money than some of the other kids, which meant that I could buy my own fags, and drink, and get invited to everything. My early taste of leadership was in running the smokers' club behind the sheds. I started at a very young age, and apart from a brief period of abstinence whilst I recovered from various unpleasant illnesses, I've been a committed tobacco-devotee ever since. It was the main reason why I never became a prefect – that, and the fact that I thought all the prefects were dicks.

I can distinctly remember three of my teachers at Queen Elizabeth who had an impact on me. Our PE master was called Eric Shirley, and he always seemed to like the boys who were not only good at sport, but also the most noisy and obnoxious. My Latin master was a chap called (something like) Ferdy Finett, who I admired because he was such an unusual man. He actually *spoke* in Latin. He was a very sensitive, modern, switched-on guy who understood adolescent boys, and if you had a problem you went to see him, and he would talk to you in proper human-being language. But then, he'd revert back to speaking Latin for most normal occasions. The headmaster was also a rather strange, strict, anachronistic man, called Ernest Jenkins. He was ex-Royal Navy, and hated anything at all modern. He thought television and cinema were quite evil, and he would openly criticise *all* parents for their awful, useless, idle boys. Can you imagine a teacher doing that now?

I wasn't an outright rebel as such, but, for example, the school uniform rules annoyed me (as I liked quite flashy clothes, and I was the first person I knew to get an Italian suit), so I would try to get round them. And I hated to be told by the teachers that they disapproved of my hairstyle. I have never accepted that one human being might tell another human being how to live their life. I don't see what gives anyone the right to do that: partly because I don't think any one person knows what's best any more than the next person – it's every-body's first go at life. I dislike people who shout at their dogs and people in uniforms who abuse their authority. Yet I respect rank and title and order and authority, and I respect wisdom and experience. And I see no inconsistency in holding these two positions, because I'm not anti-establishment so much as anti-authoritarian. Maybe that's not surprising, being the child of an Australian mother and Northern Irish father.

My father, Arthur ('Paddy') Bell was a Belfast-raised Protestant and an alcoholic – a committed participant in both traditions. He was also quite a charmer, a natural entertainer, and even an RAF war hero. But he walked out on our family when I was five, meaning that I had no intimate knowledge and have very little memory of him from that period. I would, in due course, visit him in his new life in South Africa, where he made quite a success of himself, but that part of the story comes later. He certainly lived life to the full – and paid the penalty, when, in 1964, at the too-young age of 58, he contracted cancer and died.

Dealing with existence as a single parent, my mother – Greta Findlay – worked at a laundry at night to supplement the income needed to look after me and the two daughters – my older sisters, Jennie and Linda. She was a tough character, born in the rough Sydney suburb of Balmain, before the family came back to Britain. However, in later years, after she remarried, she became firmly entrenched in English middle-class society: things like the Women's Institute and the Royal Horticultural Society and civic functions with my stepfather – and her accent changed too. But she was always, at heart, an Aussie; underneath it all, as blunt and familiar as Antipodeans often are. Tragically, she got Parkinson's disease when she was 40, and lived with it until she was 83 – that's 43 years of frustration and shaking, and having every conceivable medication tried out on her. No wonder she ended up with a serious dementia. She had a huge influence on me, but, regrettably, I didn't see much of her in the last few years of her life: it got so that she didn't know who I was and – rightly or wrongly – I gradually shied away from witnessing the awful, grisly end of a good woman.

My stepfather – Peter Pettit – came into my life when I was about eight or nine. He was the solicitor handling my mother's divorce; a full colonel in the artillery and the head of the Honourable Artillery Company B Battery, with a DSO and the Territorial Decoration. He was a very formal, proper sort of person, and served as a Conservative on the council. In 1961, he became the Mayor of Marylebone. He had two sons, but his wife had died giving birth to the second one. He and my mother had become fond of each other when he was working on her divorce, and they eventually chose to get married – but it was more an arrangement of convenience than passion.

Before Peter arrived, my grandfather – Gilbert Findlay – had taken on the role of the male figurehead in the family. He was a very moral man. Every Sunday, we were all made to go to church; so I had a fairly well developed Christian ethic and Christian attitude towards general day-to-day living. He had very, very high standards for people's behaviour. So we would all be sent off to Sunday School, and we were all taught about the Bible and Christianity and the morality of it, as it was then understood – and most certainly not in any kind of liberal, easy-going way that you see nowadays, where all sorts of rules and commandments seem to have opt-outs built in, even amongst Catholics.

Gilbert and his wife had come back to Britain from Australia in the 1920s, and he had quickly got himself firmly in the establishment, with a top job running the Baltic Exchange in London. He had been in charge of the allocation of fuel during the War. Then there was my aunt, who was born in Calcutta and was a tea planter, and her brother, born in Argentina, working on meat import and export. So in some ways, we weren't just a North London family – an international element never felt very far away.

At home, my stepfather was very aware of politics and, given all his Conservative and Mayoral connections, was politically active, with my mother increasingly playing the role of the good Mayor's wife. So as I approached my teens, I started to become more aware of the political discussions that percolated within our family. In time, I joined the Young Conservatives: it was what you did if you wanted to be connected and meet people and get girls. I went out with the Conservative agent's daughter, Trudy. Actually, everybody went out with her and everybody tried to shag her. None of us ever succeeded, but membership of the Young Conservatives was the ticket that gave you some much-valued access to her.

Ours was a thoroughly traditional Conservative family that believed in self-reliance and making your own way in life, without looking around for help. You stood on your own two feet, with no sense of entitlement, only an expectation that you needed to earn your living. Whether people were Conservative voters or not, being unemployed brought shame and embarrassment – in a way that these days would, for most, seem incomprehensible. But at that time, there was still the prevailing judgemental attitude that people who made no contribution were entitled to little or nothing, and being on the dole was not something to enjoy talking about. We were never left in any doubt that the responsibility for finding a job or career was our own.

Our locality was entirely Conservative. If you met somebody who lived there who wasn't, they had to either be a showbiz entertainer or some kind of nouveau riche entrepreneur who made his fortune out of selling scrap. It was a very class-ridden society. In fact, there were sub-divisions within the upper class and middle class and lower class. Within the middle class were the nouveau riche, who we weren't, and the upper middle class, who we were. We observed etiquette and manners and protocol rather more than some people did and less than others. But like most people, you were embedded in your class. And we had a generational history of being the middle class.

People were embedded into their religion too. Christianity was normalised, and people were mainly either Church of England or Roman Catholic. The church was still an intrinsic part of the community and how you became part of the community. And ministers of the church could, and would, be thoroughly judgemental. We came under the parish of St Albans, and the Bishop of St Albans – an unpleasant fellow – had banned my mother from taking communion because she was divorced. I thought this was intolerable and un-Christian, and I once had an argument with him about it. But that was how power was maintained, whether it came from government, clergy, judiciary or community. And that was when I first started to think about the politics of control and motivation.

In those days, you lived in your box, and only occasionally came out of it. Because of that, people were a lot easier to control than nowadays, when there are far fewer boundaries – physical, mental or informational. Then, you could see poor people in the East End of London and rich in Hampstead – and in between were people like us. Our paths from birth to death were uncertain, but there was usually a journey of sorts mapped out, signposted by the familiar practices of home, neighbourhood, church and school. You had an idea what job you might end up doing and what kind of house you might end up living in. Meanwhile, in education, for example, the 11+ was accepted by everybody: if you failed it, you failed it, and got on with your Secondary Modern life. If somebody had a problem, they had a problem – there was no sense that they had a right to society solving it for them, and for free.

The trick that the Left and Labour would pull off, in their search for dominance, was to disrupt that mentality, and – through to the present day – create a vast client state of faux compassion, expectation and entitlement. It

started with the emphasis on 'free' education and 'free' health. 'Free at the point
of delivery' became a crafty way of avoiding the question of how any of it might
be paid for. By taxation? By debt?

Nothing is free, yet people have been encouraged to assume that it can be –
and that the Left can deliver this, and the nasty Right won't. It is the fraud that
has repeatedly been played on the population of Britain: one that has, regrettably, been adopted all over the world and continues to be perpetrated – as
shown in the US with Obama. Yet, in truth, no nation can supply its people with
free education and free health and permanent pensions growth without taxing
its citizens or raising debt – in which case, the chances are that the people will
end up with less wealth rather than more. In the UK after Thatcher, state control
of everything was discredited, we thought, once and for all. Blair's subsequent
ingenuity was to impersonate the free market, whilst appeasing people and
socially engineering the country, through a dialogue of entitlements and rights
and massive state and personal debt.

Of course, in the post-war years, we were growing up in a very repressive
and regressive era, when people's rights and entitlements were as much the
topic of conversation as they are now – but in a different way. My prevailing
memory is of early 1960s debate dominated by whether girls should have
had sex before they got married. Abortion would remain illegal until 1967, as
would homosexuality (which was never spoken about in polite company). And
like anyone of my generation, I remember only too well people fretting about
whether we were all about to die a slow death in a nuclear winter. Malcolm
Muggeridge pontificated about this kind of thing, Nevil Shute wrote novels
about it, and eventually people made films and sang songs about it all. People
were starting to kick against repression and discuss what freedom really meant.
And the political parties were trying to come to terms with this. In many ways,
that discussion still rages.

If you believe in freedom, then people are free to hold opposing views from
you and to live their life the way they want to. The paradox – indeed, the problem
– is that this freedom, as we continually see in the modern era, allows some
people a platform on which to preach its destruction. And I think this is a lot
closer to home than we think – certainly not just the monopoly of fascists and
fundamentalists. The liberal Left, for example, are as illiberal as you can get, and
will shout down any debate over anything that they think they might not like or
that might contradict their belief system (or what they do for a living). I believe
that there is a thing called society and social order is a part of that. But social

order allows for differences in people. People are not all the same. A one-tier system, where one size fits all, is clearly not right; people are not equal, and they aren't the same. The aim of the Left is to motivate people by making everyone the same (which has a certain appeal if you are looking enviously at people with more than you). It proclaims diversity and freedom – but it wants anything but.

I didn't go to university, and that never bothered me. Indeed, it was never really considered. It would have been another four years of contributing nothing to the family and living off my mother, who was already working and nearly killing herself. In those days, girls didn't work, so my sisters weren't expected to contribute to the household income. Not so for boys. I don't think anybody sat me in a room and told me, but I just understood that I'd had a good grammar-school education, and now the moment had come to go out and get a job.

One option was to become a professional musician. I am naturally good at certain things, one of which is music – although I am defeated in this regard by rather poor staying power: musicians need to be single-minded and devoted with their practice to turn reasonable into excellent, but I could never be bothered. It's been the story of my life. I had very good eye–hand co-ordination, so I was good at cricket – but never great. I could play rugby to a decent standard, and was in the school's First XV – but wasn't really interested.

But I loved modern jazz. My sisters were into the jazz scene, and there used to be a Tuesday Jazz Night at the Barnet Assembly Rooms. I played the piano, with some ability, and the trumpet, the latter to a level of sufficient proficiency to allow it to earn me small money. When I was about 16, I started a band with Michael Renvoize as bass player (my pal, who we called 'Spike', who eventually became a dentist) and Richard Williams on guitar (who went on to do film animation on *The Pink Panther* and *Who Framed Roger Rabbit?*). In those days, being a musician set you apart from other people. (It possibly still does, but now, the music world has all become too industrialised and predictable.) Music was something that you could enjoy, whilst, at the same moment, it could be enjoyed by the people listening to you – so you were in a relationship with a crowd of people; you would develop admirers, or even fans, and I never made any secret of the fact that I liked the feeling that this gave you and the sense that I was 'somebody' – that I could command a bit of an audience. I didn't want to be one of the cannon fodder. I wanted success – although I wasn't yet sure what 'success' meant, and possibly I'm still not. But I did, even then, measure it by visibility and awareness. That, I suppose, was a presage of my subsequent career.

My trumpet-playing days have more or less vanished – the flexibility in the lips falls victim, like a lot of things, to the atrophy and attrition of age – although I still dabble with the piano. Back then, in the late '50s and early '60s, for a while I played as a 'professional' (in a manner of speaking). You'd get £10 for a gig at the London Palladium, £20 in Manchester with Tommy McQuater's Pick-Up Band (so you made a £10 loss, given that a return ticket to Piccadilly by British Railways was £30), or do the Marquee Club for nothing but fun and exposure. It was not a particularly glamorous life, and it was not a living income as such. So I was continually questioning whether I ought to get a 'serious job', and if there was any doubt about that in my mind, my mother put me straight.

As soon as I'd reached 18, she said it was time to go and get a 'proper' job – and it never even occurred to me that I might argue with her over that. Teaching was an option, but I disliked the idea of entering a student world of pipes and duffel coats and bone-idle coffee-bar discussions, and disliked the idea of a teaching one even more – with its lazy, whingeing, *Guardian*-obsessed staff-rooms.

So as a first step to a job, my mother took me to the Stella Fisher Employment Agency, in Fleet Street (and you'll note that, in those days, 18-year-olds were taken by their mum to get their first job). They offered me three interviews: one with an insurance company for post boy, one with a publishing company for post boy, and one with a television station for post boy. I was a polite, well-spoken, well-dressed chap, and all three companies said that they'd have me (although the insurance firm warned me that I'd be bored stiff within a few months – which I thought was rather an odd motivational approach).

In fact, it was no contest. Anything, no matter how lowly, with 'television' in the title was a draw. So I went to work at the third on the list – ABC Television – where my title turned out to be not 'post-boy', but 'Chart Boy', which meant that, as each slot in the commercial break was allocated, I had to put a label onto the board saying who had booked it. I was the lowest of the low, but I didn't care, because I felt that I was at the centre of a vibrant new world, and had no doubts at all that I was on the road to somewhere modern, glamorous and exciting.

We were based at Vogue House on Hanover Street, right in the middle of London's throbbing, brightly lit West End, where theatre-land met porno-joints and old money met new. On my first day at the television station, I'd barely been there an hour or so before I walked through a door and behind me was the actress Jean Shrimpton – so I held it open for her. And behind her was a rather long-haired David Bailey, to whom I think at the time she was engaged, so I held the door open for him too. ABC were helping promote Sammy Davis Jr. on the channel's *Sunday Night at the London Palladium*, which was a very popular show at that time. They were holding a press conference in the lobby, and I walked in on it, and there he was. I was literally entering showbiz, and – despite the poor pay – I was euphoric.

The thing was that I had found a way into a world that, for most people, could only be accessed through the box in their sitting room. And, along with my dabbling with the jazz world, it was giving me ideas about my station in life. I question whether any of these things were particularly important in terms of formulating what I'm like deep down – but they gave me a sense of how life is a string of opportunities, and that the key is taking hold of those opportunities when they arrive. ABC was one such opportunity. But it did not seem long before a new one was being passed to me – quite literally.

2

Advertising

My first advertising agency was Colman Prentis and Varley. I was playing rugby for the ITV staff team against this agency, and a guy called John French, in their media-buying office, offered me a job. He claimed later that it was so that he could get me on his rugby team, but I don't know whether that was a joke or not. It was 1961. I was 20 and would be earning a mere £20 a week, doing the least prestigious job in the least prestigious department.

But CPV were an extremely prestigious agency, dating back to 1934. They had a raft of top accounts – including Austin Motors, BEA, Fortnum & Mason, Knorr, Pepsi, Ryvita, Shell, Sunblest, Unilever, and, of course, the Tory advertising account (which got them fame when Macmillan came back into power in 1959, and involved one of my favourite campaigns, showing various ordinary people, with the line, 'I'm a Conservative'). They were one of the largest agencies in the country, and it was another piece of good fortune that had come my way. But it was also an opportunity I would seize with both hands.

At that stage in my life, I really didn't have much idea what I was doing: I don't think you do. You've just got a job, you're being paid, and you're mixing with some nice people and having a bit of fun. It felt jolly nice being in advertising, because in those days everybody was talking about it – a sort of fairly new industry, itself a consequence of the new commercial television. As time went on, I'd go to the pub and people would ask me what I did, and it felt wonderful to tell them that I was in advertising – they would be fascinated, and would want to know all about it and what it was like. I was in a business where you could enjoy yourself at work and enjoy yourself at play and the two seemed to be one and the same thing. Most of my contemporaries had gone to university, and it looked from my perspective as though they were going nowhere. In contrast, I'd got a job and I was earning real money.

The eponymous founders of the agency, Colman, Prentis and Varley were ex-Army officers. Indeed, at that time, the advertising industry in Britain was full of ex-Army higher ranks. When these kinds of officers had all been demobbed, the government had tried to work out what to usefully do with them all, and as they were very good at doing lunch, and being charming to important people, advertising seemed the perfect place to send them. Colman was part of the mustard family in Norfolk. Terry Prentis was an accountant, but he died quite early on and his wife manipulated the shares. And Arthur Varley was a colonel – a round, curmudgeonly fellow in a tweed jacket, smoking a pipe – who had married Elizabeth, the sister of Edward (Lord) Montague of Beaulieu. In those days, it was still the case that you often got the business because you went to school with someone or because you knew their relatives or you married somebody or you were in the same regiment. Colman, Prentis and Varley were very proper, they spoke properly, and behaved properly, and this brought in the work. That's how it worked.

As we emerged from the 1950s, the country was at the crossroads of austerity and prosperity. Following the war, newsprint was rationed, and agencies were allocated space and competed for that allocation. Everybody went out to lunch, got drunk the whole time, and the more you drank and the more drinks you bought for the other person the more extra space you got. There were few photographs in advertising, and many ads still used illustration. The art director was a bloke who drew pictures. I distinctly remember a Yardley cosmetics poster: a detailed colour drawing of a gun-belt, but instead of cartridges, it had lipsticks in it; the copy read, 'A woman's ammunition. Go great guns with Yardley lipsticks'. These days, that would be a photograph, without them even thinking about it. However, in those days, it was illustration as the default position. A photograph would be very expensive and unusual.

CPV, however, were effective on two fronts. First, they spotted very quickly that commercial television was going to transform the industry. And, in addition, they knew how to sell hard and find the right people to do that. I fitted in well, because I was fairly keen to make a mark, and learned very quickly how to get clients and contractors to like you and close the deals.

My boss in the media-buying department was a guy called Frank Monkman. There was a rigid and palpable class-based hierarchy in the advertising industry at the time, which meant that Old Etonians became account directors, the slightly mad ones from art school became creative directors, and the remaining, more lowly types became media buyers. I was a bit of an anomaly, as I was not identifiably downmarket – I spoke properly and I went to Norfolk at the weekends, and I got on perfectly well with the posh account directors and crazy creative people. Amidst all this was Frank Monkman – a Cockney who spoke with a posh voice and liked to use vulgarity and swearing for shock value.

And in an office where all the secretaries spoke with the most high-pitched, cut-glass, finishing-school accents, Monkman had an assistant who amused himself by playing the Cockney oik. Clients and suppliers would ring up and say, 'May I speak with Mr Monkman?' and he'd say, in a very strong Cockney voice, 'He's gone ashore for a brown load' – which meant that he was in the lavatory.

Before long, I found myself with a serious income, and the ability to buy things that previously I could never have imagined. I bought an Austin Devon (the forerunner of the A40) as my first car. Then I got a Morris Minor that, in turn, I upgraded to a Morris Minor 1000 with a soft top. I was married by the time I was 23, and Sue and I bought a house in a place called Brookmans Park (or 'Elstree' – a good 10 miles away – if you were trying to be posh). We even started going to Norfolk at weekends. My stepfather had bought a cottage there, because he was a birdwatcher and there was a sanctuary at Cley Marches. Norfolk was where the middle-class professionals went: well, you either went east to Norfolk or south to Kent and Sussex, depending on your place in the pecking order; Sussex was where the very rich people went because you went past Windsor and that's where the Queen lived most of the time, but Norfolk was next best, because she lived at Sandringham some of the time.

When John French left CPV to join another agency, Hobson Bates (which later turned into Ted Bates), he took me with him. And when he went to Geers Gross, in 1966, the same happened. In those days, the idea that people would help you to get a job was far more readily accepted. It still goes on, of course: it's a perfectly natural and normal piece of human behaviour. But now, we have a culture of envy and entitlement and artificial equality that will see an employer accused of favouritism, nepotism, prejudice, racism, or some other -ism, just because they have chosen someone whom they know is right for the job. One of the reasons why I find Socialists so offensive is because they talk about perfectly common-sensical human behaviour as though it is abhorrent. If you want to help the people around you and help the people close to you, so what?

In time, I was offered the post of Deputy Media Director, and started making some fairly serious money. The Geers Gross agency was headed by two Bobs: Bob Gross, who was a New York Jew, and Bob Geers, who I think came from Wisconsin – both fresh out of Madison Avenue, and very much of the *Mad Men* stable. They became most famous for the Homepride flour-graders, the

Kennomeat dogs (Albert and Sidney), and Arthur the Kattomeat cat, which might lead you to think that they had a certain formula to their creativity – and you'd be right.

They were chalk and cheese. Gross was an asthmatic, and he barked and coughed all the time; he would get excited and begin great coughing fits, during which you were terrified that he was going to expire at any moment. He was an aggressive, bullying character; very difficult to deal with most of the time, but every now and then, he'd smile and everybody would be enchanted by the novelty of him being nice. Then, because smiling was so unusual for him, it would trigger another terrible coughing fit and you'd think he was about to fall over. Geers was entirely different. He was the incredibly laid-back Southern boy – 'Thanks y'all'; that sort of thing. In his private life, he parachute jumped and did all sorts of strange dangerous extreme sports; an adrenaline junkie.

It was a new agency, based on these two ex-Benton & Bowles Americans in London – and because of that, didn't fit in with any pre-existing creative movement. It just felt quite fresh. We were a small group and so we all had to do everybody else's job: you began to learn the whole industry; every side of it – production, media, account handling and so on. I remember a bodybuilder chap who they employed called (I think) Sid Robeson, who appeared in their cider commercials; he was married to a teacher in the East End. What sticks in my mind is that, once, when somebody was telling a joke, they started by saying, 'This is a really funny story …' And he said, 'Do you think you could let me make my own mind up whether it's funny or not?' And that incident has stopped me from ever saying, 'Here's a really funny story …'

There was only one office, with barely more than a dozen people in it. There were two secretaries there. One was called Jenny, married to Paddy Hopkirk the rally driver. When the second girl had arrived for an interview, the first thing that Bob Gross said to her was 'Show us your tits'. That was typical of the way he would behave at times. But she did. Just like that. He even called us all in to look. And she couldn't give a damn. Nowadays, he'd be in court for sexual abuse. We were based in Soho, in Richmond Buildings – where, in one of the most famous of Soho gangland killings, Jack 'Spot' Comer was shot by his rival Billy Hill.

The whole period represented a wonderful stepping-stone experience for me; I loved all the people and it was fun and mad. I don't know that I learned anything in particular. But it was a platform from which I became well known. That was when I was written about for the first time; when Reg Collins wrote about 'The Young Lions of British Media' in *Ad-Mag* – supposed to be one of the more cerebral trade publications at that time. My job was to buy slots on the ITV schedules at the most competitive rates. There was quite a bit of wheeler-dealing involved, and I became very successful at it – but, in the main, my success came because I was polite, hard-working, and reasonably good company. In truth, life does not need to be much more complicated than that.

Although it was about to be. And by some margin.

3

Brothers

It always felt to me as though the 1970s started on Monday 14 September 1970. That was when Saatchi & Saatchi launched. The day before, the new agency had placed an enormous press ad in *The Sunday Times* – they had it signed by the management guru Robert Heller and it had cost almost a quarter of all their start-up capital. It promised a 'new kind of advertising'. For me, it would deliver a new kind of life.

One Monday morning, whilst I was in the office at Geers Gross, somebody rang me up and said, 'Hello, my name's Saatchi. We're thinking of starting an advertising agency. Would you like to come round and have an interview?' That's quite a cold call to take at the start of the week, and my first reaction, as you'd expect, was to think that it was a complete wind-up. Particularly as, only the evening before, I'd been telling my great friend Michael Renvoize, over dinner, that the advertising legend Charles Saatchi was the only person in the industry with whom I truly wanted to work. Saatchi's agency had come up with an ad for the Health Education Council featuring a pregnant man, with the line 'Would you be more careful if it was you that got pregnant?' The copywriter was Jeremy Sinclair, but at the time, I'd attributed the whole idea to Charles Saatchi. And I thought – still think – that this is the greatest print ad I'd ever seen. So to suddenly get that call – and get it that morning – was beyond weird. To this day, as far as I'm aware, the dinner and the call had no connection – it was simply a coincidence.

Before I write anything else, let me make one thing clear: to my mind, Charles Saatchi is a creative genius, while Maurice is a truly coruscating salesman and one of the cleverest people you are ever likely to meet. Their ups and downs – and the colourful experiences of those of us who were lucky enough to go along on that journey with them – have to be seen in the context of their unimpeachable qualities and achievements.

Months before the ad in *The Sunday Times* declared it in print, the brothers were dreaming about their 'different kind of agency'. Charles's previous business partner, Ross Cramer, was leaving to do films, so Charles's younger brother Maurice – who had been working at Haymarket Publishing – had agreed to step in. The name would change from Cramer Saatchi to Saatchi & Saatchi, which Charles thought would create an impact through its bizarreness alone – 'We're stuck with it, so let's make it an asset' he would say. Investors included Michael Heseltine, Mary and Lindsey Masters (the latter being the chief executive of Haymarket) and Mary Quant's husband, Alexander Plunkett-Green. (Charles – all of us who know him use 'Charlie' but I won't do that in these pages – did a beautiful ad for Mary, drawn by actually using make-up.)

As part of this new kind of agency, the brothers were going to get creatives talking directly to the clients (instead of through the more traditional account handlers); they were going to have a kind of supervisory quality-control team (the 'Ghost Squad') checking on delivery, and they planned to appoint a marketing director from the top of British commerce. Actually, none of these ideas got far beyond the dreaming stage, but it sounded great in the *Sunday Times* ad. In practice, I think they approached over a hundred candidates for the marketer role, and every single one worth appointing turned the job down. By the time they called me, they had given up looking for a marketing director and decided to go back to the conventional idea of a media director, which was where I came in. (Charles was now saying 'The creative function is the main one ... The other is media buying.') The star media-buyer at the time was Paul Green, but, after some consideration, he had declined. (There was a story that Charles had just posted a letter officially announcing the appointment when Green changed his mind, so Charles had his secretary go and bribe the postman to get it back when he came to empty the letterbox.) That late withdrawal was my good fortune, although I was still up against two other media candidates in Alan Rich (from Davison, Pearce, Baring and Spottiswoode) and Mike Townsend (Young & Rubicam). We all had experience, but because my name began with B, I was at the top of that list.

Very few people get to do what they want to do in the way they intend to do it. Life doesn't work like that. It should, but it doesn't. Most of the time, it's all a roulette wheel of fate and timing; so much is pure chance – as was the invite from the Saatchis. Living isn't a straight line, and human beings don't go down straight lines; they zigzag and do completely mad and random things, and then, sometimes, get back to the straight line – and sometimes they don't. And all you can do is be ready for the zigzagging, and try eventually to arrive at the end point that you set out to get to, regardless of how you get there. As I climbed several flights of stairs at 16 Goodge Street, I thought I could see a straight route appearing, but I was about to start zigzagging.

The Cramer Saatchi office was on the corner of Tottenham Court Road and Goodge Street, above a Tesco. It didn't look much in those days, but there were already some future 'names' in there. Film-makers Alan Parker and David Puttnam were working on the first floor in the same building (and were possibly partly the reason why Cramer had got a taste for the film industry). When I walked in through the door at the top of the stairs, the person I met, sitting at the first desk I came to, was this very blond, handsome, smart young chap, who I'd actually seen most mornings on the train coming into London – another coincidence. I'd thought that he was a male model, but he was in fact John Hegarty, who would, in due course, become one of the most famous creative directors of all time.

Meeting Charles did not include any introductory pleasantries – he is constitutionally incapable of them. He asked me if I'd like to join them; he told me he would pay me only half of what I was already getting – although there might be a 4.5 per cent option on the equity. I had not the faintest idea what that meant, but I agreed without too much thinking about it. They were launching with Ron Collins, John Hegarty, Chris Martin, Bill Atherton, Alan Tilby, Jeremy Sinclair and Maurice Saatchi himself, along with a freelance studio guy called Melvin Redford who stayed with them for most of his life. They also had an Australian accountant. And that was it. With me joining, that made up the ten that would run Saatchi & Saatchi in the early months.

I never really knew why they employed me. Some say it was just because I happened to be taller than the other two interviewees. John Hegarty once said it was down to me looking like Ross Cramer. Maybe it was because they were charmed by the dinner conversation story. And I've even heard it said that they were afraid of anti-Semitism from clients, so wanted a very English frontman. Whatever the reason, I was in. And I had no real idea what I was supposed to be going to do.

The new agency moved into 6 Golden Square in Soho, which was a very elegant building – on the outside at least. Charles had a brass plate made and installed, as if we were an expensive legal firm. We hired a receptionist called Jenny Lewis – the daughter of the CEO of EMI at the time – who used to arrive in the square in her father's Rolls Royce every morning. But inside, the offices were actually quite spartan – almost mean. Maurice was always worried about the finances. We took the basement and the ground floor, which had four largish white Formica desks at which sat the copywriters and art directors, then three offices at the end, with Charles on the left, me in the middle, and Maurice on the right. Downstairs was the boardroom and studio, and two loos. That's how it was to begin with. Very often, we'd have to be there 24 hours a day, seven days a week – so we all slept in the office, on the floor, in sleeping bags.

My early agencies had all been like *Mad Men* – everybody smoked, everybody drank, every meeting ended up in a long and late drinking session. There had always seemed to be the money to do anything that anyone needed in order to lubricate the wheeling and dealing. But the early days at Saatchi & Saatchi were different by virtue of what we could not afford to do. We launched during the Heath era, and the country was in the grip of industrial strife and huge economic problems. There were still power cuts three days a week. I think our start-up capital was around £25,000, of which a lot had gone on the ad. These were not the days of plenty by a long shot – although, in time, that would change.

Despite all the bullshit and hype, we really were a different kind of agency. Maurice and Charles were dramatically different from any advertising people I'd ever come across. Both of them were born in Baghdad, and had arrived in England in 1947, becoming part of a strong Jewish community in North London, centred on Hampstead Lane. We all knew of it, but we obviously weren't involved. Except for Ron Collins, who pretended that he was Jewish all the time to ingratiate himself. The Yom Kippur War was around this time, and both the brothers had actually thought about going. Indeed, a lot of their friends did go off to fight.

Almost every day, Charles came in and said, 'What accounts have you won? What have we got? What are we doing?' He'd bellow at Maurice and Maurice would shout back and I would sit in the middle, with things flying past my head (even a chair once hitting me.) I suspect that Charles had always bashed him up, since their childhood. He used to say to Maurice, 'I can't believe you came from the same womb as me.' Maurice has a book called *Brutal Simplicity of Thought*, and that is what they were and are – brutal and simple. (Not brutally simple. They're brutal *and* simple.) And Saatchi & Saatchi was brutality from start to finish. It began with aggression, had aggression in the middle, and had aggression at the end. Maurice had this saying that for us to win, others had to fail, and he was right after a fashion. But this approach was not something that I had come across before. And they were even happy to set staff against staff if it suited their purpose. They won't like me talking like this incidentally, but it's the truth about them, as everyone who's met them knows.

Tempers were always being exercised. Maurice and I used to compare notes on how far we stormed off after losing our temper before we regained our sanity and stopped. Once, I'd got from Golden Square to Hyde Park Corner before I calmed down. He got to the Victoria and Albert Museum. Then you have to come back, which – like the aftermath of any quarrel – is boring and humiliating.

Before Saatchi & Saatchi, Charles's agency already had the account for the Health Education Council, which we kept – a government quango (part of which was the Family Planning Association, which had commissioned the 'pregnant man' ad). It was run by Lady Alma Burke – Health or not, she was a regular smoker – who was responsible for the phrase 'milk-snatcher Thatcher'. Along with that account, the first clients were Granada TV Rental (because it was owned by Brian Wolfson, who was a distant cousin of the brothers) and the Citrus Marketing Board of Israel (that is, Jaffa) headed by Max Levine, whose son had been Charles's best friend at school. We won that account with a great strapline that went something like, 'The Lord sayeth, "Let there be oranges". Jaffa: the Chosen Fruit!' – but, inevitably, the ITCA rejected it as being anti-Semitic, even though every Jew we met liked it. Nonetheless, we kept the account.

After these two new clients came Escalade, run by an American called Paul Young, who had decided to launch a department store on the Brompton Road in London, which would open seven days a week, all night long ('for the luxury of midnight shopping', ran the blurb). Charles added another part of the strategy which was that if anyone found the same article cheaper, they would give the original to you for free. As a consequence of the pre-launch hype, the first Sunday opening caused gridlock in Knightsbridge at about 4.00 a.m. After that, the store never really sold anything else and went bankrupt. But the owner was impelled by this mad belief that all you had to do to succeed in business was capture the imagination of the public with a few great ideas – a philosophy that Charles loved. In one instance, Charles knocked up a jeans ad for them in about five minutes, with a few Franglais lines and a random picture of a romantic French couple ('pour un homme et une femme') and, lo and behold, it got an award.

Next, we got Avalon Promotions, run by a man called Alan Cluer (who set up the business after he won a lot of money on the football pools). They ran these full-page ads offering bulk-buy scissors for under five shillings. In those days, before strict trading laws, they would wait until the money came in, and only then go and buy the stock. But soon he went bankrupt and left us to deal with a £1 million bad debt. I had to go and negotiate the non-payment of bills for the space that he didn't occupy. Charles was livid. That was probably the first time I saw his really violent streak. He got an iron bar and actually went round to where Cluer worked, found where he'd parked his Maserati, and smashed the car to pieces.

Truth be known, for most of the time in the early days, none of us really knew how to run the agency. Usually, it was left to me to make it all work – learning on the job, learning from mistakes, learning from competitors even. I did everything apart from writing and rendering the ads. And I certainly tried to get a degree of business discipline into the company. I used to handle the client relationships, did the media buying, the marketing – and so, after a time, I self-styled myself the managing director. The brothers never, ever called me that. To them, I was always the media director. But half the time, people in the company just made up their own titles. And the press had started calling me 'the third brother': you can imagine how well that went down.

Maurice had his own articulation of advertising as being when an idea that captures the imagination of the public makes them change the way they think, feel or behave – and then choose. He felt that, at the time, the problem with the industry was that most of the agencies had forgotten that fact and were only concerned with pleasing the client. An account man's job was to take the client to breakfast, lunch, dinner, take his family out, play with his children, flirt with his wife – that's what you did, and that had seemed to be the central purpose of the industry, with its output almost a by-product of that. It was encapsulated in the well-known saying that when the client asks what time is it, most agencies ask what time the client would like it to be. Saatchi & Saatchi turned that around. For us, creativity quickly became God. We only had creative people, we were about creative work, and we were quite happy to declare that we weren't about anything else at all. We used to say that if you want market research, go to McCann's, but if you want an ad that's going to change the world, come to us.

Charles, meanwhile, would often just growl that he thought that the whole advertising industry was a waste of space and that clients would do better if they buried all their money in a hole in the ground – one of his less helpful pronouncements (although I guess that a similar, if milder, 'ineffectiveness of most advertising' sentiment was the basis of our first *Sunday Times* ad). Despite that random view, it was clear that we were approaching a golden era for advertising. Other agencies, such as BBH (with our ex-creative John Hegarty), would soon begin championing the importance of creativity too, so that it would be much better understood. We became probably the most talked-about industry in the country. Some of the television campaigns of the day – Hamlet, Carling, Smash, VW, Levis, PG Tips, Milk Tray, Campari; everyone will have a favourite example – have passed into the cultural history of this country. In those days, through to the early '80s, advertising felt like it was the whole world.

At the time, most of the conversations – most of the things that were 'happening' – were being catalysed by advertising. And Saatchi & Saatchi was one of the main (and earliest) drivers of this cultural shift. Advertisements were bringing in famous people, famous music, famous things, big ideas, and amazing locations, and were often commanding massive production budgets. We were in an alternative entertainment industry and I was cast in the role of the impresario, with clients funding what, in each case, was essentially an 'event' in the form of a 60-second commercial. You had the comforting feeling that you were part of the flow of what was going on and you never had to explain what you did, because everybody seemed to know every new commercial as it came out. If you bumped into somebody at a party and they said, 'What do you do?' you would answer with a reference to the latest popular commercial. That was enough.

The main creative-led agency up until that point had been Collett, Dickenson and Pearce. Many of the people that eventually worked for us came from there, including Alan Tilby and Charles himself; that was where he had learned a lot of what he thought and did. But although he talked the good talk about originality, he could be completely unscrupulous about taking ideas from any rival source that came to hand – he didn't ever feel that it was necessary for him to develop what somebody else had done just to legitimise his use of it.

Charles figured that the way to become a very famous agency was to be talked about and make everyone aware of you – and that we needed to be in *Campaign* every week. The publication had been started by Maurice when he was working at Haymarket, and there were strong links. Peter Elman was the first editor, and he was reasonably malleable, mainly because, in those days, he had very few journalists, and was always in need of content, so you could always persuade him to run a story. Charles used to ask everyone in the agency to come up with news stories with which to feed the paper – and add a Saatchi angle. He'd read *Grocer's Gazette* and *The Grocer* and he'd see a launch of a new brand – the launch of a new variety of Stork margarine, that kind of thing – and he would call *Campaign* about it, and make it seem as if the agency was about to win the account.

After a while, he got bored with ringing up under his real name, so he'd hold a handkerchief over his nose and tell them it was 'Jack Robinson'. He'd say, 'I've got three stories for you this week', and one of the stories would be that Saatchi & Saatchi were about to win Cadbury's or a budget for something had been increased by a few million, or that this or that agency was on a pitch list – all of which would destabilise the clients or the rival agencies to our advantage. After a while, Charles had other directors at it, including me. I'd phone *Campaign* from a call box, and claim to be 'John Robinson'. As the paper became a more successful publication, they became more intolerant of these calls and the tip-offs. In fact, Elman once said that if he added together all of the business that he heard Saatchis had won, it was greater that J. Walter Thompson's and McCann-Erickson's turnover combined.

Maurice, meanwhile, had the intellect, and he wrote the philosophical stuff. In his mind, there was a philosophical back-story to everything that we did. He would describe advertising as the bastion of capitalism: namely, it was creating consumer choice, increasing competition and increasing consumption, to reduce the cost of manufacturing, which lowered the prices to consumers, boosting demand, so that the whole thing was a virtuous circle – the world of prosperity. He had won the McMillian prize for economics at the LSE, so he was comfortable talking this kind of theory. He had read all this stuff about philosophy, politics and economics and was very Right-wing in his thinking – but at that time in his life, he had not fully appreciated how much of it chimed with Conservative political orthodoxy.

Although both brothers wanted Saatchi & Saatchi to be different from anything else in the industry, Charles's view was not the same as that of Maurice – who valued *real* change. Charles's approach was that first, you had to match anything that was working. His argument was that if the company was as good as J. Walter Thompson, but more creative, you'll make ten times as much money – but you need to be as good as J. Walter Thompson in the first place. So if, for example, Thompson's had got lots of account men, we needed lots of account men. Charles was preoccupied with the agency's size. If we had a prospective client due in, we would bulk up the office staff pool with 'extras' – friends, family members, people off the street – and plonk them down at desks, telling them to pretend to be working. We'd give them a few quid just to sit there.

Both Maurice and Charles were ready to do anything that was necessary to get to where they wanted to be, but their respective views on how to achieve their vision were often at odds with each other. So we used to have these ridiculous arguments, with me in the middle, with Maurice in one ear, saying one thing, and Charles in the other one telling me the opposite. They were two of the most imaginative, motivated and unusual practitioners that I've ever met – and two of the most infuriating and difficult.

As we started to grow, they told me I needed more account directors, and I took that badly and personally. I felt that they were starting to ignore my opinions, and that, in some way, this was them saying that I was not doing a good enough job. When we actually started recruiting, they dragged in ten candidates all at exactly the same time, and left them in reception, all in a row, avoiding eye contact with each other and not knowing what to say. Charles walked out into the reception area pretending to be casual, and then came back in and said that he liked the third one from the left. We asked him what his reason was, and he said it was because that interviewee was the tallest. We hired him – a chap called Bill Muirhead. And – whether Charles had a sixth sense or it was just luck – as it transpired, he turned out to be one of the best account men ever.

Another highlight of our recruitment was David Welch: an ex-paratrooper – he would always wear his paratrooper tie – who was six foot five and fantastically posh. Charles had a view that account men should speak absolutely impeccable, received pronunciation English, and be very tall and thin, wear a suit at all times, and know the names of Gentlemen's clubs where they serve fine wine. In fact he expected them *not* to know anything about advertising and thought that it represented a nuisance if they did.

Now it so happened that David Welch had been chief-of-staff to Donald Stokes, the head of the newly created British Leyland Motor Corporation. Like any new agency, we wanted an automotive account – as well as a washing powder and a confectionery brand and so on. David told us that we had a chance to pitch for Triumph cars, and he set it up. The idea was that he would get us the account and we would then hire him to be the account director. Donald Stokes would be jolly pleased because the chief-of-staff that he had been so cross to lose would be back handling his business. So we were marched up to the Midlands to Leyland's headquarters to see the great Sir Donald. It was, to the best of my memory, the only occasion when all three of us, including Charles, went to a pitch. David Welch said to Stokes, 'Sir, I'd like you to meet

Maurice and Charles Saatchi and Tim Bell. They run an agency called Saatchi & Saatchi.'

'Sounds like a Chinese laundry,' said Stokes. Charles frowned and looked like he was about to strangle him, but he managed to control himself. We'd prepared a presentation for Triumph cars, and when Stokes heard it, he said that he 'thought Benson and Hedges handled that account', meaning Hobson Bates (the incumbent agency). But then we had another stroke of luck. Stokes had just hired a man called Keith Hopkins to be the marketing director (and therefore the person who would now have a significant role in deciding on the agency). He was the erstwhile public relations head of BLMC and a very heavy drinker to boot. Hopkins had taken a shine to David for his ability to drink late into the night and I'm sure this really helped us win the account. In time, he came to love us too.

As we became more successful and more serious, we were able to push the boat out on the spending – although Charles was still unpredictable on bills. In those days, the fashionable thing was to colour everything in burgundy and cream – it was the great feature of Carnaby Street. Once they'd announced that Barbara Hulanicki's store was burgundy and cream, that was it settled. So the designer Rodney Fitch (who'd worked with Terence Conran) was commissioned to do all our interior in these colours. However, they finished decorating at just the moment when the cult was turning to green and cream. Charles was absolutely livid, and wouldn't pay Fitch his £1,800 fee, and got served with a County Court Order in the small claims court to pay. But he never told any of us, not even Maurice. Every official letter he received would be thrown in the bin. Then one day, they were both out, and the receptionist rang to tell me that the Sheriff of London had arrived wanting to see someone in authority. At that time, I had no idea who or what was a 'Sheriff'. I really did have a vision of a man with a tin star and cowboy hat. When I met him, he was, obviously, just a chap in a suit, but he just said to me, 'I hereby present thee with a Garnishee Order.' I sat there holding this document, which, being in legal jargon, was unreadable. When Charles came back from lunch, I showed him it, and he said, 'What's that?' I said, 'It's a Garnishee Order, which I've taken on your behalf.' He said, 'What the fuck's a Garnishee Order?' and I said 'I haven't the faintest idea.' So I rang my stepfather, who was a solicitor, and he told me that the authorities had been to our bank and taken the money that was owed to them. When I went back to Charles with this news, he went bonkers, going on about the 'fucking police state', and the rest of it.

In 1975, the country was still in recession, and the advertising industry was suffering. At that time, we were surviving on the BLMC account and the Health Education Council, and were still making a healthy profit – around £190,000 at the previous year-end (the highest in UK advertising billings). That was all well and good, but it was not the stuff of the grand vision. So Maurice decided to go hunting for an agency that we could take over. Garland-Compton had some good fmcg accounts – like Proctor & Gamble (spending more on advertising that any other company in the world), Rowntree and United Biscuits, plus a wide global network – but they lacked our creative abilities. Maurice pitched it to Ken Gill, their chairman (who had been looking at BMP and CDP, and who he had met back in 1973), and persuaded him that it would be a great merger – although we all knew that, really, we were swallowing them up. The deal went ahead in September 1975.

It was officially called Saatchi & Saatchi Garland-Compton. That was agreed in the documents, but we simply instructed the switchboard to answer the phone as 'Saatchi & Saatchi'. Then Maurice crossed out the word Garland and put Saatchi & Saatchi Compton. The brothers had a way of agreeing to all sorts of things and then just amending and varying what they had promised to suit whatever they wanted. The biggest shock the Compton's people got was on the day of the announcement. Gill started getting all sorts of calls from other London agencies – who didn't like us – saying that he would come to regret the move. And then he saw the *Campaign* headline which read, 'Saatchi swallows up the Compton Group' (which Charles had briefed, obviously). Some of Gill's friends said that it brought him close to tears.

We'd sold them Saatchi & Saatchi in exchange for the majority of shares in the new company. In those days it was called a reverse takeover, but we had already made several acquisitions before that, which is what enabled us to move into some new offices in Lower Regent Street. We'd bought two small agencies, the first called E. G. Dawes and Notleys, then the larger George J. Smith agency for £90,000, which was something of a dud (being, as was soon discovered, largely insolvent, which gave Charles another reason to verbally beat up Maurice), but all this did was inspire the brothers ever more in their thirst for acquisition, and give them some practice for the bigger fish. And with the new deal, the brothers had succeeded with what they came to regard as their most successful ever business stratagem – a masterstroke.

However, the process had filled me with uncertainties. Although I had been introduced to Gill and some of the Compton people during the discussions, I only knew half of what was in the brothers' minds. You were never told what the strategy was. You gleaned it from whispers and conversations: most of us used to sit around until late at night trying to work out what they were trying to do. There was no point in asking them, because they would never have told you the truth – if they even knew themselves what the truth was. 'Let's be number one' – that's all Charles ever used to say. But of course, in the end, that's exactly what they got to be.

4

Golden Era

The Garland-Compton deal brought us a conventional agency. It also brought a lot of heads of things – joint media directors, joint creative directors, joint managing directors, joint chairmen, joint everything. And assimilating that lot was a fairly brutal process. Some people left; some just got obliterated; some got so humiliated that they had to flee; some were just cut off at the knees.

There were two completely different dialogues taking place: one amongst the Saatchi people who talked to each other in a particular way, completely condemning everybody from Garland-Compton; another amongst the Garland-Compton people, who hated us back. Everybody plotted against each other. On the second floor was a row of deputy chairmen, none of whom had any power or anything on which to work. It was known as 'death row'. Any of the Garland-Compton people who we didn't like were made deputy chairmen and put up on the 'row'.

But we were now the fifth largest agency in the UK, with over a hundred employees, necessitating another move, this time into new premises in Charlotte Street. Straight away we won the Schweppes account, which no one had expected, especially as we had been up against big players in JWT and CDP. But the Schweppes managing director, Keith Holloway, who was a friend of Gill, thought that we had the magic creative spark, the lack of which in his incumbents, Ogilvy & Mather, had made him call the pitch in the first place. I presented with Jennifer Laing, who had come in from Garland-Compton. We had an idea with the line, 'You can always spot a rotter by his total lack of Schweppes' and then 'Drinking Schweppes straight'. It led to one of the great campaigns, and great account relationships in advertising at that time, and one that lasted over a decade. That win transformed the agency, and turned us into *the* creative shop *par excellence*.

I became joint managing director – although Maurice and Charles never said that to my face – and in came a guy called John Spratling, who thought he'd be the deputy managing director, but I wouldn't let him. The creative director from Garland-Compton was Bob Bellamy. We used to call him Mr Knee because he would sit next to you and put his hand on your knee, and leave it there whilst he was talking to you. Keith Nicolson was the media director and Ron Rimmer was the managing director. The unwritten rule was to go in and kill your opposite number – which we did. Jeremy Sinclair took the creative director position and Roy Warman became media head.

We were having a party where I'd had God knows how much to drink. Suddenly Rimmer appeared and said he'd got to talk to me about Spratling being so unhappy that he was thinking of leaving. So I was dragged out of this party to sit and listen to what we could do for Spratling, how much money we could pay him, and so on. When I told Charles, he said, 'Why the fuck is he talking about that when we've just won Schweppes?' The next morning, we were having a board meeting, and Charles mysteriously told me not to attend. He went in himself – which he never normally did – and there and then just told Spratling that he didn't look well, and that he needed to go on a six-week cruise for which Charles had already bought the tickets. That's how he was got rid of. They never, ever called anybody in and fired them, because if you did that you had to pay them lots of money, and Charles certainly wasn't going to do that. Then Rimmer himself left, to go to McCanns. It was a symbolic moment, because Rimmer had been, as MD of Garland-Compton, the very first person Maurice had rung to make enquiries about merging. Maurice and Charles needed a replacement with a more specific financial brief than Rimmer's, and in the end, for that role, they hired a certain Martin Sorrell.

By this time, I'd got myself a chauffeur, because I had to go out to lunch and drink a lot and entertain clients (although both Charles and Maurice drove themselves). In fact, sometimes I could hardly speak after lunch, so it was better to be driven back to the office than nod off in a taxi or something – but that's a different point. The industry imposes enormously on your private life, so you've got to make it palatable. So by the same token, I tried to make life easy for the Saatchi staff. We had nice offices, they had proper facilities and if they wanted a newspaper, you delivered newspapers. The company paid for everything, and that created an atmosphere where people thought it was a nice place to work and that they got more from it. We helped people out with all sorts of things – their mortgages, their debts, all sorts of stuff. Our view about money was that if you get up in the morning worrying over the bills, you're going to produce crap work. You had to provide people with some self-esteem

– even if it was just through a spurious job-title, so they could tell people who they were.

I never had a closed-door policy – because it was good management practice not to, but also because I wanted to know what was going on. The last thing I wanted to discover was that somebody had been having a word with somebody else and I didn't know about it. Knowledge is power. If you know what's going on, then you're in a powerful position. If you don't, you become irrelevant, or you wake up on the street. I knew most of the ins and outs within the agency but, at the same time, knew very little about the brothers' minds. The more I became the central figure, the more I became detached from them. In many ways, I was running the place, and they were happy for me to do that, because it took all the flak away from them – whether it was internal management issues or external accounts and client issues. In fact, Maurice and Charles were becoming ever more detached, more interested in looking outwards, plotting and scheming their next corporate takeover.

They kept such things from me. They would avoid me, or dissemble without any scruples. They operated entirely on the basis of mushroom management. In fact, Charles's great line was, 'Why tell the truth when a good lie will do?' I used to quote the line to people and there was many a time when I would adopt the same philosophy – although never with the chutzpah that Charles managed on a daily basis. The only thing you knew about Charles was whatever he wanted you to know – which, more often than not, was either a downright fabrication or some kind of incomplete truth. I'm not sure he particularly wanted to have any connection with reality, partly because that was too dull and too boring and partly because it required you to do things. In a way, there is a sense to that: a lot of the client problems that seemed a nightmare on Monday had gone away by Wednesday if you just shut up and ignored them.

The most striking example of the brothers' disingenuousness occurred in 1982 (around the time of their takeover of Compton USA, by which time I was increasingly being left out of any kind of discussion) when I was sent to re-pitch British Caledonian. I had persuaded BCal to pay David Frost £1.5 million to appear in their advertising campaign, and it had been a complete disaster, so we were in danger of losing the account. They were an extremely difficult client, but we pulled it round. When I came back, I trudged into Charles's office and told him we'd kept the account. All he said was, 'Well done', and didn't seem to want to talk further about it. At the time, I didn't think much of this because it was quite normal for there to be no thanks or congratulations.

What I didn't know was that, throughout all this, Charles and Maurice had been secretly pitching for the rival British Airways account. They even told *Campaign* before they told me. The way I found out was deeply embarrassing. The director of public affairs at British Airways – a man called John Perry – rang me up, out of the blue, and suggested supper. I sat with him for three hours at L'Etoile, whilst he burbled away about how we were going to be working together, with me looking bemused and trying to bluff it that I knew what he was talking about. When I confronted Charles and Maurice about it, they told me that I must have been dreaming. In fact, they would never – even at some future date – speak to me about what had really happened. In the end, it was Lord King, the BA chairman, who told me the whole story, a long time later. The media world can be a ruthless one, but the brothers took that to a new high – and one element of that would be that accounts would be resigned without any loyalties whatsoever if something better showed up. It meant freezing me out; all part of the bargain. That's how they worked.

And then there was the issue of Charles's modern art, which I hated – so he put a sign on my door, which read 'Phil E. Stein'. He'd hung a Schnabel on my wall and I loathed that. It was a sort of large, rectangular thing made of mud with a tin lid stuck in it, plus half a Coke can and some footprints. He told me it was an absolutely fantastic work of art and I just had to put up with it. On one of the days when he was coming at me, I went flying against the wall, and landed on the painting. He shouted, 'You're destroying the fucking painting. It's worth £100,000 more than you. For God's sake, stand up straight and stop falling on my things.'

Sometimes, however, I happened to be on the right side of Charles's sharp wit, as on one occasion when Granada Television were launching UHF aerials for the new 625-lines system. Their marketing director, Mark Floyd, had asked for an ad, and his brief was that he didn't care what it looked like as long as it had the word 'free' in it three times. John Hegarty and Ron Collins were the creatives. Hegarty, who was the more pragmatic, produced something that said, 'Free UHF aerial, fitted free, free'. But when I took it to Mark, one of the three 'frees' had been left off, so I had to write it back on. When I brought it back, Hegarty showed it to Collins and Collins went absolutely berserk. He stormed into Charles's office yelling, 'That fucking account man has written on my layout!' But Charles simply replied, 'Who the hell do you think you are, Ron? Michaelfuckingangelo?'

Throughout all these times, the excitement far outweighed any moments of despair. Working for Charles Saatchi, you didn't have any time to sit and think about whether it was a good idea or not. He always used to say, 'Success creates success', and we did indeed breathe in the air of success. Something happened every day that was good. In terms of billings, we had flat periods, as any agency does, and I probably doubted myself a bit during those times. But basically, we had a phenomenal sense of vision and I probably became better at selling that vision than the brothers who'd had it in the first place – because that's what I do. I know how to talk to people; how to sell other people's ideas.

It took me a while to grasp that about myself, but as the agency grew, more and more creative people came in and produced campaigns, and I sold more and more of them. The only reason the creatives liked me was because I sold their work. If you failed to sell it, they didn't speak to you. We progressed neither through structure nor procedure – it was all about personality and drive and imagination. Yet at the same time, I learned the most extraordinary amount working with the Saatchis, not because they were teaching me, but just because of the experience – and thinking about what had happened, and why.

I was having a very enjoyable time, and that meant having a lot of fun. Long lunches, big nights, irrelevant expenses. Sometimes, I got through on a wing and a prayer. Sometimes we made it up on the spur of the moment. For example, we used to make up research results all the time. Of course, there were times when Maurice and I would spend hours working out how to pitch things and how to present them, but so much of it was about the art of communicating something. Sometimes, it all just seemed like common sense to me, but that was my skill – I had the knack of being pragmatic and plausible, which can be surprisingly lacking in our industry. The more success we had, the more we repeated the things that we had done before, albeit with a bit of embellishment, but only if we thought it necessary.

Despite the endless arguments, we made for a superbly well-balanced trio – especially in the earlier years when we would be together more. Charles brought the creative energy, Maurice brought his academic understanding, and I turned all that into some kind of practical dialogue that clients could understand and that inspired them to give us their accounts. At times, we were incredibly impressive. The joy of it was that we'd started with a blank sheet of paper, without any conventional structures. We didn't start with a media plan or a marketing plan or an account man's strategy document – we just made ads. Then we'd retro-fit the strategy and the research insight. It was all back to front, and that was much more satisfying and far less restrictive. When you actually haven't got the resources, it can be quite a challenge to hide this fact from the clients, or explain it away. But in the early days, that's what I had to do, and I was extremely adept at it. Which is why the brothers liked me – and needed me. I was skilful in taking a disadvantage and making it sound as though it was an indispensable part of our offering.

Charles hardly ever used to attend client presentations, but he would sit in the projection box and spy on what was happening. You could see him all the time and it was horrible – you'd have those eyes looking at you. On one occasion, we were presenting about 20 different ideas to Campbell's soups, and the guy said that our preferred route (which Charles had done) was too soft and that they needed something nearer to a hard sell. At which point, I heard this terrible noise and Charles stormed out of the projection box, into the room, and came right up to the guy's face. 'You want a hard sell, do you? Well here it is.' And he banged his fist on all the work, shouting 'Hard sell, hard sell, hard sell, soft sell, mid sell, hard sell – there you go, take your pick.' The Campbell's guy said, 'Yes, your work is all very well but I prefer Sam's work. [Sam was another creative.] I think he does much better work.' To which Charles replied, 'Well, for your information, *he* is a *she* so what the hell do you know about anything.'

Outside of work – although most aspects of my life at that time were actually just extensions of work – I was indulging myself. My first significant car had been a Fiat 124 Sport. It had belonged to Bob Gross, when I worked at Geers Gross, and I'd told him so many times how much I liked it that he finally gave it to me. I'd always had a penchant for fancy cars, although in the early years of Saatchi & Saatchi, we were bought Minis. Charles liked big, classic cars, so this made him very bad-tempered and grumpy – coming to work in a Mini and going home in a Mini. So Maurice and I met and agreed to buy him an old Rolls. He lent it to me to drive down to St Tropez, but on the way back to Calais I took a bend far too quickly and rolled the car over into a ditch. So I had to ring Charles up and say, 'I'm afraid, I've wrecked your car'. He never really forgave me for that, although he didn't particularly care about the car itself. He just went and got a new one. After that, I bought a whole stream of Ferraris and Maseratis, although mainly second-hand. I started off with a Maserati Indianapolis – a penis substitute, quite obviously, especially as it was metallic pink. I drove that for a while, then had an Aston Martin. Then when I had children, I switched to a more sensible Bentley. I used to collect my daughter from school in it, and she would describe it as a 'Loser Cruiser'. Now I don't give a damn. I hardly ever drive and I couldn't care less about it. It's one of those things you go through. It's just part of growing up.

By now, I was sharing a flat with Roy Warman, our media director – in St John's Wood and then Belsize Park. This was after I'd separated from my first wife Sue – which was unfortunately one of the horrible repercussions of my indulgent lifestyle. Roy and I used to be known at the 'odd couple' because we were so very different – he was an ex-football centre-forward. It was a true bachelor flat. He loved fishing and he used to keep the bait in the fridge, and every now and then you'd open the door and bluebottles would fly out because the eggs had hatched. He used to get takeaway pizzas from supermarkets and he'd cook them with the cellophane on. He never tidied up or did any house-keeping, so I would take all the dirty cutlery and crockery and put them in his bed. Then he'd come home drunk and just get into bed with them and sleep. Nothing made him tidy anything up or put anything away. I was neat and tidy and kept the place smart, and he permanently made it a pit. Nonetheless, it was easy sharing with Roy because we worked in the same place. He had a blue Porsche and I had a red Ferrari at the time. On one occasion, he parked his Porsche in the back of my Ferrari. He came in and said, 'Some fucker has driven into the back of your car.' I looked out the window and I said, 'Yes, it's you.'

People thought it was glamorous because we lived on our own and we could do exactly what we wanted, like adolescents. I got to know everybody in the industry – not least because life was a relentless sequence of social functions and miscellaneous escapades. At the time, the advertising industry was a community where everyone was making loads of money and having seemingly unlimited fun. Servicing clients wasn't only about producing advertising campaigns; it was about getting tickets for events, getting jobs for the clients' children, getting tables at restaurants that were full, arranging for top tailors to make their suits at a discount – all that stuff. I remember the beginning of the series of fights between Muhammad Ali and Sonny Liston. Charles had a friend who owned a cinema and we used to go there in the middle of the night and watch these fights live from the US. You had to do things that put you in the swing, so having seen the latest fight was essential to your being an essential part of what was going on. *Campaign* was so successful because it was the village paper and everybody read it to see what everyone was doing. And Saatchi & Saatchi dominated it. We were the pioneers of the industry – the Young Turks.

It's now quite a worry because I've gone from being a Young Turk to an old fart. Some agencies are still run or owned by or connected with the people who were the bright young things of their day – David Abbott, Martin Boase, John Hegarty. They were all starry-eyed romantic fantasists in the '70s, and

I see them from time to time. Some of them aren't as big as they used to be, whilst some of them are even more famous than they were then. Unfortunately, we've reached the point now where if you talk to a 30-year-old in the industry, they've often never heard of any of them. The role models have disappeared. David Abbott was undoubtedly the best copywriter in the business, but now if you meet copywriters and you say, 'What do you think about Abbott's copy?' they say, 'Who's Abbott?' The truth is that a lot of the fun has gone out of the business. Everyone now has to be so terribly serious and boring – which is why you get so much serious and boring advertising. The reason we did such exciting, exhilarating, entertaining stuff is because that's what the industry was.

At Saatchi & Saatchi, we were quickly building a newsworthy business – not just in terms of order-book or revenue, but in terms of building a community with a spirit and an attitude of mind and a relationship with each other that worked. Saatchi & Saatchi had the most extraordinary atmosphere in it, both collegiate and competitive. The traditional corporate structures and hierarchies weren't there, but there was a fiercely political competitive spirit – directed externally against all other rivals, but also from one employee to another. Yet everyone loved working there. Years later, when I was leaving, Charles said to me, 'The only thing I'll never forgive you for is making such a happy company, because we could never get anybody to leave.'

Despite all this, I didn't find it as satisfying as it might have been – at least up until the later work for the Conservatives. You don't really get into any depth of any kind in anything except the work, which is all you think about, analysing and understanding why people buy things and how to get them to respond to advertising messages to buy something different. All your friends are in the business, doing the same. You actually can't be bothered with the diminishing pool of friends outside the business, because there's nothing to talk about if they're not in advertising.

We were on a rattling train, but I was probably going too fast. I was married when I was 23 and had walked out of that marriage when I was 28. For a while, before sharing with Roy, I'd lived in hotels for about a year, including the Piccadilly and the Mayfair. I was the guy who would sit in the bar at 4 o'clock in the morning talking to the barman. I could get up at 8.00 a.m. and be in the office ten minutes later. Weekends were not relevant because you worked all the time. You pay a price for working this way. You're going at such a speed that people can't keep up with you, so you lose your friends – you lose touch, you're not there, you keep turning down the parties – because you are spending all your time on business or with clients. You live a minute-by-minute existence, with no pre-planning, never knowing what you're going to do. You can't agree to anything in case you get a better offer from a client. In terms of marriage, for a time, it had become easier on my own.

You become so involved in what you're doing that you lose track of how it fits any life plan. Your absolute focus is your business, and anything connected with business. You miss sleep and you eat at wrong times; you eat the wrong food, drink the wrong drink, and too much of it. I smoke like a train now and I smoked even more like a train then. Eventually, one day somebody will offer you something to help you get through the night and like a fool, you join in. You become a bad friend because you're not interested in other people's lives because you're so interested in your own. It makes you a racy boyfriend because you've got loads of things to attend, to which you can take girls and impress them. I once bought my girlfriend a Porsche for her birthday. She loved it all. It was very exciting. Eventually I married her. Virginia Hornbrook.

I'd met Virginia when she was working at Capital Radio for Hal James. So she was in pretty much a similar business to me and she had her own life. She went to all the right parties and got involved with people like David Briggs who invented *Who Wants to be a Millionaire?* and Simon Booker, who later married Kara Noble. So she had her own friends and had a similar lifestyle, with the drinking and partying, rushing everywhere, never having any sleep. We'd get home at 4.00 a.m., get up at 5.00 a.m. and be somewhere at 7.00 a.m. Everybody drove round with a change of clothes in the car – it was that kind of lifestyle. You didn't have a normal private life. I had moved away from all my early friends, who lived in North London and in Barnet and round there, who were estate agents and insurance reps. I was the boy in the glamorous trade and after a while you get bored with talking to them about it because they don't understand what you're talking about and they sit there open-mouthed and say, 'Surely you didn't do that?' 'Of course I did.'

When I was much younger, I had three ambitions. First, I wanted to be earning £1,000 per annum by the time I was 21, and £3,000 a year by the time I was 30, so I actually achieved that one fairly easily. The second ambition was to be moderately well known. Jeremy Paxman once asked me why I didn't go to university and I said that it was because the universities were full of people who smoked dope, wore duffel coats, had long hair, and were utterly boring, whereas I felt that I belonged to a more modern world of sharp suits and thin ties. And then I added, 'I wanted to be one of those people that, when you walk into a restaurant, people know is somebody.' And the third ambition was about my family. When I got married, I decided that I wanted my family to be able, if they so wanted, to live the life experience that I'd had – in the fast lane, travelling first class, in expensive cars, wearing expensive clothes, going to expensive places, paying silly prices for lunch and mad prices for a bottle of champagne. If they wanted to. My second wife Virginia was quite a few years younger than me, and I always assumed that I would go before her (I just didn't expect her to throw me out, beforehand) and I believed that I should try and leave my children with a cushion, because I knew how difficult it would be for them to get decent, satisfying jobs, however clever they were.

In terms of what the years at Saatchi & Saatchi brought me, I managed to achieve all of these ambitions – at least to some reasonable degree. But it was not what I'd regard, in retrospect, as a satisfying process. The brothers never allowed you to feel that way.

When Ivan Fallon wrote his book, *The Brothers*, I was given the original draft, and he had called me 'the only really nice person in their story'. But Charles had copy approval, and had things like that taken out. It's just the way they both are. Yet the time working with the brothers, building the agency from practically nothing into arguably the world's best creative shop, represented a once-in-a-lifetime opportunity. What's more, I knew this at the time, and they gave me something for which I will always be grateful. But during those early Saatchi years – with all the exhilaration and excitement and highs and lows – there was still something more that I wanted, and needed: something more meaningful than advertising alone could bring. Fortunately – and with the kind of seren-dipity that I have experienced on several occasions in my life – that something was just about to arrive on the scene.

5

The Calling

I've been interested in politics ever since childhood. It's amazing how many people claim a lack of interest in the subject, especially given the enormous influence that politicians have on your life. Which is why saying that you will abstain in an election is just plain nonsensical. And I've always been a Conservative, which belies the view that you start out more Left- and get more Right-wing as you get older. I'm not somebody who used to be Socialist and then grew up and became a Conservative. I've been a Conservative since the day I could say the word.

I was influenced by my grandfather, who raised me from the age of four (after my father had cleared off to South Africa, leaving my mother behind to fend for herself), and who was the Secretary of the Baltic Exchange – an incredibly proper man who believed in right and wrong and ran the huge trading exchange with a rod of iron. To me, he represented the basic tenets of Conservatism and what I think is the best way to live your life: that is, being self-reliant, taking responsibility for oneself and one's family, and being decent to others; things that are fundamental to creating a civil society. I believe that I have lived my life this way. I've paid my taxes and paid my bills. I've never tried to cheat anybody. I've done plenty of foolish or wrong things, because I'm not a saint, but I've always taken responsibility for them. That's why I don't like football: because it's the sport that has, to my mind, become all about who can cheat their way to a penalty or getting someone sent off without anyone ever taking responsibility.

In recent years, politicians have got themselves lumbered with a terrible reputation for lying and cheating. There is some justification in this, but I don't think that politics today is riddled with moral badness in the way that a lot of the public seem to think – although I do think that Blair and Campbell brought in a whole new level of cynicism. Politics is not all about lies and deceit. But neither was it ever about telling the whole truth and nothing but the truth.

I'm sure that's why, when we won the Conservative account in 1978, Saatchi & Saatchi were so suitable to the political environment in which we found ourselves. We knew how to play the right game.

Saatchi & Saatchi were pioneers in the rapidly advancing art of getting a simple message across to a lot of people. In a way not dissimilar to how we ran our commercial advertising, we would work out what we thought that the Conservative Party ought to say, and how to say it – then, if necessary, we retro-fitted the facts to get it approved. We could, in those days, find statistics that proved anything, no matter what it was. People think that nowadays we live in more duplicitous times, but with the availability of information, you actually have to be a lot more careful – in what you say, what you print, what you advertise – because anyone can check everything. For a dishonest politician, it's now a lot harder to tell lies.

The paradox, however, is that this has stopped politicians making a clear-cut case about anything. My view is that politicians are now probably more careful about what they say than they ever were, so they end up saying a lot less. They fear the noise of the counter-argument, which will be powerful and instant-aneous, because of Twitter and the like; so they approach any media interview with the intention of saying as little as possible – and certainly aiming to avoid revealing what they *personally* believe – with a carefully rehearsed platitude that allows for wriggle at some point in the future. But it just makes them seem vacuous or slippery, and makes people find politics so tiresome. Politicians daren't tell a lie, and daren't tell the truth – so no one says anything meaningful at all. It's a vicious circle.

As for actually getting anything done, that's the least of anyone's ambitions. Politicians certainly can't do – or daren't do – what they know should be done. Take taxation, for example. I have absolutely no doubt there should be no income tax, just a very high purchase tax, which would be the fairest and most progressive system. In such a system, those with the most money, buying the most goods, pay the most tax; people with the least amount of money, spending less, pay the least amount of tax. This would be better than taking a percentage of people's income, which penalises earning, and can act as a counter-incentive to work, as seen by the fact that countries with lower levels of income tax get higher revenues into their exchequer. Everybody knows this. Yet politicians would never try it because they doubt that they could convince the people of their argument and they think that the mere suggestion would lose them votes. Another reason is that, for politicians, it is counter-intuitive. Arguing that we need less taxation – and indeed, less politicking and less government – is alien to them. They can't help themselves. They want to tax; they want the huge bureaucracy giving bureaucrats something to do; they want to interfere. Margaret Thatcher's three principles were ever-greater liberty, free trade, and a small government, but even she failed to do a very good job of the last.

Politicians are risk-averse for all sorts of reasons, but the most avoidable one is that most of them are rotten communicators, which makes them unconfident at persuading people over an uncomfortable policy. Sure, they can make speeches and argue the toss. But they're not good at listening to, or understanding, real people – who they think are represented by the talking heads in focus groups or characters on television soaps. So if they have a radical idea that needs 'selling', chances are that they will fail – or not dare bother. Look at the mealy-mouthed way in which deficit reduction was sold to people. When it comes to the art of persuasion, these days, there is no one who has what it takes; no one with 'selling' skills in the right area; despite all the communication resources that are now at their disposal – which has probably made them even more lazy and inept.

Last night, I was sitting talking to three Cabinet Ministers, all of whom were banging on about how the party was not communicating its case and how the BBC has its Left-wing agenda. So if they know what the problem is, why can't they do something about it? But they don't know how to, or don't understand it, or have a tiny bit of knowledge, which is arguably worse than none at all – so they'll mismanage Twitter or Facebook and get embarrassed. On the same day I was having that conversation, all three parties had been found out trying to delete recent speeches from the internet. They stupidly never realised that they would be spotted doing that, and, further, that indelible copies remain available on archiving sites – so they haven't got rid of anything, just drawn attention to it.

Time was when people would enter politics because of their convictions, and they saw it as their prime task to turn those convictions into a reality – even if there was a risk of failure, or even of losing votes. You would get people from a variety of past experiences, some battle-hardened by past failure, but who would enter politics to make a real difference, and had a view on how to do so. Margaret was one such person: determined to succeed in her vision, but with plenty of bruises from what she had been through. She was an outsider – by sex, by upbringing, even in her largely non-collegiate approach – and, in many ways, she remained an outsider as far as many in the Tory Party were concerned. She was not one of them, and over time they increasingly let her know this. The phrase 'one of us' which she coined would have precious few to whom it could refer.

But I was one, and proud of it. In several senses of the expression, because, like her, I was an outsider. Not public school, not even university. Certainly not establishment. In fact, I've been an outsider all my life and I've liked being so. Sometimes it brings kudos; other times, you can use it as a defence mechanism. When I started working for the Conservative Party, I was an outsider because I came from the advertising industry – which, to politicians in the '70s, seemed like the rock music industry with added insanity. I understood *their* world far better than they understood mine. I had experience, not least because I'd actually been a Young Conservative and I'd gone to Conservative functions. My local MP had once been Reg Maudling, whom I knew reasonably well and for whom I'd canvassed. I'd read political books, read the newspapers, listened to *Today in Parliament*, and I'd been to Westminster and sat in the gallery. I went and saw people like Iain Macleod speak, and canvassed for him as well. That experience was, of course, limited – a sort of semi-casual acquaintanceship. But it was a world that intrigued and inspired me. I'd been in the same room as Churchill and Mountbatten. In fact, I'd already met Margaret Thatcher before she became a minister, when I was a member of the Hampstead Conservative Association. To me, at that time, politicians seemed like big people who made big decisions and had a big influence on things. Some were towering figures, the like of which we don't seem to see any more.

So politics was important to me, and I probably had a bit of a feel for it. In fact, I'd once been on the Elstree town council, and I took the canvassing very seriously. It taught me to put expectations to one side. It was a middle-class area, but a lot of couples were not married. You'd knock on the door and there would obviously be a bloke living in the house – sometimes he'd answer the door, or be standing there in the hallway. But if you asked if there was, say, a Mr Smith, they'd say, 'No, only Mrs Smith lives here.' You were too polite (or too scared) to say, 'Well, who are you?' or 'Who's that, then?' It stemmed from the war. Many widows didn't get married again; they just 'lived in sin', as it was called in those days. There was a Married Tax Allowance and the Married Woman's Property Act that meant a benefit if you could prove that you were married, but it could be impossible to say who was whom. There were blokes who lived with blokes and women who lived with women – whether they were in the same beds or not – and you suddenly realised, even in those days, that the conventional picture of suburban middle-class family life wasn't even the half of it.

The bloke living next door to me was a bricklayer. He had a physically enormous wife called Val, and when she got pregnant she went into hospital because of the complications of her weight. One day, he knocked on my door and asked me if I'd drive him to the hospital. The hospital food was, in his words, 'so crap' that he would take her a thermos flask full of cooked mince, which he gave to her as soon as we went in, and she gobbled up the whole thing with a spoon in front of me, which was not a good thing to witness, I have to say. I'd never seen anything like that before. That kind of lifestyle – and behaviour – came as a complete revelation to me. And yet it was – just about literally – right on my doorstep. I never sat in judgement, but I came to realise not only that there were extraordinary differences between people of different classes but that the conventional idea of a working-class man, a middle-class man and an upper-class man was not the whole picture. You'd find just as many upper-class people living in a hovel as you would working-class people living on a very expensive private estate – because some blue-collar workers could earn a lot of money by doing overtime. I learned about a lot of those things, and it struck me how completely irrelevant the detailed explanation of a political party's philosophy was. Westminster was a completely foreign land, and – in those days before television exposure or the internet – no one even had much idea of what happened there. Nor did they care much either.

Neither by upbringing nor philosophy was I a figure of the establishment. But as far as Saatchi & Saatchi were concerned, I most certainly was. To Charles and Maurice (and to the mainly Labour-voting staff), I was the loyal and traditional Conservative thinker on the payroll, and a template of an Anglican establishment male. By early 1978, I guess I had some of the trappings of respectability, with a house in Hampstead (which the agency had purchased for me) and a steady girlfriend. But I was in need of a new challenge, and elsewhere in London, circumstances were coming together than would supply that for me and change my life forever.

In 1978, Gordon Reece was the Tories' Director of Publicity. He'd been to the Republican Convention in the US and studied the American political approach, including Johnson and Nixon and then Carter versus Ford in 1976, and loved the glamour and salesmanship of it all – but without first realising that we had many more restrictions on us in the UK that would preclude us doing a lot of that stuff. (It was typical of Gordon to be a bit casual over a rather important point of detail.) However, he realised that the next election would be a televisual contest

– something that had been very successful in securing the recent Australian Liberal Party's victory – and that you had to decide early on what the central issue would be. He would also be behind the rather smart move, very early in her election campaign, of switching Margaret Thatcher from doing the heavyweight political programmes – given that there was a Left-wing bias from many of them, and that in one-on-one interviews, she could seem hostile or defensive – to some of the more populist shows, which had less of a hostile agenda. Once he had her on *Jim'll Fix It*. In those days (before people knew the grim reality), the host had a saint-like status, and commanded a huge Saturday evening audience. And, in 1978, as one of the first steps in that radical message modernisation process, Gordon decided that he needed an ad agency that was good at television, and that was up-and-coming and hungry for the fame, rather than comfortably established. Everyone he asked pointed him in the direction of Saatchi & Saatchi.

So he rang them up and went to meet Maurice, who didn't know what on earth it all meant; I'm pretty sure that Maurice voted Labour anyway, because that was what most of the Hampstead Jewish community did in those days – and Charles was just an intellectual anarchist. But Maurice could always sniff a commercial opportunity, and he spotted straight away that this account had the potential to bring the fame and connections that were part of their own Saatchi vision. Maurice rang me – I was away on holiday in Barbados at the time – not least because he knew that I was *the* Conservative on the payroll. I lived from time to time in Norfolk and, as far as Maurice was concerned, that's where Conservatives live (and which was completely different from the Jewish community in Hampstead Lane where Maurice lived); I spoke received pronunciation (almost), I had table manners, I knew some grand people … In the brothers' eyes, I was truly the face of the Conservative establishment.

In fact, Maurice used to check matters of behaviour and etiquette with me. When he had breakfast with the old Lord Rothermere, for example, he asked me where he should take him, and I told him to go to the Berkeley in Knightsbridge. He actually hired a Rolls Royce to take him there, which was funny, because Lord Rothermere was never going to see it – and, in the event, it was better that he didn't, because Maurice went bling and ordered a white one, rather than a black one. I'm not sure that matters went that well inside actually, because we later heard that when they sat down in the breakfast room the waiter came across and said, 'Would you like a croissant, my Lord?' Lord Rothermere took offence at this and called the manager. 'That chap came out and offered me a croissant', he said. 'If I want a croissant, I'll go to Paris. This is England. Bring me some eggs and bacon!' I think this was Maurice's earliest introduction to aristocratic eccentricity, of which he had no understanding in those days. Maurice was, however, very good at picking things up and making useful friends – even people who were so different, like Lord Rothermere. Maurice would check the detail with me: 'Tim, which suit?' 'Tim, what's the best restaurant?' I didn't know much more than he did, but I just used to make it up or try to remember what I thought I'd heard people say. The truth was that I was not much more clued-up than he was.

After the Gordon Reece enquiry, Maurice rang me up and asked what I thought, and I told him not to take the account, because, I felt, it would disrupt the whole agency – as it had done when I had been working at Colman Prentis when they had handled part of the Tory account. But by the time I came home, they had just ignored me – as they often did – and had signed the account. My reaction was to say, 'Well, fuck you', and wonder why they'd asked my advice in the first place. But my view changed completely when I first went to see Gordon.

Gordon Reece looked a bit like Ronnie Corbett; he'd done National Service, so there was a bit of *Carry on Sergeant* in his DNA. He smoked huge cigars, drank unbelievably expensive champagne, and everyone described him as dapper – indeed, he was always immaculately dressed, with crisp shirts and shoes that he permanently kept so shiny that you could see street furniture reflected in them as he walked. He loved the whole media world, and fitted in perfectly. He'd read Law at Cambridge, but decided that there would be more money as a journalist. Then he moved into television, doing *This is Your Life*, *Emergency Ward 10* and various religious programmes. He was a very devout Catholic – sometimes he would go to Mass several times in one day because he liked it so much – and had six children from his marriage. His wife was an Anglican who used to debate his Catholicism with him, much to his annoyance. He would say, 'We don't spend all night fucking; we spend all night arguing about the difference between Catholicism and Anglicanism.' It really annoyed him. He loved all the editors and of course, the great influence in everything was David English of the *Daily Mail* – who was a close friend – and Larry Lamb from the *Sun*. Gordon was a man of great principle, and when life made him counter his principles – which happened when he got divorced – it caused him terrible upset.

He met Margaret when she was the Opposition Education Secretary and he was commissioned as a freelancer to produce a Party Political Broadcast. He saw her as, like him, a person of unimpeachable principle and he was magnetised by it. He became absolutely devoted to her, and, in time, helping her to be successful was all that mattered. During her leadership campaign prior to the second ballot (with Willie Whitelaw the favourite), Gordon did a film of her washing the dishes, which they put on *World in Action*, and it was so successful that Whitelaw's people thought they might have to make one with him doing the same, possibly wearing a pinafore, which would have been quite a sight.

After she had won the leadership, Margaret made him her full-time adviser. He set to work straight away, on her image and especially how she came over on television – which when she first really came into the public eye seemed very shrill and bossy. That was when he had the hairstyle and the wardrobe altered, and took her for some vocal coaching with Sir Laurence Olivier, which was when she developed the husky thing.

When I met Gordon, just after Saatchi & Saatchi had been appointed, I absolutely loved him. We struck up a wonderful conversation. We were both on the same page: Conservative, traditionalist, with a respect for the great national institutions. Truth be known, we both had a soft spot for the flamboyant lifestyle – drinking fine champagne, smoking great cigars, going to very expensive restaurants. But we also understood our role as tradesmen and I don't think we ever got above ourselves. Indeed, the Party came to treat us with suspicion and envy in synch with Margaret treating us as her confidants. Gordon once said to me, 'You will never be invited by any cabinet Tory to their home for dinner, because they will always regard you as a tradesman. Neither you nor I will ever be asked.' He was absolutely right; nobody ever did. With two exceptions: Kenneth Baker and Margaret – because they didn't see people in that way, and didn't treat people like that.

The Chairman of the Party at that time was Peter (Lord) Thorneycroft, with Janet Young and John King (of BA fame) as his deputies. It was Gordon who had sold to him the idea of using Saatchi & Saatchi, and he immediately liked Maurice and me; he also liked David Welch with his paratrooper's tie (who would salute and call him 'Sir'), and he liked adverts. Peter used to say to me, 'Oooh, it's like going into a sweet shop. I used to go in with my dad and he'd point to all the glass jars on the top shelf and ask me to choose one, but I wanted them *all*. You come in here to your agency with all these ideas and I want them all – but I can't afford them all. It's like the sweet shop again.' He liked me because he regarded me as a proper Conservative.

Margaret had created a new career for him – brought him back from the dead, after he'd been thrown out along with Selwyn Lloyd during the night of the long knives when they got rid of half of the Cabinet. He had actually been Chancellor in 1957 under Macmillan. He adored Margaret and he loved Gordon because he saw Gordon as stylish. Thorneycroft was an old-fashioned Etonian Tory who spoke like an aristocrat (which he wasn't); he would talk about 'huntin' and 'shootin' and 'fishin' without sounding the 'g', which you don't if you're an aristocrat. He'd once been thrown out of the House of Commons for calling someone a liar, after he'd been accused of owing half of Scotland. Once we knew that story, we made him a T-shirt which said, 'I'm not an aristocrat. I own most of Scotland.' He absolutely adored that T-shirt, and used to wear it to the meetings with us. He'd put it on over the top of his waistcoat and shirt.

Lady Young was in charge of the money, and didn't at all like the idea of it being spent on us – especially Gordon and me. She had a very parsimonious approach when it came to money – she once vetoed a swimming pool in her constituency, saying that people could always swim in the river. She thought that we were flash and superficial and probably an unnecessary expense – and she was never happy at Gordon's spending, including his penchant for champagne and eating at his club. Famously, when she complained about his expenses, Alistair McAlpine, the treasurer, said, 'You don't understand, Janet. As you have to run your car on petrol, so you have to run Gordon on champagne.' I think this was emblematic of the change in the way the Party was now having to come to terms with the way the world was changing. And Margaret was the most obvious symbol of that change. As I found when I went to see her.

6

Iron Lady

Although I had met Margaret Thatcher once, very briefly (when I was a counsellor), my first meeting as the newly appointed Saatchi & Saatchi's account man was when Gordon took me in to be introduced to her in the Leader of the Opposition's room in the House of Commons. I was greeted first by Airey Neave, who was head of her private office and who had been an incredibly loyal adviser during her leadership campaign. He was a rather shambolic figure (he often wore a crumpled Columbo raincoat) who had an impenetrable Irish accent which meant you couldn't make out a word that he was saying. He led the way into an anteroom where the two secretaries were sitting typing. In time, I would get to know them well: one was Alison Ward, who later married Lord Wakeham, and the other was Caroline Stephens, who went on to marry Lord Ryder. One of them (I can't remember which) called me the 'man from Starsky and Hutch' and I don't think it was intended as a compliment. When Gordon arrived we went in, and Thatcher was there at her desk, head down, writing something. All she said was, 'Sit down.' There was a brown velvet armchair and a brown velvet sofa, so I plonked myself down in the middle of the long sofa, where there was no arm support, so I just floated there looking like a complete prat.

She said, 'What's your favourite poem?' and I said '"If", by Kipling'. She frowned at me really suspiciously, and said 'Who told you?' I said, 'Nobody told me. It's my favourite poem.' Then she said, 'What's your favourite speech?' and I said 'Abraham Lincoln's State of the Nation', and I quoted him. '"I fail to see how making the rich poor makes the poor rich."' 'Who told you?' she said. 'Nobody. They're my favourites.' She said, 'Well, we're going to get on.' Then she said, 'I want you to understand three things. First, politicians have very, very large toes and very large fingers, and it's easy to tread on them. I have neither. You will always tell me the truth, however painful you may think it might be to me. Secondly, if you have any tricks that will get me elected, don't use them. Because if the people don't want me, it won't work. And finally, you will get a lot of abuse for working for me. I hope you're a big boy.' I said, 'I hope so too.' She said, 'Right. Well, we'll get on then. Take him out, Gordon.' And, at that, we got up and fled.

Now can you imagine any modern politician saying that second point and meaning it? The answer is no, because now they actually do want the bloke with the box of tricks. They want the Wizard of Oz. They want David Axelrod and Alastair Campbell and they want the people who can fiddle around and confuse the audience and publish dodgy dossiers and set up attack dogs and do all those things. That was not how we worked. And that was not the way she wanted us to work. She saw it in terms of a battle between Right and Left, but also a choice of right or wrong – which meant that ambition did not trump honour.

She was completely dedicated to what she saw as 'proper' Conservative thinking and was totally opposed to state control, state management, the state telling you how to live your life, what to do with your money, any of those things; they were all wrong in her eyes. They weren't just slightly wrong. They could not be half-implemented. They were all unequivocally wrong. And wrong not just in the political sense, but also in that she regarded them – as I do – as intrinsically evil. Our job was to demonstrate that to the voters.

I believe that getting people to realise the inherent failure in Socialism was her proudest achievement. And it's easy to forget that she converted Labour into having to accept market dynamics, which was what Blair knew he had to do to get the Party back into power – in due course to be unpicked by Brown and his successors.

There are all sorts of theories about how she had won the 1975 Leadership Election – and whether it was by default because of weaknesses in the other candidates. The inadequacy of the opposition – Heath, Whitelaw, et al. – was obviously part of it, but it was also because Airey Neave had conducted a superb campaign. Airey Middleton Sheffield Neave MP, DSO, OBE, MC, TD – shabby raincoat and accent and all – was a figure that the Tories adored: an Irish ex-Eton, ex-Oxford, ex-Colditz prisoner, war hero, on the union side of the Irish political argument, and brilliant in the corridors and in the tea rooms. He'd go round and chat, and would identify exactly who could vote, who was pissed off with Heath, who'd missed out on a job, who'd been demoted, who hadn't got their own way, who was in trouble, and so on – and he would slowly but surely coax people onside. A great character whose life was soon to encounter tragedy.

Neave had suffered a heart attack in 1959, and it was said that when Ted Heath heard this, he told him sniffily, 'Well, that's the end of your career.'

Neave never quite forgot that remark, which had added extra piquancy to the leadership campaign. When he wasn't being churlish, I'm not sure Heath spoke to anyone. Heath seemed to dislike all the MPs, he loathed the Party, he loathed government, and seemed to loathe everything except sailing and classical music. He mellowed a bit in his later years, but for most of the time he was in a state of permanent angst.

At the time, the climate as regards people's sexuality was very different. The Montague case in 1954 had begun a shift in public opinion, so that by 1967 consensual gay sex had been legalised. But it was still next to impossible for a publicly accountable figure to be upfront about it. Heath's problem was that he didn't fit in. And television was not kind to him either, even before the Mike Yarwood thing. The Tory Grandees had chosen him as the new meritocratic middle-class image for the Tory Party, hopefully as a foil to the artisan Wilson, but the latter was much craftier and more quick-thinking.

By the time Margaret came along, Heath had become a grim parody of himself, and she won the leadership by a mile. Compared to Heath, she was dynamic, exciting and aggressive. The Party had never come across anybody like that before, let alone a woman, and they certainly didn't know what to make of her. But they needed someone to save them from Heath. She won the first ballot by 11 votes which forced Heath to resign, but it was not a sufficient margin for her to assume command. However, by then she had momentum, and she easily won the second ballot against Willie Whitelaw, while the other candidates – Geoffrey Howe, Jim Prior and John Peyton – were never going to do anything.

In the early exchanges across the Debating Chamber, Callaghan talked down to her as though she were just a silly little woman. At first it was tough going for her, and many in the Party doubted her abilities. But over time, that started to work against Callaghan. He patronised everybody and he played everything down, and in the end, that would be his downfall. It was as though he couldn't take anything seriously, no matter how bad things were.

However, when she was asked by the BBC to do a television debate with Callaghan and Thorpe, Gordon and I vetoed it without telling her. Gordon's fear was that she would tear Callaghan apart, and people would see her as an arrogant bitch being disrespectful towards this jolly nice older avuncular figure. It would also give disproportionate airtime to the Liberals, just as happened with Nick Clegg in the 2010 election. (And now, they keep thinking about debating with Farage. It's amazing how politicians make a mistake and repeat it over and over again.) The BBC then sent a second request, which she saw before we could get to it, and worked out that we'd made a decision on her behalf. She was livid. She brought Gordon and me into her office in Flood Street and fired us both on the spot. We were literally shown the door – thrown out. Although on the way, Denis, who had had a few gins and had seen all this before, just said to us, 'Don't worry. She'll be fine in the morning!'

Gordon wept all night. We sat up in his flat, drinking champagne, with him just crying, 'Oh, she's never going to speak to me ever again.' Eventually he fell asleep. Next day, we woke to a phone call from Margaret's office, telling us to get back round to Flood Street. I got him up, made him put on a clean shirt and we went straight back and – exactly as Denis had predicted – she didn't mention a word about it: like it had never happened. All she said was, 'Hello. Let's get on with the work.'

That's how she was. She had no time for any kind of emotional stuff getting in the way of what she felt she had to achieve. She could be brutal, make snap personal judgements, and behave like the worst kind of bully, but, so often, this was the flip side of her determination to grasp the big picture. And in that sense she was absolutely fabulous. It is the kind of thing that comes with greatness. And possibly as part of the same set of characteristics, so many aspects of 'personal' interaction were just of little concern to her. She found women and feminine small-talk utterly tiresome. 'How boring', she would say. 'They're going to ask me about my hair and my dress and talk to me about hem length and pregnancy and knitting.' Ultimately, she wasn't really interested in anything other than politics, was intolerant of any points of view that differed from her own, and took a fairly dim view of the people who dared hold them.

You loved her or hated her. You thought everything about her was fantastic and enchanting – or you saw everything about her as some kind of vicious personality thing or class thing and despised her; the irony being that there was absolutely nothing upper-class or elitist or pretentious about her at all. The voice never did her any favours, but she hadn't started out from Grantham speaking in that way; she'd taught herself the cod-RP whilst she was at Oxford and done a rotten job.

She had one or two very loyal women – but they were not friends as such: like Janet Young, with whom she got on quite well, though she thought her a bit of a prude. Then there was Dame Guinevere Tilney, her unpaid wardrobe mistress – married to Sir John Tilney who was an Admiral, whom Denis had bumped into somewhere. Guinevere chose Margaret's clothes, which is why, in the early days, she looked like a sort of Victorian remnant, because that's how Guinevere dressed. Guinevere must have been 70 and Margaret was about 50, so you had this 20-year difference – it was hopeless. Margaret disliked fuss being made over image issues and, in those early years, she simply wasn't too bothered about how photogenic she was, in a way that would seem unprofessional these days. Take the hair. It obviously had to be immaculate all the time. But being Margaret, she did it with Carmen rollers: she saw that as sensible, quicker, easier, cheaper, and her secretaries could do it – so they were all shown how to do Carmen rollers. On image issues, Gordon and I could only get round her one item at a time.

In truth, she could be a very straightforward person, even when surrounded by security and the rest of it. One time, she decided she would visit the Saatchi & Saatchi offices in Charlotte Street. Everyone except Charles came down to meet her. I greeted her as the car drew up. Once inside, she went up to each and every person and said to each one, 'Hello, I'm Margaret Thatcher.' When she finally got to the lift, there was a chap standing there waiting. She said, 'Hello I'm Margaret Thatcher, what do you do?' He said, 'I'm the sales rep for *Titbits*', and she said, 'What's *Titbits*?' I think he just told her that it was a weekly newspaper, without explaining that the title was a few tits and bits more literal than she realised.

She loved the atmosphere of the agency, she liked both Maurice and me and she quite liked the creative people – because to her, they were exotic and funny; they dressed oddly, they had long hair, they were all a bit weird, like squawky jungle birds in an aviary. And she quite liked David Welch as the officer and gentleman in the mix. Maurice meanwhile was an expert on economics, so we endlessly talked about how you can't spend more than you earn – he knew all the macro-economic lingo, so that went down very well with Margaret. Of course, she had no sense of humour, but she liked being made to laugh; perhaps she so liked laughing because it was so hard a thing for her. Of all the advisers, Gordon and I just knew how to make her laugh, which was less about being ironical or using parody, and much more about just smiling and being colourful. She sometimes described us as the 'laughing boys' (a term that originated from one day when we turned up and Margaret, Denis, Mark and Carol were all sulking after a four-way family row, which we knew nothing about when we arrived in the jokiest of moods) – in many senses of the expression, that's what we were and that's what she often needed amidst all the frustration, grief and hatred she had to endure.

But the person who probably made her laugh the most was actually Ronnie Millar, her speechwriter. He adored her too. Originally a playwright, he was a very theatrical character, living with his mother, who had been a chorus girl. He was gay, but not overtly so. Margaret would always say about him, 'You must be careful with Ronnie, dear, because he's very sensitive.' He'd travelled around with Noel Coward, and when it came to the speeches, Ronnie saw his role as expressing Margaret's points of view in a partly theatrical way (which could cause problems, as you can imagine) and partly in a more commonplace fashion – in the same way that he would write plays that were both intelligent to clever people and intelligible to ordinary folk. He once spent ages trying to get her to deliver one particular line about people being 'parents and children of the nuclear generation' and she eventually got so fed up, she said, 'The trouble with you, Ronnie, is that you think I'm Anna Neagle.' The funny thing was that he did. He would write monologues for her picturing in his mind a grande dame in front of a packed West End theatre hall. It was Ronnie who had written the speech where she compared James Callaghan (returning from the Commonwealth Heads Conference) to Moses, with the invocation: 'Keep taking the tablets.' And she said to him, 'Ronnie, nobody calls them tablets any more. We'll say, "Keep taking the Pill".' She neither understood what Ronnie wanted her to say, nor the unintended implications of her own alternative. She just didn't naturally do humour. This made it next to impossible for her to deliver funny lines – such as when she tried to mirror the John Cleese dead parrot sketch – where she had not the slightest understanding of the joke nor the inflexions needed to deliver it. None of this, however, prevented her from loving being made to laugh or being entertained.

There was another story about her use of the term 'pussy', which she had started to use about people who couldn't organise things. We all had this fear that she had a mind to say it (publicly) about Jim Callaghan: 'The trouble with Mr Callaghan is he couldn't even organise pussy.' Some of her ministers, jealous of my popularity with her, set me up, by asking me, in front of her, if there wasn't some phrase that I didn't want her to use on television? Of course, that got her to ask me, 'What's wrong with "Pussy" dear? What do you think it means?' So I was made to look a fool trying to explain to her what it meant. It was a piece of humiliation for me. But on the other hand, in a way, it cemented our relationship, because I was bold enough to tell her. The Shadow Cabinet people liked it because I got my comeuppance, but, in the event, it just reinforced her opinion of them as fat, comfortable, complacent men who weren't used to having a woman taking charge and who were trying to make her out as naïve and to ridicule her adviser.

As we came into the summer of 1978 – still in opposition, and before any election had been called – we were really motoring along. The strategy was to emphasise dissatisfaction with the incumbent Labour administration and thus to get the electorate to crave a modern Conservative alternative. We had no idea when the election would be, but we were on a permanent war footing. Most people were dubious about whether it would be called for the autumn because historically, the incumbents seem to lose elections held then. But it was always possible; more so as the industrial landscape of the UK was in a terrible state.

We wanted to avoid any debates on health, education, and social services, which were Labour strengths. Above all, we wanted to talk about the quality of our leader, compared to Uncle Jim Callaghan, who could be portrayed as old, boring, patronising, and without personality. That level of personalising of the campaign was quite controversial (and Margaret was never wholly certain about it). For all his faults, Callaghan had a residual popularity and, in the early days, she came off a good second best in the Commons debates. Not least because behind her she had a Party that was divided and not convinced about who they'd chosen to lead them. ('We're stuck with her now', as Nicholas Fairbairn would not altogether helpfully say.) Many at the time thought that we should do the opposite of a personal campaign and neither attack Callaghan directly nor indeed mention Margaret – especially as some people couldn't accept the idea of a woman PM. The Party still tended to defer to its origins in the upper classes and the managerial classes and ownership classes. Until the late 1950s or early 1960s, it was indeed completely out of touch with the working man. Heath had somehow got elected in 1970, very narrowly, and people in the Party had even thought that he was quite a novel idea, being a grammar school boy, not a toff. Margaret was grammar school stock, although her advantage over Heath was that she was married with children. She, at least, had a semblance of a normal family background.

So our main strategy was to make people more and more fed up with the current situation. The clever bit in that was that the longer Callaghan went on, the more dissatisfaction we could leverage. In the event, we believed that Callaghan had made a terrible mistake by not calling the election for October, when, we thought, he might have scraped home. But on 7 September 1978, Callaghan had blinked. Maybe it was because of our advertising; or maybe he thought the delay would bring an economic upturn. But his decision gave us six more months to continue our attrition, and produce even better work. We'd already got five Party Political Broadcasts (PPBs) in the can and, with more time, we were now able to do four new ones for the campaign. By the time he lost a vote of no confidence in the late spring of 1979, he was coming to the election as a beaten man.

Our target was very wide: the younger, first-time voters without blind affiliation; the skilled C1 and C2 manual workers, who were fed up with industrial stagnation; and female voters who had tended in the past to vote Labour, but who were now similarly fed up. To put it another way, we wanted *Mail* readers, but we also needed *Sun* readers; the broadsheets would look after themselves. After what he'd seen in the US, Gordon was convinced that we could sway these groups with an emotive campaign, rather than just hit them with cold and rational arguments on economic policy or industrial legislation. And creating single-minded, impressionistic advertising was stock-in-trade for us at Saatchi & Saatchi.

The first time that Margaret really seemed to be moving the polls was in April 1978, when she delivered a speech on immigration. It wasn't a 'Rivers of blood', but her standard Tory fare of British jobs for the British shifted her into a four-point lead. I was commissioning market research, and if we didn't have the right data, we'd just make it up. It was my job to brief some particular subjects, get them verified by the Conservative Research Department, and then get them turned into ads by the creatives and sell the ads.

Most of that creative work was overseen by Charles, invisibly, and Jeremy Sinclair, very visibly. Unlike every other creative I've ever known, who reads the *Sun* or *Mirror*, Jeremy read the *Financial Times*, looking at his share prices and checking the stock market. Chris Patten was the Conservatives' Head of Research, whose job it was to approve advertising ideas, which he found next to impossible. He would tell us that we couldn't say something because it was not true, which, in his view, seemed to apply to everything we tried to say. We would come back and tell him that 'we're not saying it's true; we're saying it *could* be true.' You could argue that we were always trying to stretch the truth, but then everybody was at that time. We came from an industry that said 'Tide Washes Whiter' – always depending on which water you used, what washing machine, etc. What we did was write ads that made the sort of claims that we'd heard in conversation – things that we would like to say. So we tried to say them. Patten couldn't cope with it all, and he certainly didn't like me. He thought I was a Flash Harry. We'd go to the Café Royal: Chris Patten, Larry Lamb, Gordon and I, and we would all be wanting to talk about something different, like a dysfunctional married quartet. Gordon would be talking about the problems with Catholicism and the Pope; I'd be talking about the latest record release and what it meant to the younger audiences; Larry would be talking about the working-class supporting the Conservative Party; and Chris Patten would just sit there, flummoxed.

As part of our plan to make it easier to get things through, we tried to befriend all the ministers. Typical advertising smarm tactics obviously; that was my job as an agency account man. For example, when there was a question on law and order I had to go and supervise a meeting with Willie Whitelaw, as Home Secretary, and ask him what the policy actually was on that brief. He answered something like, 'Ah, glad you asked. What a good question, yes. Our policy on law and order is short sharp sentences.' So, like a good account man, I asked, 'What does that mean?' Angus Maude, who was then the Deputy Home Secretary, took his long cigarette holder out of his mouth and said – after a dramatic pause – 'Hanging!' But you could never anticipate what they might say: in truth, at different times, different people would each say something completely different.

It was often very hard to take it all seriously. The only consolation, sometimes, was that the Labour opposition were, we knew, in a far less organised state than we were. In the run-up to the election, there were weeks when we were convinced that we couldn't lose – we didn't believe that anybody with a brain could possibly vote Labour. When we met people who did, it just confirmed our belief, because they actually did seem stupid, or they voted Labour because their dad always had done. Meanwhile you had to remember, when you met a Tory, that the opposition was not always Labour. Some parliamentary candidates were being done in by the Liberal Democrats, so we had to go through different conversations depending on local circumstances. In this respect, we were just brilliant at tailoring our conversations to our audience, and it worked, mainly because they'd never met any people like us. It's all commonplace nowadays, but back then, they had never seen anybody produce ideas and pictures and storyboards – and they were amazed. It was like introducing jewellery and mirrors to jungle natives. And then came our first Party Political Broadcast – which was a triumph.

Our line was 'Britain is going backwards'. It featured people walking on Waterloo Bridge, Stephenson's first locomotive, the Comet jetliner, people climbing Everest, and so on, with the film running in reverse. The voiceover said, 'Backwards or forwards. We can't go on as we are.' Then we cut to Michael Heseltine, who said that, while people often vote the way they've always done, it was now no longer like that. We then showed a very simplistic economic circle, running from a grocer (just like Ronnie Barker in the brown overall) to a housewife (who looked exactly like a suburban housewife) to a husband (like a banker) and then there were the three children. It said something like, 'If I charge more, she has to ask him for more, and I might have to ask him for more, and if I ask him for more, that's not going to do the economy any good'.

You can imagine us showing this to Geoffrey Howe, who just said, 'You can't describe economics like that'. So I returned with a piece of paper that Maurice had written, which said, 'We're affecting the demand side of the economy as opposed to the command side of it. We'll do a subsequent film that will show the command side of it.' They couldn't do anything else but agree with us because we had all the right words. There was something both hilarious and clever about the way we, the agency, tried to bamboozle them with creativity and panache – and we succeeded. Because they knew we were good.

We all knew about the incredibly memorable 'Girl on the Hill' film (sometimes called 'Daisy') that Lyndon Johnson had used in his victorious 1964 Democratic campaign attacking Barry Goldwater, produced by Bill Bernbach, which had started with a small child picking petals from one to ten, followed by a ten-to-one countdown ending with a nuclear mushroom cloud. That ad was only aired once, but became our template for much of the work we were trying to produce: strong imagery, high emotion and a simple dramatization of the key political issue. If, like the Johnson ad, it also generated controversy, providing we were in control of that, so much the better. The best example of this is probably the most famous political poster of all time: 'Labour isn't working'.

We were sent to present a stack of potential ideas that had been filtered by Jeremy and then by Charles. My job was to sell them in, and, at the very least, get one accepted. Or, as Charles would say, 'Don't come back if you don't.' The actual 'Labour isn't working' idea came from Andy Rutherford, and I know there is a story – true or not – about him finding it rejected, and sneaking it back into the art-bag just before we left. Howsoever it got there, as soon as Margaret set eyes on it, she said, 'What's so clever about that?' and I told her that it was a double entendre. 'Really,' she said, with great irony. 'Tell me, then, Tim, what that double entendre is that I'm not seeing?' So I said, 'Well you know, it means there's high unemployment and at the same time that the Labour government isn't functioning …' She then said, rather sarcastically, 'I'm sure that's very clever,' as if she still didn't get how it worked. I took a pasting from her, which I knew always meant that she was about to say she liked it. In fact, as soon as the meeting was over, she said to me that she thought it was 'Wonderful'.

That wasn't the end of it though. Shortly afterwards, we were summoned back to Central Office and Peter Thorneycroft told us that there were doubts coming up, and that she was having cold feet about it. This time, when we met her, she came out straight away and asked why the first word on the poster was 'Labour' and whether we really thought it a good idea to put our opponents' name in the headline. Given her earlier positivity, I was completely unprepared for that, so I burbled some reassuring rubbish about it being bang on our dissatisfaction strategy, and that it would be all right. What you learn about politicians is that they have to go through a lot of hoops. She liked it and wanted to do it, but somebody else had told her that they didn't. So now she had to deal with the objection, which she could do by looking stubborn and saying, 'I'm doing it regardless of what you think', and give herself a heap of angst. Or she could say, 'I've gone back to the advertising agency with your concerns, etc., etc.' Truthfully, my answers didn't matter, as long as she could go back and claim that it had been confirmed as being fine. And so it was that the photo-shoot was set up, the artwork completed, and in August 1978, the poster went up on a mere 20 sites across the country.

Denis Healey, who at the time was the Chancellor, went ballistic – which was his first mistake, as it made him appear to be panicking. He said that we were selling politics like soap-powder and that it was phoney because we'd used Saatchi & Saatchi employees. He wasn't quite right, because they were actually Young Conservatives gathered together by Michael Portillo (who I think might be one of the people queuing in the picture), but that point was lost anyway. Healey had instantly made matters worse for his Party: he generated a huge news story and, from a spend of around £50,000, we ended up with a level of free media coverage that would normally have cost us millions. I can understand how it might be offensive having unemployed people portrayed by stand-ins, and these days you'd probably make sure they really were unemployed. But in the end, our casting corner-cutting would not matter. The ad captured the imagination of the media, who rightly thought that it was really smart. With the media story growing by the day, soon everyone in the country knew of the poster. Plus, I think it did a number of things that people underestimate.

For a start, it was quite witty, and at the time most political advertising was unbelievably boring and devoid of humour. And it was so beautifully laid out – visually, a very striking advertisement. Few people realise how much those creative craft skills transform the degree of impact that something has, and as it was a big and bold poster, it meant that when the media saw it, it wasn't physically a little thing – it was a big thing. When the controversy hit, the newspaper editors were forced to physically go and look at a 48-sheet poster in situ, on a hoarding – these being pre-internet days – where it really hit home. Everyone saw through Healey's rage, and understood that it was all about him not liking the poster because it was so effective and truthful. And we were clever enough to let the controversy run and run. We never revealed who the people in the photograph really were, and that just kept the controversy alive, to our advantage.

That ad did feel like it represented a turning point of sorts. However, there was always a feeling that Callaghan might pull it off when push came to Election Day shove. I think that was our insecurity up until the second week in 1979, when his relaxed approach really did catch him out. On 10 January, Callaghan had been to a summit in Guadeloupe, whilst the lorry drivers were on strike and all manner of industrial chaos was taking place back home in the UK. Unlike Margaret, who could get by on very little sleep, Callaghan was famous for how much sleep he needed – you never kept him up late, and you never saw him early in the morning, and he used to sleep on planes. So when they landed at Heathrow, he was ill-prepared and cavalier as was often the case. Of course, the press were lying in wait, and when he came to the top of the aircraft steps, he just did what he often did, which was to do the 'Sunny Jim' bit about his swimming in the Caribbean. Then, to make matters worse, he started talking to an *Evening Standard* reporter about how other people around the world did not actually have a view of Britain in 'mounting chaos' – by implication, wondering what all the fuss was about. Gordon Reece and I didn't really think there was much of a story at first, but when we discussed it with Larry Lamb, the editor of the *Sun*, we added a bit of dramatic licence, and gave him the line – even though Callaghan had never actually said it – 'Crisis? What crisis?' And that's what Larry used.

But Callaghan was a canny and accomplished politician, and he could convey a degree of warmth and security when he was in front of the camera. By contrast, we had to keep Margaret away from cameras, unless we had complete control over the actual image that was being projected, as she could unintentionally rub people up the wrong way. There was never any conscious conversation or conscious strategy planning about this. But like the Party itself, the public needed time and help in getting used to the presence of a woman leader – and her character. Her strength, of course, was that she was everything that Callaghan was not: she could seem clear, visionary and determined. So after Callaghan's disastrous bout of apparent complacency, we knew that we had an opportunity, in the next PPB, to be the foil. The plan was to talk of urgency and unity – in the national interest. At first, Margaret thought that this was a soft option, and that she ought to be going directly for Callaghan's throat in an aggressive confrontational attack. But Peter Thorneycroft and I talked her out of that. 'Margaret. It's not you being any weaker. It's just you putting your country before petty Party politics.' And she liked that.

She wanted it filmed in the Leader of the Opposition's office in Westminster, and kept insisting on bunches of flowers in the background. Ronnie Millar tried to get rid of them, as he rightly thought it was completely out of character with the subject of crisis and spirit of determination, but oddly, she was having none of it. So I told Ronnie to stop arguing with her and I just told the camera people that, after a couple of minutes, they should cut in close, taking the flowers out of frame – and she'd be none the wiser.

There were some great lines in that PPB – written by Ronnie and Chris Patten. 'This is no time to put party before country. I start from there.' Those words were quite similar to those that Thorneycroft and I had used to sell the idea to her in the first place. 'In the national interest,' she said in the broadcast, 'surely government and opposition should make common cause on this one issue.' She was talking directly to camera for about ten minutes and suddenly, people in their homes were seeing a stateswoman and potential national leader. The sentiment was, of course, spot on, but it was also a great example of an emotional pitch, Margaret coming over as the 'wise female' trying to be reasonable and sort things out for the sake of the country. The unions were, by implication, the squabbling kids, with the Labour government just looking like it either didn't know about or didn't care about what was going on.

The broadcast turned out to be one of the killer punches of the campaign. We leapt to a 19 points lead in the polls and Margaret's personal rating went to almost 50 per cent. I happen to think it won us the election. The next day, Callaghan told her that he wished he'd done it, and, for once, she didn't think it was him being the patronising sod that he could be, and that he actually meant it.

All the time, our aim was to make the C2 audience realise that they could solve their dissatisfaction by voting for us. We always had in mind the old campaign (from the CPV agency) that ran in the late 1950s which showed milkmen and miners and people with the line that read, 'I'm a Conservative'. So our media strategy centred on the *Sun*, and we got Larry Lamb to meet with

Margaret on many an occasion, which finally convinced him – and, in turn, Rupert Murdoch.

Larry Lamb (his real name was Albert) was the canny son of a West Yorkshire blacksmith, but he hated the unions, especially as, at the time, they could make it hell to get a newspaper out. We made ourselves popular with him by drip-feeding him gossip and 'secret' insights. He once wrote that Margaret thought Callaghan was another Stanley Baldwin – a compliment – which was actually something that we'd fed him. In truth, there were an increasing number of editors who thought Margaret was the Messiah. David English at the *Daily Mail* was obviously on our side, and would practically run word-for-word articles that we'd sent over, such as the 'Labour's Dirty Dozen' lies list, which we timed perfectly during election week. And throughout all of this, Margaret was developing her rapport with the 'ordinary' voter, dredging up what she remembered of her childhood as an ordinary grocer's daughter – which worked a treat. Even some of the Left-wing papers rather liked her as well. The *News of the World* liked her. But we only mixed with editors where it was directly relevant and profitable in editorial terms. Otherwise we were mates with the political journalists because they were easier to work with. And we were always keen to keep the debate in the media as an emotive one.

As time went on, we often suggested doing some stronger anti-Callaghan stuff, but Margaret generally disliked overtly personal attacks – possibly because she had suffered more than most from them. I remember once when a researcher came in and said that he'd discovered the dynamite revelation that Callaghan owned three different houses. To which Margaret replied, 'Yes, it is wonderful, because we would like it if everybody had three houses.' She was not at all comfortable with us starting out with the idea of smearing anyone. Can you imagine that today?

The polls were strongly in our favour at that time, but she was always unsure of whether any lead she had was significant, and whether people would, at the final moment, be swayed by the familiarity of the 'Sunny Jim' persona. As the Winter of Discontent dragged on into spring, the backbenchers were pushing her very hard to table a vote of no confidence – but she resisted. She knew that it would always be a difficult vote to get through, and that, if she failed, it would have negative implications for the opposition's credibility. So she resisted – until 28 March.

When the debate did eventually take place in Parliament, she was actually quite subdued, and Callaghan delivered, by any yardstick, the better speech. But by that stage, I don't think that anyone was listening to him. There was very little he could say to swing it. In the end, we got the vote, albeit only by one member. One of the Labour MPs died that night, and there was a story that they tried to get the dead body through the lobbies to cast its vote – but that was just a silly story. Britain was in a shocking state at the time, and even the House of Commons catering staff were on strike. Maybe that helped us. But we got the vote and an election date was announced. It was a very brief celebration for her, because just two days later, the Irish republican paramilitary group INLA assassinated her great friend Airey Neave, by setting off a huge bomb underneath his Vauxhall as he left Westminster. She hid it well, but that affected her enormously, and for a few weeks, she was very low. Ronnie tried to lift her spirits by taking her to a few West End shows, but I don't think that did anything at all to help.

As we went up to polling day, Charles's view was to run the 'Labour isn't working' poster again and again. Maybe we could change it to '*still* isn't working' – which is what we eventually did, in fact. We knew we had the best poster, so we wanted to get some use out of it. But then there developed a concern that we were becoming a hostage to fortune, because everyone in the Party, including Margaret, knew that the policies that a Conservative adminis-tration would introduce would increase unemployment and we would be hoist by our own petard.

Gordon was especially into visual messages, and took her all over the place, including the bizarre trip to a Norfolk farm where they gave her a two-day-old calf to hold. I'm not actually sure what the hell the message here was to be, especially when this mad struggling calf was given to her. We were terrified it was going to crap itself. She said, 'I'm not going to hold this for 20 minutes', but in the end she nearly did, and Denis said something like, 'If you don't put the thing down, it'll soon be a dead calf.' Our unbending belief, however, was that we would win through communicating a 'feeling' (be it of despair at Labour, or hope for a better future), rather than a rational argument.

This kind of approach seems run-of-the-mill in today's terms, but in those days, it was much more innovative, because we were bringing the best of the advertising world into the political one. It was a pioneering approach to political communication, and in no small measure got her the victory on 4 May. I don't think I'd really ever doubted that we would. Or maybe I had just not dared consider what might have happened next to us all – every man, woman, and child in the country – had she not won.

7

Power

On the night of the Election – 3 May 1979 – Saatchi & Saatchi were having their party at Charlotte Street and Central Office was having one at Smith Square. By midnight, the former had turned into a rubbishy wallowing drunken affair, so by the early hours of Friday morning, I'd flitted over to Central Office. Margaret had gone back to Barnet Town Hall for the Finchley declaration. The newspapers were already writing their front pages and the big rumour was that Heath was going to be made Foreign Secretary, which was giving Gordon and me hysterics; it was so far from what we knew she had in mind. At the final count, we achieved 339 seats (with Labour well down on 269, and David Steel obliterated). A swing of 5.1 per cent was the greatest since Labour's Clem Atlee beat Churchill at the end of the war. Once we'd reached 316 seats, which were what we needed for a majority, Callaghan conceded. Oddly, Margaret herself was not confirmed as MP for Finchley until after 2.00 a.m., because they lost a ballot box there.

The first person to telephone her was the Australian Prime Minister, Malcolm Fraser. He would actually be the first person to officially call her 'Prime Minister', but that passed her by. She just asked, 'What does he want?' And Caroline said, 'I imagine, to congratulate you.' Margaret had a very old-fashioned view of the way information and communication worked, so she found it odd that he had learned the news so quickly. Not so long after that, Ted Heath rang to offer congratulations. She wouldn't take the call. It seemed a very brutal thing to do, but I think she had never forgiven him for being sullen and rude to her many years earlier when she had won the leadership.

When she returned from Finchley, she took a very short catnap and then began work on her Cabinet list, ticking off the ones that had won their seats, and crossing out any that hadn't, so, in effect, her mind was already in Prime Ministerial mode. I'm not sure she ever took a second to reflect on what she'd done – not at that stage, anyway. Ronnie Millar reported to us that he'd seen

her a bit tearful, but you could never tell with Ronnie what he'd seen and what
was in his dramatic imagination. When Peter Thorneycroft arrived and started
trying to get her to celebrate, she just wasn't interested.

Ronnie had come up with the St Francis of Assisi quote ('Where there is
discord, may we bring harmony ...'), which he said was Churchillian, but
which Gordon and I thought sounded a bit too pious. In the end, Ronnie's idea
trumped our anxieties, probably because of his Churchill allusion, and she went
with it. The other thing that people forget is that she also invoked her father,
Alfred Roberts, and how his simple entrepreneurial values had been 'the values
on which I've fought this election'. Saints and grocers – in her mind, there was
no difference. If the vision is right, it is so regardless of its parentage.

When Thorneycroft came in, we did have a few drinks and celebrations.
Margaret thanked everybody and went downstairs to see the Party workers.
But all the time she kept saying, 'I must get on with the job.' She was getting
worked up about all that she felt she needed to do. As though she needed to start
running the country at that split second. That was the way she treated things.
Anyway, she needed to go to Buckingham Palace that afternoon. I was actually
quite used to that kind of mood, which, albeit on a somewhat less grand scale,
is part and parcel of agency pitch life. Whenever we'd won a piece of business,
I'd say to Charles, 'So what are we going to do next?' Once you've achieved
success, you move on to the next thing, not sit and wallow or indulge yourself.
Then there is the fact that, on the day after an election result, everybody wants
to know who's going to get what job and there are loads of people ringing up
offering congratulations, but usually in the hope that they will be remembered.
Back at Saatchi & Saatchi, Jeremy Sinclair was over the moon, because he was
a staunch Tory. But quite a lot of the creatives who clearly weren't Tories were
trying to think about how they'd explain to their wives and girlfriends and their
pals that they'd helped elect the she-devil.

Margaret was very well aware what her members thought of her. And,
in return, she could do the manoeuvring and the manipulation and all that
the game-playing required. By that time, we all knew the members who had
been disaffected, who had been passed over, who Heath had upset, who were
a drunk, who took drugs, who had a mistress, who had an illegitimate child,
who had been found out – we knew all that. In those days, the Whips knew
everything that went on, and so we could always make the calculation about
votes and how they would work and who had to be Whipped and who didn't.
She unashamedly used privilege and reward and promotion and so on. She

was a capitalist and understood that people were motivated by money – and that when you made somebody a Parliamentary undersecretary, they got a rise (financially and emotionally), and they'd be very grateful to you. She saw it in very simple, straightforward terms. And above all, she knew who was 'one of us'. She was also aware that most ministers thought, at the back of their romantic minds, that one day they might be Prime Minister. So they were all a threat to her. And nothing has changed.

From the day I met her, and she said what she said, it became very clear to me that Margaret had very few friends. She was quite lonely, which is why she leant so much on Denis – and at some level, on Gordon and me. She was friendly with Peter Thorneycroft, but she wouldn't have shared the inside of her soul with him. She would have told him something of what she was thinking and what her options were, but equally, she was careful not to say something that he could use against her, should he at some later date plan an attack. That applies to most of one's colleagues in politics. You don't really ever trust anyone. Whereas I wasn't a politician. I had no political ambition whatsoever.

I think one of the problems that politicians have is they have to go to lots of meetings with lots of people who they don't particularly like or know or agree with. Almost by happenstance, Margaret had found, in me, someone with whom there was an honest (rather than calculated) agreement with her over most things. We had similar non-establishment, grammar school backgrounds, and she liked me at a personal level. I wasn't being paid, so I wasn't doing it for money. I wasn't expecting to be given an award of any kind. I didn't long for any special status. She knew exactly where she stood with me. I didn't want any of those things. I had absolutely no ulterior motive, apart from the fact that I absolutely loved, if I'm honest, sitting there at the seat of power, and I loved her, because she wielded her power in such an extraordinarily accomplished and visionary manner. I was so sick of all the waffle that went on – in politics, in media, in advertising – and she just sliced through that waffle.

Of course, I'm quite good at being charming and I treated her like a woman. She didn't behave in any kind of conventional feminine fashion – she never responded to compliments, for example – but it was a mistake to respond in kind and not to treat her as a woman. So I never stopped complimenting her. She didn't want to be surrounded by people saying 'Now you're the PM, you're going to behave like a man – let's all belch and fart and drink pints, so that we know we're all really men.' I bought her flowers and chocolates and I commented on her hair and her dress. None of the Cabinet or her Ministers did that. They were all too baffled or too frightened. One of them once said it was like leaving home and finding that Nanny was at the office.

For the next few years, after that first election, I was in euphoria. They call it the 'aphrodisiac of power' and it really is. Suddenly I was mixing with people that I admired and people that had been my heroes. It was very heady stuff. The added attraction was that I was far more interested in politics than in advertising – although I can see a very close relationship between the two. It seemed to me that anything we did at Saatchi & Saatchi after that which was not part of the Conservative work was going to be a bit of a case of 'after the Lord Mayor's Show'. So, in the short term, with my immediate duties over, I had to steel myself to going back to doing the job I'd been doing before and deciding to lead the team and trying to do the best pitches.

Of course, the brothers could see the opportunity that our involvement in the campaign had provided, especially as it might make them more famous. Also, the Conservative Party would clearly create a better business environment for companies like Saatchi & Saatchi. And there was also a belief that, having won the election, we would be allowed to do some fairly radical, mad campaigns for the Conservatives, as we went forward with the account, rather than have to do very boring things.

Meanwhile, the only reason Maurice and Charles were happy for me to carry on handling that account was because I knew how to talk to the Tory Party and I could get things through. Maurice had meagre interest in other people's backgrounds, so would never have got on with Thorneycroft, who could only really be understood if you knew his story as a posh Etonian, cast out onto the scrap heap, but brought back by Margaret. I knew exactly what to say to him and how to treat him and how to get the most out of his link with Margaret, because I knew how grateful he was for what she'd done. Maurice and Charles would not have been able to handle the nuances of the relationship.

At the same time, I wasn't sure if we'd get any business as a result of it. In fact, I thought most of the big government departments and the big clients who were Tory donors would not want to be seen hiring the Party's agency and might actually avoid us. Indeed, the Manpower Services Commission abandoned us straight away. Maurice always had the view that we could say to anyone that we got Thatcher elected and they would give us the business, so he was rather offended when things did not turn out like that as often as he would have liked. Clearly, being near the trappings of power was an advantage, and I did get to know some important clients through the political work, such as Hector Laing

(United Biscuits), Keith Showering (Showerings drinks company), and Basil Collins (Cadbury–Schweppes) and the like, so we did win a few new business pitches in this way. I think it helped with clients like British Leyland when you could get them a visit to Downing Street, and that probably helped when we had to do a re-pitch at the end of the '70s. But I can't think of anybody who automatically walked through the door and said that we could have their account because of what we'd done in the political village.

For me, 1979 was the start of a political connection that lasted until Margaret's death. During those early years, there were not many people who became close to her, but I regard it as one of the great privileges of my life – possibly the greatest – that I was eventually one of them. Denis was obviously her main source of comfort and greatest ally, but we tried to go some way – Gordon, Ronnie and I – to help where we could. We had no hesitation in thinking that Margaret was a fabulous woman and leader, the like of which we might never see again. I don't think many others felt quite that way, at least at first. They preferred their superficial assessments. They felt threatened. And it was easier to hate her than it was to like her.

Because of that, she was a very isolated figure – and that must have hurt her. From the very early days, she had to deal with the glowering hatred from Heath, which you could feel when he was in the room. And you could always sense the simmering dislike of her from within the Party – a sort of 'What the hell is a woman doing here?' I remember a conversation that we had in which she said, 'I can either try as hard as I can to be just like a male Prime Minister, or I can try to be a very different Prime Minister because I'm female, or I can mix the two together' – and the last is exactly what she did. She used her femininity when it suited her – she could cry, she could look coquettish, she could be emotional when others were being rational, all of which were her instinctively female attributes. But then there was the 'iron' in her blood, wanting to run the country, get the job done, defeat the enemy. She knew that nobody else was going to do her job and that she had to get on with it. She was very proud to be British, but she was not in any sense gentrified or grand. She had a house in Flood Street, but it was fairly ordinary, and the furniture wasn't exotic.

Denis was one of the few people who knew exactly how to treat her, and when he died, I don't think she recovered – her rock had gone. Denis was always frustrated by the amount of overwork and stress through which she put herself, and he couldn't be bothered with the complications and manoeuvrings that the position brought. Sometimes, he'd say, 'Sorry, dear, but I've had a difficult day too. You don't need to tell me about yours.' He thought that the pressures of office were ridiculous, and, of course, saw what effect it had on his wife; it saddened him, although he remained utterly phlegmatic – most of the time – about what she had to deal with. He was a lovely gentleman, who hated fuss and bother, and just told it as he saw it – extremely un-politically correct by today's standards. He would never take things as seriously as people wanted him to, and you could never quite feel safe when the press were in earshot, but fortunately, he mainly stayed well away from the media. He had no vanity, he never sought any publicity, and he sought no credit at all for his role in Margaret's achievements. His view of the press was quite simply that, if you didn't like it, don't read it. Yet many journalists quite liked him and the way he behaved.

He was fiercely loyal, and if Margaret argued with anyone, he would back her judgement without question. They would go through conversations where Margaret would say that someone was awful and he would say, 'Yes, you're absolutely right, they are.' This led to the occasional awkward moment, when he would stray off-message: Margaret could change her opinion over people and decide that they weren't quite so awful. Sometimes, Denis hadn't quite kept up, so he would still be going on about how ghastly they were, and Margaret would scowl at him now inadvertently disagreeing with her revised opinion.

Margaret was his second wife, because his first had left him at the end of the war, but he would never talk about that, and didn't even tell Mark and Carol, who only found out through the media. Denis was retired and a millionaire, but he was of the very careful generation and hated waste of any kind. He'd kept his Rolls Royce, but he wasn't allowed to drive it (except at the weekends, incognito, when he played golf), in case it gave the wrong image, so it was kept in a garage for five years.

I liked Denis and he liked me. I don't know why particularly, but we became very good friends. Our backgrounds could not have been more different. Partly, it was because I was prepared to go to the ends of the earth for his wife. Men often like it when they see the woman they love admired by somebody else. He was very astute. He would say to her, 'Don't bother asking any of them, Margaret. Go and ask Tim' or 'Go and talk to Gordon.'

Of course, it's well known that she needed very little sleep. She could go a whole day without apparently going to bed, which annoyed Denis. He really did constantly say to her, 'Go to bed, woman!' She regenerated her energy by catnapping. She'd sometimes go to sleep whilst you were talking with her, but it only happened with people with whom she was totally at ease. She didn't sleep with the enemy. Sometimes, you'd keep talking – out of embarrassment – or sometimes you'd just stop talking for a bit and hope you didn't fall asleep as well. On one occasion, at Chequers, I did, and when I woke up, she had wrapped me in a blanket and was reading me poetry out loud.

There's an old saw that if you haven't been Conservative at some point, then you haven't got a heart, and if you don't become a Conservative, then you haven't got a head. For me, Conservatism was both head and heart and always had been. I make the joke now when I say I'm a man of the Right because it is, and I like to tell people that the Latin for 'left' is *sinister* – but these are actually what I believe. Of course, I know many on the Left, and am friends with them. Even when I was living in North London, I knew George Brown very well. He lived down the road from me and I used to watch him staggering home late at night, tripping up, and falling over, with his tie hanging down. He was a terrible old drunk. I knew quite a few Labour MPs; mainly those who were quite nice, and who were on the Centre-Left. There have been many very moderate Labour Members of Parliament from the '50s and '60s with whom I have had many long and fascinating arguments. Primarily over what I see as the three fundamental dividing principles between Left and Right: individualism versus collectivism; the creation of wealth versus the redistribution of wealth; and the general view that we all have a choice in life to expect support or to seek to support ourselves.

The Left hold the view that large tranches of the public can't look after themselves, so the state must look after them. It is also convenient for the Left to argue that people who don't accept this view are somehow, de facto, uncaring. That was the attack that was made on Thatcher – namely, that she didn't care. Indeed, that attack came from her own side – from cowardly MPs, wanting to safeguard their own seats in any way they could – as well as from the opposition benches. In return, she believed that she had to persuade people, so that they could work to a common vision. If you asked her why the government should communicate, she would say that it was so that people understand what the government is trying to do and then they can help you do it. The debate at the time was based on principles, and it was probably the last era when politics was conducted like that.

Margaret used to say, 'If you want to make an omelette, you have to break eggs.' These days, politicians are terrified of breaking eggs, because they think it will lose them votes. All it does, however, is demonstrate that they don't believe in anything. She was very different in that respect. Even in those days, she was surrounded by fear and refused to let it dilute her own vision – even if that meant she'd have to go it alone. She had few people on whom she could truly rely. Perhaps as well then that she was, at heart, one of the most self-reliant people I've ever met. It saddens me that her legacy has largely been lost, or rewritten – overcome by a modern-day preoccupation with entitlement and faux compassion to which Centre-Right parties now seem to have to pay deference.

Many years ago, I came across Ayn Rand's famous book, *Atlas Shrugged*, which, to my mind, sums up in the most effective way imaginable the notion of self-reliance. Rand is another of my heroines (unsurprisingly, given her philosophy). I always loved her eccentricity and intelligence and extraordinary life story: a Russian Jew who had lived through the revolutions, she found her way to Hollywood and a job as an extra working for Cecil B. de Mille. She became a successful author and screenwriter before, in the '50s, moving to New York, where she gathered around her a group of followers and intellectuals and began to develop her philosophy of self-reliance. She invented the notion that the closest society ever gets to a superhero is the individual self of each member of that society. It's the very opposite of Socialism which denies the self, and appeals to the collective; Socialism looks down, not up. Margaret never thought of herself as a superhero, but she wanted to inspire people to regard themselves in that way. That's why she was not interested in the kind of faux compassion that, as far as we were all concerned, defines Socialism and the Left. She was unique. Rand was unique. That's their point.

8

Going Further

Whilst Margaret Thatcher was revolutionising Britain, I was getting quite a lot of credit to which I was not entitled for achievements that weren't mine. If I'm honest about it, I quite enjoyed basking in the glow of it all. But then it's quite difficult living up to the artificial expectations that people have of you. The same thing happened to Alastair Campbell, who – rightly or wrongly – became regarded as instigator of anything Tony Blair did. The press push the Merlin or Svengali image; they like to add a layer of alchemy into the story; people like to imagine a magical and mysterious process pulling the strings of power. That is the whole basis of superstition. Anyway, for a time, I was getting praise, and I lapped it up.

One consequence of this was that, not so long after the first Tory election victory, I was invited over to the US. The presidential election was to be held in November 1980, and Bill Brock, the Chairman of the GOP National Committee, had asked for a presentation on how Thatcher had won in 1979. They thought that the main issues were inflation, unemployment and the trade unions; that is, the same as had confronted Thatcher. I never told anyone at Saatchi & Saatchi because I was afraid that if Maurice found out, he would send himself instead.

So it was off to Washington, DC, all expenses paid. At the time there were five nominations for the Republican candidacy, and when I walked in to give the presentation, they were all there, sitting behind one huge desk – a quintet of formidable American statesmen reeking of power and authority, and just the one of little me. It was surreal. They were magisterial, pleasant and curious in equal measure: giant and wise elephants who'd noticed that a strange little Dumbo had wandered into their midst. There was Gerald Ford, the incumbent President, so he knew all about protocol and correct behaviour and was therefore very charming. Then there was John Connally, the Governor of Texas, who seemed to me likely to be the next President; he had these dark eyes and just seemed extremely sharp; he was probably the most assertive of the lot;

polite but intimidating; he'd been travelling in Kennedy's car at the time of the
assassination in Dallas, and took the ricochet full-on into his chest. Howard
Baker was the most studious-looking, although he kept losing interest, getting
up to take phone calls or go to the washroom or whatever. John Anderson just
peered out from behind a pair of huge black-rimmed glasses; he was the oldest
and probably the least impressive, who, in the end, stood as an independent
candidate.

Plus Ronald Reagan. All I'd heard about him was the Hollywood stuff, so I
hadn't expected myself to take him seriously. But he immediately struck you
with his conspicuous physical presence. He was huge. He dominated the space
around him. Yet he was also a very nice human being – which was all the more
surprising coming from a man of such power and aura. (It shouldn't have been.
But it was. Why is that?) He had an enormous glass jar of jellybeans that he kept
offering me. In retrospect, it was easy to see why so many Americans adored
him.

So they sat there facing me whilst I gave the presentation. At the time – not
being an American, not being very up to date with American politics, and not
having done enough homework – I had no real sense of their expectations and
requirements. As a result, I wasted the first 20 minutes of it trying to explain
the difference in the electoral systems – which, of course, was of no concern to
them at all, and which bored them rigid. It was a slow stage-death: really embarrassing. Once I got on to winning elections, I was able to recover somewhat,
and, by the end, I think they felt they had got their money's worth. Indeed,
when Reagan was chosen as the GOP nomination, his people offered to pay
my expenses to go back and see him again in Washington and make comments
on the election campaign. I went a few times. He had his own advisers around
him, and I quickly learned that there was no point in making any smart-arse
comments about what they were doing because I had nothing that I could
possibly add to improve their campaigning – which was more sophisticated
and far better resourced than ours in the UK. So I would sit there and say, 'This
looks great; fabulous. You're bound to win', which they were happy to hear. And,
of course, he did win, so at least my reputation came out of it intact.

In truth, we got on because his political philosophy was exactly the same as
Margaret's, and that was exactly the same as mine – so we were common souls
talking about the same things. One time, Gordon Reece and I went and had
dinner at the White House with the President and Senator Pete du Pont (Pierre
Samuel du Pont IV, actually), who, at that time, was being seriously looked at

as a future Republican presidential nomination. There was Gordon, myself, Nancy and Ronald Reagan, and du Pont and his wife Elise. Gordon and I were put on either side of Nancy Reagan. Gordon knew that she loved black-and-white movies, from her own era, and he loved them too, so they spent the whole evening engrossed in this bizarre conversation about how old movie stars used to smoke a cigarette in a certain way and how they used to have one foot on the floor when they kissed in bed, and do this and do that. I couldn't get a word in. Gordon burbled on and on and she grinned her way through it. If I ever chipped in with the odd remark, she would politely smile at me (I suspected that she couldn't do anything else *but* smile, because of all the facelifts) and immediately turn back to her more interesting conversation with Gordon.

The thing that singled out both Margaret Thatcher and Ronald Reagan was their sense of a single-minded vision. Neither was motivated by the rewards or the power from the title. They just had this incredible sense of an achievable ambition for their respective countries. Reagan was unlike Thatcher in that he didn't do detail, whereas she did. He was sometimes criticised by his aides, and indeed, by our Foreign Office (who called him a 'Bozo'), for this, and for being willing to drop everything at the end of the day and go watch a movie with Nancy. Margaret was the opposite, in that she rarely left her work behind. He could do small talk, and do it very well, with anyone – so he was very easy to love. She couldn't; and wasn't.

But they both had an absolute determination to make their respective nations the greatest in the world. And they both, incidentally, were quick to spot the desire for policy reform in the Soviet Union. They got on astonishingly well together – he'd send her informal messages when he knew she was feeling the strain, such as during the miners' strike and after IRA atrocities – because they had this shared mentality and similar world view: although the idea that they were in each other's pocket is ridiculous. One occasion in particular demonstrated that.

Grenada was a member of the Commonwealth, located in the Caribbean off Venezuela, with a recently installed Marxist government. In 1983, there was a violent coup, where the Deputy Prime Minister seized power, killing his leader in the process, and putting the Army in charge: it was really a case of one Marxist faction overpowering another. Then in late October, Reagan decided enough was enough and agreed to a major US armed deployment to restore order – but ignoring international law in the process. I also think he never fully understood the significance of the Commonwealth and the fact that, Marxists or not, their Head of State was the Queen – so that, he was effectively invading one of her sovereign territories. Strangely enough, on the night of the mission, Margaret had been at a dinner in honour of the US Ambassador in London. When she got back, she got a message telling her that Reagan had given the operation the green light. She blew up. She came over and said, 'Tim. Go to the study. Immediately.' I wondered what the hell had happened. When I met her there, she said, 'Can you believe what he's done? Ron has invaded Grenada. Well what are we going to do about it?' I said, 'I haven't the faintest idea. I think you think I'm Geoffrey Howe.' They then found Howe and Heseltine, neither of whom had the foggiest notion of what was happening. I think at about one in the morning she called Reagan and had a right old rant and rave at him. Indeed, for quite a while after that, she really sulked with him. She started going round saying that the Americans were getting as bad as the Soviet Union. 'After all I've done for that man [Reagan]', she'd say. It became so bad that the Americans began to hit back at us, claiming that we were being unsupportive and that she was being 'prissy'. So after a while, she had to cool down and try to rebuild bridges – which she did as Chair of the G7, when the French and Canadians were whinging about US economic policy, and she came to Reagan's defence. Mitterrand and Trudeau turned on her, but she later whispered to Reagan that they would never hurt her because 'women know when men are being childish'. It signalled that the two of them were strong again.

Over the years, I had regular, enjoyable and fruitful meetings with Reagan. Naturally we agreed on so much. He had a plaque on his desk, which read, 'There is no limit to what a man can do or where he can go, if he does not mind who gets the credit.' Another said, 'It *can* be done.' (Long before Obama appropriated the 'can' word.) He was what I would call a real Conservative – a man who you could call 'great' without any sense of hyperbole.

I worked with him on several occasions, but without getting personally very close to him. I think that, in general terms, Americans are easier to be superficially friendly with, but harder to get to know well. With American politicians, that phenomenon is multiplied a thousand times. These people have a wide emotional moat around them – an essential by-product of the impossibly treacherous lives they lead and personal threats they face. Even with Thatcher, it was many years before I began to break through, and that was made possible when I started looking after her family.

There is a great loneliness in power, and these people usually deal with it by being very careful in giving of themselves. They have very few people whom they can truly trust, or with whom they can share what is in their hearts and souls. That's why Denis was so essential to Margaret, and Nancy to Reagan – real, irreplaceable consorts, who became part of the stories of greatness.

Meanwhile, the international stuff was burgeoning, and by 1980 I was getting to see more and more political leaders abroad. One of these was the Irish prime minister, Charles Haughey. Saatchi & Saatchi had acquired a Dublin advertising agency called O'Kennedy Brindley, which had the Fianna Fáil government account. It was a fairly Right-wing party in those days, and Haughey was coming up to an election in 1981. The agency thought it would be fruitful if I could go across and, as with the US Republicans, talk to them about the Thatcher election. He met me in a hotel in Dublin – because it would certainly cause trouble if the media caught a British advertising Johnnie going into an Irish government office. Anyway, I was sitting in the hotel waiting for him in a designated private area, when suddenly, about a dozen garda rushed in and started searching everywhere – on the terrace, behind the curtains, around the bar – presumably for spies or bombs or paparazzi, who knows? Then in strolled Haughey, with his foreign minister, Brian Lenihan.

Now rather oddly, Brian Lenihan was the spitting image of my natural father (who happened to have been a Northern Irish protestant), and this completely threw me. With the accent and all, it was like my father had just come into the room and was talking to me. For the first few minutes, I was dumbfounded. The first thing Haughey said to me was, 'So. You're Mrs Thatcher's image maker are ya?' I didn't think it was any use trying to split hairs and argue with him, so I just nodded. 'Right,' he said, 'I want a new image.' I said, 'I don't believe in new images. The skill is to get to know somebody, find the real person, and get that real person in front of the people so they can decide.' At which he frowned at me and said, 'OK, then. Do you know anybody who does do new images?'

In the end, I did get to work for them. That day, after we'd been we talking shop for just a short while, Brian Lenihan said, 'Have you ever drunk Irish whiskey?' to which I replied, 'No, I don't think so.' And that was it. Off we went, sampling what felt like all the whiskey bars in Dublin. By the early evening, I was completely legless. Lenihan drove me to the airport in his minister's car with motorcycle outriders, through immigration, onto the plane, and had me dumped in a seat on the plane. It was then, as coherent reality began its fight back, that I realised I hadn't even checked out of the hotel or got my bags. When I told the stewardess, she said, 'Oh well, we'll contact Mr Lenihan.' And the plane was made to sit there on the runway, whilst Lenihan's people went back to my hotel, packed my suitcase, no doubt paid the bill, and brought all my belongings to the aircraft. I felt like a god, except that, by that time, I was sobering up, and felt as ill as no god has ever felt. Anyway, Lenihan and I became quite good friends after that. I used to see him occasionally and once I even told him how much he looked like my father – although he probably thought I was just buttering him up, because he replied, 'Well, whoever I bloody well look like, I'm not going to pay any more of your bills.' He was a lovely man.

Rather different were the Russians. Very many years later, I was asked over to Moscow to meet with what was called the 'propaganda committee' (that's how it translates anyway) of the Yeltsin presidential campaign. It was being run by a man called Igor Malashenko who had been the managing director of NTV, which was the first satellite television channel to broadcast in Russia, owned by a colourful media tycoon called Vladimir Gusinsky, who later was put in prison and stripped of his assets.

I met with Malashenko and Anatoly Chubais, the economics adviser to Yeltsin, along with a man called Alexander Korjakov, a former KGB general and the head of the presidential security service (the PSB). When Yeltsin did his speech from the top of a tank in 1991, resisting a hard-line coup, Korjakov had been the large tough-looking bodyguard standing next to him. These guys were always doing bad things to each other: in later years, Korjakov would organise an armed raid on Gusinsky's bank headquarters in Moscow, and release documents about Chubais's financial dealings; that kind of thing.

We went there in 1995 or 1996 (by then as Bell Pottinger consultants) with a proposal for a campaign for Yeltsin. We suggested several campaign strategies, based on our other presidential campaign experience which by then included UK, USA, France, Malta and Columbia. When we were presenting these ideas, Korjakov interrupted and said, 'What do you know about Russia?' and I said, 'I know absolutely nothing about Russia, but I know a great deal about democratic elections and you know nothing about democratic elections, as you've never had one in this country.' I continued, 'Yours is based on *organising* the vote – you put the vote into lumps and you organise the industrial vote, the Oligarch vote, the media vote, the elite vote and all that stuff. Whereas, what we do in the proper democratic elections as we have them in Britain is *ask* people if they'll vote for us: we don't tell them; we ask them.' He said, 'You don't understand anything about the Russian people.' So I asked him to explain what it was that I didn't get. He said, 'It's simple. You need to understand that asking to be liked won't get you any votes. The

Russian people were born to be unhappy.' I replied, 'In that case you should win by a landslide.' At that, he did his deep, sinister Bond-villain voice and said, 'No jokes, English.'

Unfortunately, coming back on the plane I bumped into a journalist from *The Times* and I stupidly told him the truth, which he printed. Before long, Yeltsin's people rang me up and said that I'd leaked my involvement, and so they didn't want us to work with them any more. That taught me never to tell journalists anything at all, because it only hurts you. But it's a rule I've failed to keep.

The strange thing was (Russians notwithstanding) that I often got on better with people outside the country than back on home soil. Certainly, even back in 1981, after less than two years working with the Tories in government, enemies were popping up all over the shop. For Margaret, politically, things were getting tense. All the indicators of economic success that mattered – inflation, interest rates, unemployment level, balance of trade – were moving in the wrong direction, and the visits from the men in suits had begun. Thornycroft, Harrington, Atkins, Howe et al. In effect, they were telling her, 'It's time for you to go. It hasn't worked. You've got your place in history, the first ever woman Prime Minister, but now we want you to drink of this very large cup of poison and clear off.'

It wasn't entirely personal; they didn't blame her; they said it was unfortunate; but it had all gone the wrong way and now they were in office, it needed to go the right way. Of course, it didn't help that a replica of their nanny was telling them how to proceed. And as it was impossible to persuade her that she was wrong, they thought that it was probably the easier option to get her to give in and go, and everything would go back to the cosy world of their imagination. They were in a quandary of sorts, because they agreed with her in principle. But they didn't like the effect of agreeing: which was that the public – and their constituents – had started to grumble at the mid-term medicine meted out to the sick country.

With this in mind, and our awareness of the pressures coming from within, the internal coping strategy was based on leveraging their fear and greed: fear of what they'd get with a rival like Howe or Heseltine in charge and greed for the good they'd get if our incumbent stayed put long enough to turn things around. On many an occasion we were seeking gratitude for favours yet to come. So often, however, our schemes and machinations were pre-empted by Margaret just getting fed up with all the nonsense. Many a time, she just said to them, 'Go away!' and they always just skulked off, craven, weak and frightened of her. One day, a long way in the future, they would smell her cuts, and stay, like a pack of jackals near a wounded antelope. But not for now.

Margaret wouldn't ever show it to their faces, but this had already cut her deeply. One time, her secretary, Caroline Ryder, rang me up and asked me to come round because she was at such a low ebb and needed a lot of cheering up. On the way, I stopped at an art shop in Grosvenor Street and bought her a painting of an owl sitting on a tree branch outside Scotney Castle, where she used to stay. It was quite expensive – from memory, it cost me around £4,000, something like that. When I gave it to her, she said, 'Oh, I'm the wise owl am I?' to which I politely nodded. (As a peer, I have an heraldic crest, and as a reference to that moment, it has owls in it.) I think there was a Rembrandt over the fireplace, which she took down and replaced with this owl. 'Now, my owl will stay there for *ever*', she said, in the manner of a George Eliot heroine. It had cheered her up for a few minutes. But by the next day, it had gone, of course. There is a lesson for us all in there somewhere.

9

Enemies Without, Enemies Within

The two events that tend to be used to define Margaret Thatcher's time in office are the Falklands War and the miners' strike. I had a lot more to do with the latter than the former. Indeed, I was very uncomfortable with the Falklands War. The idea of anything being resolved through international conflict seems to me, if you look back at history, to be quite flawed. With a few notable exceptions, rarely has anything been resolved in this manner, which is far better at winning territory or riches than at winning hearts and minds. There's no doubt that the Falklands was one of those exceptions and set her apart from most other politicians, because she did something that nobody believed was possible and that few other politicians would have risked. She sent a task force across the world, defeated an illegal aggressor, and stood up for Britain. Everybody now understands how bold a decision it was on her part, and how it changed the course of the election in 1983. But I was never at ease with it.

It also gave me a few dilemmas in terms of loyalties. One such occasion was when my friend David Frost interviewed the Prime Minister (a couple of years after the war) about the controversial sinking of the Argentine battleship, *Belgrano*. Whenever David was doing politicians, he used to telephone me a day or so before and say, 'Tim, I need your help. What's the gut question?' He had a photographic memory and a great attention to detail, but he also always wanted to work out the gut question.

This time, I said, 'Well it's probably about the *Belgrano*, and whether it was on its way out of the exclusion zone.' So then he said, 'Well what do you think it was doing?' So I told him that I'd heard from the admiral at the time that it was heading out. 'Great. Right. Thanks.' So when he interviewed her, he pushed her hard on this, but she gave him a very hard time back, and they went on and on for ages about battleships zigzagging and whether the heading mattered given the ship's intent, and on decisions that have to be made in an instant in the heat of battle. She had always been in an invidious position, not least because there was a lot of secret information (about the sophistication of British intercepts, for example) that she could not reveal, subject to the 30 years disclosure rule. On the day the ship was sunk, I know for a fact that she was up all night in tears at the 321 deaths. But she called David 'bonkers', and said, 'Isn't it extraordinary? ... You choose to spend so much time [discussing] one day and one direction. [But] you're welcome.' David was really cross with me afterwards, as he thought I'd set him up and made him look stupid over the zigzagging thing. I said, 'David, you're a great friend of mine but so is the Prime Minister. What could I tell you?' And he just said, 'OK. On this occasion, I forgive you.' He was like that over any disagreement. He was such a balanced and great and good man. Margaret didn't take his questioning at all personally, and she was happy to do a second session with him at a future date. (It was more than could be said for Henry Kissinger, who refused to speak to Frosty for about 20 years, after he asked him about bombing Cambodia.)

I believe that to see the Falklands War in simple terms as the reason for the 1983 Conservative election victory is a mistake. On balance, it did indeed give an enormous boost to Thatcher's credentials as a great leader, both to her own Party and to the voters. But the key factor was that it also had a significant effect on her own self-confidence. After that, she was different; she performed differently; she was much more sure that she was in the right – which was helpful in some respects, but it fed the hubris as well.

Soon, it started to get ever more difficult to manage the perceptions of the public who couldn't abide the hectoring, headmistressy persona that came naturally to her. There were times when I would play focus group films to her, showing ordinary people complaining about her style, and I was probably one of the few people from whom she would take it – comments that could be hurtful to anyone. Maybe it was because she trusted me as the spokesperson of the national mood. But it had an emotional effect on her, and her mood swings were only too evident – the effect of running a country and running for a second term. It is hard to overestimate how difficult that is. The election victory of 1983 was unquestionably influenced by the war, but we were also helped by economic policies beginning to bear fruit just in time. Unemployment, inflation and interest rates weren't good, but they were becoming less of a concern.

Although during the Falklands War the US had mixed views (because for some in power, US self-interest favoured Argentinian appeasement), Reagan was 100 per cent supportive, in a way that could not be said about some of her predecessors and successors – of whom you would expect greater loyalty.

Margaret stood up for Britain and was not willing to compromise. You may call it single-minded or you may call it bloody-minded, but she certainly knew what she had in mind for her country. Reagan was exactly the same about the United States of America (and I think that history has judged him as one as the finest Presidents).

At the same time, Margaret genuinely believed that the Labour Party didn't like Britain. Not in the sense that they were traitors, but that they saw no great virtue in being British or in British values, culture, or way of life. I've always felt the same way. The Labour Party are, I believe, inclined to want to change Britain – part of this is ideological, and part is about tinkering with immigration and social engineering to create an electoral environment more inclined to Labour voting. Successive Labour governments have easily done enough to suggest this. We tried to say as much in an ad that we did around 1992 about Blair and his Party wishing Britain were like some other place – a bit of Sweden, a bit of India, a bit of Russia, and so on – which is passed off as being in the cause of diversity or tolerance or openness. But it's not. If it's not electoral manipulation, it's a sign of embarrassment with our own culture and history and way of life. Labour have been apologising for the Empire since 1946. Margaret never apologised for it, because she was proud of it. These days, it is hard to remember what a poor self-image we had of our own country in Britain prior to 1979, and, indeed, of the capital city, which was in very poor health. She transformed that, laying the platform for the self-belief and pride in 'Great' Britain that prospered in the decades following – something that Blair used as his launch-pad.

Few people fully understood the magnitude of what she was attempting at the time. She was not popular: many people didn't like her, they didn't like her appearance, they didn't like her manner, they didn't like her voice, they hardly liked anything at all about her. But it was hard not to afford her respect. After she died, how often did you hear people saying that, although they didn't agree with her policies, they admired her determination? At the 1983 ballot box, you had a choice between, on one hand, a woman who – against formidable odds and uncertainties – sends a task force across the world and achieves a remarkable victory against an unpleasant aggressive state, and on the other, a Labour Party run by Michael Foot – talking about abolishing the army and marching with the CND and heaven knows what. The nuclear debate at that time was incredibly intense, with marches in the street, but there was no contest in the minds of the electorate as to who made them feel the safest on the world stage – whether they liked her voice or not.

Michael Foot was probably the most extreme Socialist the Labour Party has ever had and their manifesto for that election was – as famously described by Gerald Kaufman – 'the longest suicide note in UK political history'. *The New Hope for Britain* was all about nationalisation, abolishing the House of Lords, getting rid of the nuclear deterrent, and giving a free reign to Clause IV Socialism. A lot of voters rejected this, not simply on the basis of the policies themselves, but because of the overt ideology.

The contrast between Foot and Thatcher was dramatic – even though both suffered criticism as ideologues. As time went on, she became very conscious of how she came across in the media, but had no interest whatsoever in image, and had in no way come to terms with the visual demands of the television age. I don't think it was a case of Foot eschewing it; I'm not sure he even recognised it. So when he turned up at the Cenotaph on Remembrance Sunday in 1981, wearing an old green coat (which came to be known as his 'donkey jacket'), I doubt that he had even remotely considered that this would look bad and be interpreted as disrespectful. Image – clothing, even – didn't matter to him, and he assumed that it didn't matter to voters either.

We designed an ad featuring a picture of Michael Foot walking on Hampstead Heath in his donkey jacket with a stick. The line was, 'As a pensioner, he'd be better off with the Conservatives'. She was absolutely incensed. Foot was a frail man and looked all of his 70 years, and I don't think the voters liked that in a potential leader, but – credit due – Margaret saw it as nasty, vicious politics and was having none of it. To be absolutely honest, I don't think we'd actually thought about how insensitive this might have been on a personal level to the man. Indeed, I'd thought that the concept as a whole was brilliant: we had photographs of Labour MPs like Tony Benn, all with the similar headline ('as a rate-payer ...', 'as a parent ...' and so on). But when she saw the photograph of poor old Michael Foot with his walking stick, she was appalled and threw me out of the office.

It was interesting behaviour when seen in the context of, for example, how far Ken Livingstone was willing to go during the GLC elections and the personal attacks that rained down on her head and on her family from Labour in later years. Cecil Parkinson (who was running the election campaign) didn't like the ads either, but I think his view – which again probably had merit – was that the Labour Party was doing enough damage to itself, without us encouraging the voters to feel sorry for them. However, some Tory campaigning did get very nasty when she wasn't looking. The Party's own bulletin called Foot an 'amnesiac'; a 'clapped-out … half-witted … invalid'. I think that made our idea look quite restrained.

Within the 1983 election team, we absolutely and profoundly believed that the people would vote Tory for fear of the alternative – which came across as an unattractive soup of Communism, Socialism, collectivism, redistribution of wealth, and higher taxes. Parkinson had a decently sized campaign budget, and we were starting to use some of the methods I'd witnessed in the US, with computerisation and direct mail taking a much bigger role. I worked in the advertising industry, which is the bastion of capitalism, and promotes the idea of brands that are dominant in the market; that the larger your share, the lower your cost; an industry that believes in choice, in competition, in all those things. So the message that we needed to get over was intrinsic to my own home-industry. We thought that all we had to do was emphasise the degree to which Labour had moved to the Left. We even bought 1,000 copies of the Labour manifesto and mailed it out to wavering or lapsed Tory voters, to frighten them. One of our best pieces of work in this respect was an ad we did that put the manifesto of the Labour Party and that of the Communist Party side by side, above the headline, 'Like your manifesto, Comrade.' Even some of our cleverest ideas seemed to emerge quite naturally. I won't say it was easy to keep coming up with ideas, but we were blessed with a very easy target. That said, at Saatchi & Saatchi, most of the creative people were fairly Left-wing. Certainly, they weren't in the least bit Conservative, so any slightly cerebral brief we gave them with a broadly Right-wing principle – such as 'Caring that works costs cash' – tended to either irritate or stump them.

In the end, Labour and Michael Foot were no real match for Thatcher. Disastrously, the opposition vote split between them and the SDP–Liberal Alliance, and on 9 June 1983, the Tories came home with an increased majority of 144. Labour was at possibly its lowest ebb. But an inestimably more ruthless and powerful Left-wing adversary was on the way. Immediately after the election came the second great defining event of her office. For the next 12 months or so, a significant proportion of my time would be spent dealing with the miners – and Arthur Scargill.

Long before she won the 1979 election, Margaret had developed an instinctive understanding that the unions in general, and the miners in particular, would need to be taken on in what would be an at times literal fight for survival. Heath had suffered total humiliation in 1972 and 1974 (when Margaret was in the Cabinet), which had led doves like Jim Prior to believe in industrial appeasement as the only option. Margaret had always believed that such an approach was only going to give us more of the same industrial shenanigans that we'd seen during the past twenty years. In the case of the previous Conservative government, as soon as Heath lost the support of the public, he was as good as defeated.

In contrast, Margaret was buoyed by the belief that she had been chosen by the electorate over Callaghan in 1979 – reaffirmed in 1983 – on the basis of non-appeasement being the only way forward out of the mess. She had kept an old strategy paper called *Stepping Stones* (written by two businessmen called Hoskyns and Strauss) that described the choice ahead as being one of 'shit or bust', and she knew that a massive confrontation would have to be had. She always knew it – but where she differed from Heath was that she knew how important was the timing.

Margaret had a reputation for being a decisive leader – but actually, she was just as likely to take her time over a decision, to the point of even seeming hesitant on occasions. In the case of the miners, for a long time there had been something of a phoney war going on. The first Employment Act of her government was far less dramatic than had been expected. But then, slowly but surely, she began to make her moves – first by getting rid of Prior over to Northern Ireland (which is where you put people you want out of the way), and then giving Norman Tebbit the Employment brief. (Coming out of the election, unemployment was still over 3 million, with the reduction of inflation the priority.) We actually had the first pit dispute in 1981, when the miners – led by Joe Gormley (the President of the NUM, who was relatively moderate compared to his successor) – rejected a closure programme, but, on that occasion, the government quickly had to back down, because the coal stocks were too low. The miners then elected Arthur Scargill – an unashamed Marxist – who, from the start, was hell-bent on toppling the government. By this time, however, Thatcher was far better prepared.

Like an army preparing its food supplies for war, her government had been stockpiling coal, so there weren't going to be any dark moments with electricity turned off. This was the crucial factor to avoid what had happened to Heath. Within days of the second election victory in 1983, she appointed Peter Walker to Energy; he was a bit of a wet, but good on media management. And, in the same year, the American industrialist, Ian MacGregor was put in charge of the National Coal Board. In the spring of 1984, the NCB announced that twenty collieries were to close with a loss of some 20,000 jobs, and, on cue, out came the miners. Doing so in spring, when fuel demand was light, was their first tactical mistake. Nonetheless, the strike would be the longest and bloodiest in British industrial history – even leading to people getting killed.

Ian MacGregor had just turned 70 at that time. He had lived in America for much of his life, but was, by birth, a Scot, born in Kinlochleven. He was actually very proud of being Scottish – but had a pronounced and at times incomprehensible American accent and dialect. He had a good degree in metallurgy from Glasgow University and had been an expert on weaponry during the war. Callaghan had brought him in as non-executive director of British Leyland, and then, after the election, Keith Joseph suggested to Margaret that he would be the ideal chairman of the heavy loss-making British Steel, with a brief to take that industry into privatisation and profit. After that, Margaret thought that he might be the man for the yet greater challenge of coal. Arthur Scargill called him the 'Yankee steel butcher', to which MacGregor would say, 'I'm the plastic surgeon' (his metaphors were never ideal). Either way, he set out on coal as he had finished on steel, by planning closures and redundancies, and immune to any thoughts of taking any prisoners. But I really liked him.

We used to call him the block of granite because it didn't matter what went on in a meeting, he'd just sit there, showing no concern for, and not much interest in, what anybody said. He was hopeless in dealing with people, politicians or media. In fact the British news industry was a compete mystery to him. He was used to US regional media, where most stories stayed local, and where rogue media outlets could easily be leant on. The power and scope of the British national media confounded him, and he became paranoid about them and thought that they were all communists. But, in his defence, I doubt that many English businessmen would have taken on what he did. It needed someone from outside the British system, who had no scruples about the use of a proverbial knife, whether it made him butcher or surgeon. It needed MacGregor to do it.

It did not make the job easy for us though. From the moment I was brought in, it was obvious that MacGregor had only limited interest in the PR battle and trying to explain his decisions was either not in his skill set or not in his nature. He said what he felt. Scargill's position that no pit should close (unless exhausted or not geographically viable) was clearly nonsensical, but MacGregor was useless at explaining a counterposition. For a start, he looked and sounded old, alien and inarticulate. Scargill ran rings round him, even sometimes calling him insane – an allegation to which MacGregor lent credence to by doing weird things like pretending to faint and trying to conceal his face from press photographers by putting a paper bag on his head. Nor did it help that MacGregor was incapable of showing sympathy. The press was full of stories about miners' families starving and going to the soup-kitchens. MacGregor would act as if it wasn't any concern of his – which it probably wasn't. As the strike intensified, Margaret and her Cabinet – who understood only too well that winning the PR battle was the first imperative – grew increasingly worried about this. Even if an unlikely compromise were reached, any post-deal meetings would see Scargill declaring victory and MacGregor (and the government by implication) looking like the loser. By April 1984, the problem was acute. MacGregor was a figure of hate or ridicule or both. Which was when David (Lord) Young asked me if I would go in as a PR specialist, alongside another adviser called David Hart.

David Hart's role in this story is not so well known, but he played an inestimable part in our successes. He was the Eton-educated son of the family of Polish Jews that owned Ansbacher, the merchant bank – but he'd lost all his money trying to make films, and had become an undischarged bankrupt. He looked like a cross between Lord Lucan and Oliver Reed, eccentric and flamboyant, the father of five children by four different women (he had ex-wives and mistresses all over the place), who lived for most of his time in London out of a room in Claridge's, but had lots of other properties. He'd read all sorts of obscure political philosophy, and had a lot of weird extreme views: Margaret's ministers were very suspicious of him and called him a spiv (he had a WW1 fighter-pilot moustache), yet he was an affectionate and likeable man – with astonishing generosity. He got on well with Ronnie Millar, who had got him in to see Margaret in the first place, and the relationship went from there. Hart's brother had worked with MacGregor at Lehman Brothers in the US.

Like many of us, he had reached the conclusion that Scargill was only concerned about a Marxist revolution and political supremacy, and Hart was determined to frustrate those plans. So, later in the campaign, he would disguise himself and go drinking with the miners: oddly, they regarded him as one of their own because he took snuff, as many of them did (because smoking was banned underground). He worked tirelessly on developing an anti-strike movement in the coalfield areas, helped fund a breakaway democratic miners' union, and set up military-style protection for non-striking miners and their families who were threatened by vicious NUM gangs. He developed something called the Gulliver Plan, which aimed to tie down the NUM with a multitude of legal actions – something that indirectly led to Scargill seeking a donation from Colonel Gaddafi, which did not play well with the public. In later years, Hart came to the view that Michael Portillo was the future of Britain, and financed his leadership campaign, before Portillo pulled out. It was typical of the things that he would do: such a colourful character, for whom tragedy struck, in later years, when he developed motor neurone disease. The last Christmas card he sent me had a picture of him as a paraplegic, in his wheelchair – wearing a red Father Christmas hat.

In the first months of the strike, MacGregor was given a very clear instruction, which was to not give in. He had handled the American Metal Climax strike in the US, which bore some similarities, in that a powerful union was trying to topple the establishment. I remember first seeing him at a board meeting. None of the NCB members had ever experienced anything like it before. He would sit down and they would all stare at him, and he would stare back at them, and there would be long awkward silences. They were always expecting him to tell them what to do, and he would expect them to tell him what they had done – usually not that much.

When he arrived, the NCB was almost entirely run by Left-wing people who frankly were not much different from the union bosses. The Deputy Chairman's name was Jimmy Cowan: to all intents and purposes, a Communist, who oversaw the Scotland area – where the miners were some of the most aggressive of them all – and whose modus operandi was generally to give the miners whatsoever they asked for. The management would just do as they were told – so if the union wanted more money, it got more money, and if it wanted to stop working for a while, it would stop working for a while. In the '70s – the days of Red Robbo at British Leyland – it had been continual farce. The NCB public relations guy, who MacGregor thought was just too weak, was called Geoff Kirk: MacGregor writes in his autobiography that Kirk was first described to him as 'the industrial PR man best liked in Fleet Street' which set the 'alarm bells ringing'. Kirk was quick to tell me that I was neither needed nor wanted and that he would not co-operate with me. He famously said, 'You can't use him … He works for the Tories.' Given the two election victories, MacGregor regarded that as a strong credential, whereas for Kirk, it made me a two-headed monster.

The industrial relations director was Ned Smith. MacGregor once described him as the 'old style of Hobart House'. He was professional, but again rather conciliatory-minded. I remember one time when he got up and said, 'I've got a meeting with Scargill and one or two other union bosses next week. I think I can find a settlement.' MacGregor said, 'What would you want to do that for Ned?' Ned replied, 'Well, I'm the industrial relations director, so it's my job to reach a sensible settlement.' To which MacGregor replied, 'Well, Ned, why would you do that, because when you come back to me with the settlement, I'm just going to say "No"? What are you going to do about that?' This kind of thing just led to Smith getting more and more cross – he suffered from bad back problems, which didn't help matters – and in the end he resigned.

MacGregor had a vision about how the pits could be, and he even took some of the working Nottinghamshire miners to pits in America where they had burger bars and coffee bars underground and where they wore white uniforms because they didn't have any coal dust. The main strategy was to keep the working miners (such as those in Nottinghamshire) working and encourage more miners to strike-break and return to work. We engineered a massive propaganda programme, appealing over the heads of the union bosses, getting the Fleet Street editors onside, and running stories about what Scargill was really like, and how MacGregor wasn't the bogeyman he had been portrayed as. Working with Saatchi & Saatchi, we came up with ads featuring lines like 'How the miners have been misled' and 'Come off it, Arthur!' which we had to pretend were Mac's own ideas, because we were not using the official NCB agency, which was CMP. This kind of adversarial campaigning would really upset Geoff Kirk and Ned Smith, who were being sidelined more and more, and could only think about negotiating a settlement on the miners' terms. It got to the point where Ned Smith wouldn't talk to me at all.

My brief involved trying to help MacGregor perform better when he appeared in public, putting the modernisation argument across better, so that people weren't just reading about miners and their families suffering, but would understand that there was a genuine economic case, and that, without change, the ultimate suffering would be greater. I would visit MacGregor every morning and every evening to discuss with him the progress and tactics. He called me 'Doctor Bell, the spin doctor'. He lived just round the corner from me in his apartment at 54 Eaton Square with his wife – the sort of lady that you only ever called Mrs MacGregor. Even he called her Mrs MacGregor. We'd have supper in what he called 'the oily spoon' – an Italian restaurant in Elizabeth Street called Memo's. And despite all his weaknesses in communication, I grew really fond of 'Mac'. He was a really nice man, who had made a career out of doing the most difficult, shitty jobs imaginable.

He would tell us stories about the industrial disputes in the US and the Mafia and the FBI. He'd say, 'Y'know, back in the US, when these guys get out of control, they just get hung from the nearest lamppost. That's what you guys need in this country. You're all too soft and moderate.' It terrified me that one day, he'd blurt that out in front of the television cameras. It was a good job he had a thick skin, because he was roundly abused and insulted. Mick McGahey, the Scottish miners leader, called him the 'alien whose clan does not even have its own tartan' – which I think is meant to be a terrible insult, although I'm not exactly sure. The press coverage of MacGregor was particularly offensive and one-sided, especially the television and particularly the BBC, with a predictably partisan approach which often favoured the Left over the Right.

I only met Scargill a few times, although there was absolutely no point in talking to him. He didn't listen to a word anybody said. There were never any pleasantries, not even 'Hello'; just an entire conversation in polemics. As soon as you met him, he would just launch into self-righteous vitriol about the evils of profit and how it must all be stopped. He had twinkly blue eyes, but there was a deep deadness in them. I don't think he was really interested in people – the miners or their families – just consumed by a mission to start and win a war. His aim was to generate chaos, force the troops onto the street, hope that a few people would be shot, and thus bring about a full revolution. I think a lot of the miners knew this, but he was their leader, so there was no option but to let him lead. At that time, I wasn't anybody of any significance, so when we were in meetings together, I don't think he had any idea who I was or why I was involved – nor did he care. He probably regarded me as MacGregor's man, which made me an irrelevance because I had no decision-making power. He and MacGregor couldn't even be in the same room, there was so much mutual loathing.

In the end, there were probably two all-important factors that set public opinion against the miners. First, the NUM refused to hold a ballot, which made them seem undemocratic and hypocritical. Then there was the increasing and often irrational violence. The public may have had sympathy for the individuals and communities involved, but when the mobs started burning their own houses down, setting fire to the pits, smashing all their own equipment, stealing all the crops from the farmers, and damaging their land, it all started to change a bit. They were torching their own credibility.

I went up in a police helicopter on a few occasions, to observe the pitched battles, but my field experience was thankfully quite limited. My office at the time was in an old room in Maple Street, rented by Saatchi & Saatchi, and with David Boddy and Rod Tyler helping me out. I was not a very visible member of the NCB team, but I still received all manner of threats and peculiar warnings – poison pen letters, mad ramblings, sinister claims that I was being watched and that I would be killed next time I ventured out – but that was par for the course, and anyway, I've had a lot of that kind of thing over the years. Nothing surprised me. The Praetorian guard were unbelievably violent people, and they had a very clear philosophy that the way to get what they wanted was by threat, intimidation and action – so they smashed things and destroyed things, and came after individuals, and whipped up the mob to do the same. But I was relatively detached from the kind of things that were visited on some of the poor folk who lived in the heartlands of the dispute and were deemed to be antipathetic to the Scargill cause. Every now and then MacGregor would get slightly worried – he had experience of being on the receiving end of violent attacks in the US – and would insist that we all had more security. But he couldn't have done the job if he let it all get to him personally.

I was, however, instructed to have a bodyguard. There was a 24-hour rota system, but the main chap I had was an ex-SAS officer called John, working as a freelance for the Conservative Party, as opposed to being a serving police officer or military. All he ever told me was that he shot a Sheikh in Aden. He had sat on a hillside for about three months with a high-velocity rifle, waiting until this particular Sheikh that they wanted rid of walked out of his house – then he blew him away. John used to sit in the passenger seat of the car. I would ring down when I was leaving the house and wasn't allowed to open the front door until the car had stopped outside; then the door would be unlocked, John would get out, look up and down the street and peer up into the air – presumably for snipers – and I would go and get in the back of the car, and the door locks would click down. If I went to a restaurant, he used to go in first and look all round and then sit on another table watching. If I went to a friend's house for dinner, he would get out of the car first and walk round the perimeter of the house. The whole thing was absolutely horrible. For the first day or so, you think it's exciting and that you're POTUS, but very quickly it becomes utterly oppressive. You can become paranoid, and start to think that the whole fiasco will actually draw more attention to you. If some nutter gets out of bed in the morning and wonders who he can assassinate today, he's more likely to kill somebody who's got a bodyguard in the car than somebody who hasn't. You don't want to be reminded all day long that you might be a target. It takes away yet more of your privacy. And it's embarrassing as well. There's only so much smalltalk you can have with your bodyguard.

We were once going to do a pitch and we were in two separate cars. Terry Bannister, who was the account director, was in the car behind which had caught up with us, and when we stopped at some traffic lights, he started walking up to our car to ask me something. Before he could open his mouth, he was having his face pushed into the bonnet by the bodyguard. I kept saying, 'No, no, he's my friend, please don't kill him.'

I sometimes thought that MacGregor felt the same kind of irritation with me shadowing him like a puppy to protect him from saying the wrong thing. If MacGregor went to speak or do an interview, I would go too. But you can't turn somebody into someone they're not and MacGregor was a boardroom street-fighter who cared not one jot about any unsympathetic image he might be communicating. Of course, the mine workers wanted to personalise it, because they knew that both MacGregor and Thatcher could easily be portrayed as uncaring, unsympathetic and out-of-touch with working people's lives. MacGregor was perfect material for Scargill (whose colourful nature was adored by a lot of the media) in this respect. We tried all we could to make MacGregor seem less belligerent, but that was his character, and he was never going to look like he was the miners' friend. Eventually we decided that there had to be somebody else to do the job of speaking for the Coal Board, because MacGregor just couldn't do it. So we brought in Mike Eaton, from the Yorkshire region. If MacGregor didn't do avuncularity, Eaton piled it on in shovel-loads: he got on like a house on fire with the more moderate miners, and even the Yorkshire ones thought that he was a decent bloke. He smoked a pipe, drank frothing pints of Webster's bitter, and was a sort of carbon-copy of Harold Wilson. The problem was that he was too much of a good thing, and liked his ale so much that he was often a few pints on the wrong side of drunk. So when he went on television, they'd put him in the green room, and he'd be pissed rotten within ten minutes. I used to meet him at the Goring Hotel every day, because we didn't want people to see us in discussions at the NCB headquarters in Hobart House, and he was always likely to start drinking even first thing in the morning.

I'm not sure I ever thought we'd be on the losing side, but, at a late stage in the dispute, there was a very tense (and well documented) time with the NACODS deputies: they were the pit safety people, and moderates, who had originally defied Scargill by not striking. In fact, they had never before, in all their long history, been on strike. The acronym stood for 'the National Association of Colliery Overseers Deputies and Shot-firers'. They used to take canaries down the pit to see if there were any poisonous gases – that was something that was a hundred or so years old and had never been modernised because that's what they'd always done and always wanted to keep doing. In October 1984, they ran a ballot, mainly over something called the Colliery Review Procedure. MacGregor regarded this as a phoney grievance cooked up by the TUC, who were still hurting from Scargill's criticisms of them for their poor support, and saw NACODS as a way to redeem themselves in his eyes. NACODS were led by their President, Ken Sampey, and the General Secretary, called Peter McNestry – we called them 'Scampi and Chips'. Keeping the NACODS people at work had been essential (although MacGregor didn't agree), because if they stopped working, all the other miners who we had encouraged to stay on would have to stop on safety grounds. This terrified people like Peter Walker (who used to talk directly with McNestry), and the thumbscrews were put on MacGregor to appease them – but he just said, 'Go ahead. Go on strike. Do your damnedest. You won't stop me!'

There was a critical moment when we were in Margaret's suite at the Brighton Tory Party Conference. It was an hour or so before the IRA bomb went off. Tebbit phoned MacGregor to tell him that, on the PM's direct instructions, the NACODS had to be bought off. MacGregor was not happy with this at all, and told Tebbit as much. Norman made me talk to him, and I had to try and coax him round. Then Margaret put in a call to him directly. He finally agreed, and said he'd speak with them whilst holding his nose. Peter Walker had stayed back in London, so our job was to arrange an urgent meeting involving him and Norman Willis, TUC General Secretary, along with the NACODS team. We had authority to try to reach a settlement midway between the NACODS demands and the NCB demands.

The pressure on MacGregor was intense, but he was still very bloody-minded about what the government had told him to do and what he felt was right. It was not beyond him to agree to their faces, but then, when push came to shove, say what he really thought. I remember arriving at Walker's office, with the union bosses already all there swilling beer and eating sandwiches. Peter Walker said, 'Well, Ian, I think this is a very good opportunity for us to reach a common ground and Norman and his colleagues have come in and they've given up their time so we can see if we can reach a compromise agreement.' To which MacGregor replied, 'Well, I'm not going to do that Mr Secretary.' Walker said, 'What? Sorry Ian. I didn't quite catch that.' MacGregor said, 'I'm not going to do that, because it's not the right thing to do. I'm the Chairman of the Coal Board and it would be a disaster not to stand firm at this point.' At which point it all went nuts. Walker said, 'I'm going to make sure the Prime Minister knows what you've done!' and the NACODS said, 'Well we're not fucking well sitting here being insulted by this bloody Yank,' and they all got up and stormed out.

Of course, in the end, we had to get them back, and by 25 October, we had reached a settlement that was far better than the NUM had been offered. This was the turning point in the strike. Scargill should have sued for a similar settlement which he might have won, and which would have enabled him to claim victory. But he would not budge, and from that moment, his campaign was doomed. NACODS were settled, and more and more miners started drifting back to work. Wise generals know when to pull their troops from battle – as Margaret had done on the earlier strike. Scargill knew not. Now it was the Prime Minister who lived to fight another day.

During the strike, Bernard Ingham had made it plain he thought MacGregor was a disaster. He favoured Geoff Kirk and was unhappy when he went. Ingham was Margaret's press secretary for 11 years, after doing the job for ministers like Barbara Castle and Tony Benn. He had been a staunch Labour supporter and NUJ activist whilst working for the *Guardian*, but had become disillusioned with the unions and turned Tory. He had very little to do with us in our role as Party advisers, and that suited him. In those days, there was separation between party and government: the special advisers (which included the advertising agency) reported to the Party and were political, whereas Ingham was a civil servant, in theory, reporting impartially to government. That distinction changed for good when Campbell went on the Blair government's payroll and they effectively merged the SPADs with the government, bringing in a heap of problems and issues. Ingham was most definitely a civil servant – the government's spokesman, and never mentioned by name in briefings – although, to be honest, he was supremely loyal to Margaret and unceremoniously brutal to anyone who threatened her. He developed the use of the non-attributable Lobby system as a way of communicating Margaret's core beliefs, as well as leaking horrible things about people he (and she) disliked. Although he and I were both devoted to Margaret, we were, on the rare occasions when we came into contact, always at loggerheads. To our team, he seemed bad-tempered and sarcastic – he would do that Northerner thing and say, 'I'm honest and blunt and call a spade a shovel', which is a euphemism for being rude and dogmatic. Oddly, I think Margaret saw some of his plain-speaking straightforwardness in herself, which is probably why she had a soft spot for him and always defended him.

10

Unsettled

In the middle of the NACODS dispute, on 12 October 1984, at the Party Conference, the Brighton Bomb went off in the Grand Hotel. It was nearly 3.00 a.m. We'd had a meeting with Margaret (who was working on her speech for the following day) and Denis (who was thinking about going to bed), and I was walking round to Lord McAlpine's cocktail party. Then the middle of the hotel just disappeared – walls, floor, the lot. Oddly, it felt like there was a delay before the sound, which then seemed to reverberate about 15 times over and over again. One voice then just said, 'I think we'd better leave', as if something very minor had happened such as if the hostess at a party has just burned the meat course. It was all very 'stiff upper lip' behaviour, no screaming or shouting, just making conversation, walking down the fire escape and out onto the promenade. It was only when you looked back that you could see how much of the hotel had gone. Quite a few people still had it in their heads that there were boats in the bay that had fired missiles – probably because it was hard to imagine that a single planted device could do so much damage. Nobody had the faintest idea whether Margaret had been killed or not.

When the bomb went off, Michael Dobbs had been taking a bath. The only thing that he had been able to find was a raincoat, and now he was walking around in it and nothing else, pontificating about what was happening, as if he knew something that no one else knew. However, what he didn't know – and we did – was that his raincoat had split all the way up the back and his white hairy bottom was sticking out.

As the sun came up, a lot of people moved into the hotel next door – people were sharing rooms and so on. Alistair McAlpine rang up the boss of Marks & Spencer in Brighton, got them to open, and sent his secretary to go and buy their entire stock of knickers and underwear – because many delegates had lost all their clothes. They had volunteers standing outside the hotel lobby, with a huge pile of underwear, giving out different sizes to the women. (The men weren't too bothered, which says something about gender differences, I guess.) All day long, the M&S store in Brighton was full of conference delegates buying new clothes to get them through.

It felt like the Tory Party at war, in that everyone was determined to be steadfast, and everybody behaved in the most civilised way imaginable – this is what the Blitz must have been like. Everybody helped each other, shared stuff, got things done. As what had happened started to filter through, we learned that John Wakeham's wife had been killed, along with another MP, Anthony Berry (who was in room 659, which should have been occupied by Peter Walker, who had stayed in London to handle the NACODS issue). Norman Tebbit's wife was thereafter paralysed. Norman himself was not in a good way either, to the extent that, at one point, they weren't sure whether he'd pull through or not, although it was reported afterwards that he had been partially protected by a mattress that fell on top of him. I went into the Metropole hotel next door, where Rod Tyler had a suite, and about eight of us slept in there for the next night or so. Only a few hours later, and with negligible sleep, Margaret gave a completely rewritten – and supremely defiant – speech, about how we had all just been witnesses to an attempt to bring down the government. The bomb was a momentous event, both in terms of its audaciousness and malicious intent, and in terms of its absolute strategic ineffectuality.

Cometh the hour: I think that was one of those fleeting historical moments (I still see her giving that speech as a cameo) – a point in time when she reigned supreme and when Party and country witnessed her indomitableness. She had avoided death literally by a few metres, yet there she was, speaking from an improvised text, and, of course, there was a huge ovation when she'd finished. It was hard to imagine, at that moment, that within a few months she would be suffering one of her worst crises – over the Westland helicopter deal.

If the 1984 Brighton speech was the high water mark of Party unity, Westland was one of the lowest. Ostensibly, it was about the Cabinet disagreement over the future of the British helicopter industry, the last remaining manufacturer being Westland, who were making heavy losses and needed a rescue bid. Michael Heseltine – Defence Secretary at the time – preferred a European consortium led by GEC, while the Westland Board and Margaret favoured an American-led bid from Sikorsky. In the end, she just overruled everybody and said we're going with the latter, leading to Heseltine throwing a fit in a Cabinet meeting, storming out into Downing Street and publicly resigning – an act of the most appalling bad manners. She didn't even know that he'd resigned until the Cabinet had adjourned.

There had been bad blood between them for years, probably since he did his reckless mace-waving stunt in the Commons, as a result of which she had come very near to sacking him from her Shadow Cabinet there and then. They were certainly not often on speaking terms, and their political philosophies were so different that they may as well have belonged to different parties. He was an advocate of ever-closer European federalism and was always keen to use his Defence portfolio for a bit of social engineering, such as artificially creating jobs on Merseyside – the kind of thing to which she was viscerally opposed. The problem was that she was never quite sure how to deal with him, and it led to one of the few sagas where she could actually be said to have been indecisive. In avoiding a face-to-face confrontation, she just left him free to rampage around the media like a wounded, vengeful lion.

In all of this, I was in a rather strange position, as I was PR adviser at the time to Arnold (Lord) Weinstock of GEC, which put me in the opposite camp to Margaret. Weinstock was the son of Polish Jews. He came from very lowly origins, and was a wonderful, clever, charming, witty man, who loved horseracing, and eventually owned a lot of outstanding race winners. However, the media didn't always treat him kindly, and it was my brief to try to project a more favourable – and actually more accurate – impression of the man as a great industrialist.

The Westland affair dragged on and on all through 1985 and beyond, with shocking damage to the government, Party, and PM, and leading to Leon Brittan's resignation for leaking material. And all this might never have happened. Two nights before the Cabinet meeting, I was sitting in Weinstock's office and he said to me, 'Why can't she understand that she's wrong?' To this, I replied, 'Because she thinks you're the ones who are wrong not going with the Americans.' He said, 'Well, she's never discussed it with me.' I said, 'She doesn't believe in telling businessmen what they should or shouldn't do.' Weinstock then said, 'Maybe we can sort it out. Can we call her?' So, there and then, I rang up Downing Street, spoke to the 'Switch' as everybody calls it, and tried to get put through to Margaret. But I could only get Robert Armstrong, who was the then Cabinet Secretary. And all he would say was that she was too busy. I said, 'If she's got two minutes in the car or between, Lord Weinstock needs to speak with her urgently …' He said, 'It won't happen, but I'll tell her', and put the phone down. Arnold listened to all conversations on a big squawk box, so he heard the interchange and said, 'You see. I told you she wouldn't speak to me.' I told him that he was wrong and that she would return the call. We sat there for an hour but the call never came – because Armstrong never gave her the message. My guess is that, had Lord Weinstock spoken to her that night, he was in the right frame of mind to rethink his position and pull GEC out of the European consortium and join the American bid. She would then have had no difficulty in awarding the contract and everything would have been resolved. Who knows?

The lesson I learned in that event was that people in power are not their own masters. Other people decide to whom they'll speak and where they'll go and what they'll do. It was especially the case before mobile telephones. Nowadays, it's easier to ring the PM on his mobile and speak directly to him or Tweet him if you like, but not in those days. The Westland saga did a great deal of harm to Margaret. It made her look as though she was a liar. It was the beginning of her demise. After that, I think she felt she had to be more dishonest herself, in order to survive. She lost her straightforwardness. She listened to those amongst her advisers who were only interested in winning the argument, and beating the other side up – which, over time, amplified the worst parts of her character, the bullying and the aggression. Those were the aspects of her character that had not been so apparent before.

For my own part, as a function of the coal strike, I developed a reputation for being able to handle industrial disputes, so I got asked to help with the seamen's dispute and with British Rail. In time, I had acquired a reputation as an ad man, a reputation as a political adviser, and a reputation as an industrial relations adviser. I think it was around this time that I learned the importance of admitting one's own insufficiencies: I believe that, for example, if you don't actually know something, it is by far the best policy to say that you don't. It's odd, but people in many industries – media, advertising, and politics especially – can't say those three words: 'I don't know'. If the client says, 'Did you see that piece in the *Financial Times*?', people feel they need to say, 'Yes.' And if they haven't, they spend the next half an hour trying to work out what the fuck it was that they have just said that they knew all about.

Throughout the second half of 1984, I was mulling over the implications of leaving Saatchi & Saatchi. In the event, I resigned early in the New Year, by which time I had unquestionably had enough. I'd reached the point where I no longer wanted to stay. Whilst the miners' strike had been going on, I was meant to be running the company, but there was no interest or satisfaction in it for me. The brothers had been buying and trying to buy various global networks, which they'd then tell me to integrate and merge and so on, which I just didn't enjoy. I liked client work and the politics, and I became increasingly uninvolved in what the brothers were doing.

Charles then came to me with the suggestion that I could earn much more money by being a 'consultant' to client senior management, rather than doing conventional advertising work. That was when he created the idea of a new satellite office round the corner in Maple Street, where I would be given half a dozen people working for me, including Michael Dobbs, running this kind of global corporate advisory operation. Charles had started by suggesting that I take a 51 per cent ownership and that I'd make a lot of money out of it, but I'm sure the whole scheme was just to get me off the premises.

In my memory, Michael Dobbs is often pouring drinks. There was one occasion when we were at Chequers, and Margaret had a very bad day and was in a filthy temper. We sat down in the drawing room at the front of the house, and she said, 'Let's have a drink.' Dobbs was about to do the honours, but for some unaccountable reason, just at that moment, they brought in the newspapers. When we were in London, Margaret never normally read them. Instead, Bernard Ingham would give her an edited media-briefing file in the morning, and we tried not to let her near the actual newspapers because it sent her wild with rage, and there was always the danger she'd try to sack all her ministers or get the editors sacked. But now she got hold of them and started reading all sorts of gossip and nonsense, and was getting herself into an even fouler mood. Dobbs gave her a whisky that she drank without even questioning what it was – I'm not sure she was even aware of drinking it. Anyway, as we went on, he just kept on pouring the whiskies and she kept drinking them, and very soon became completely pissed. He kept asking, 'How much?' and she kept saying, 'Plenty!' She was sitting in her chair, and then suddenly, she just passed out. Dobbs and I wondered what to do. We even wondered if she was dead – so we crouched over her looking for signs of movement and breathing – at which point she woke up, barked, 'What do you think you're doing?' and stormed out (possibly to go and be sick). After a few minutes she arrived back, looking and sounding angry-mood-normal, and started castigating the papers again.

Michael always poured drinks for Norman Tebbit too. Tebbit was a very emotional man. He'd kind of adopted Dobbs (on secondment from Saatchi & Saatchi), who followed him everywhere – did his drinks, looked after him, the lot. Tebbit was the Left's bogeyman – they reviled him. You would go to meetings in his Chingford constituency and they'd hold up banners that said, 'We know where you live' and the like. Even before he was injured in the bombing, he faced some truly terrifying threats all the time. But he was hysterically funny, with a manic, almost violent sense of humour. He used to hang plastic chickens on the back of his door. An anecdote had been circulating that in order to keep himself as cross as possible, he would tear the heads off chickens. So Norman decided to let reality follow the myth. People would go and see him and he'd say, 'Excuse me now, I just want to tear a chicken apart', and he'd go and take a plastic chicken off the door and pull off its detachable head and then come back and sit down.

That Saatchi team at Maple Street were eventually positioned as a sort of a commando unit that came in to oversee big pitches – such as for Johnson & Johnson – and make sure that the work was exciting. It sounds a lot better than it was. Nobody really knew how seriously to take it. I didn't care that much, to be honest, as I was thoroughly enjoying life, doing things like the political work. Charles's plan never came to anything significant: like so many of the things he talked about they were ideas that he would never nail down. In my cynical view, they were his conveniences for moving people around, rather than achieving anything meaningful. Yet I was still regarded as the Managing Director of the agency by all the staff, who hadn't the faintest idea what was going on at whatever office.

In truth, all I wanted was an endorsement from Charles and Maurice. But it was never forthcoming. I wanted them to say, 'Tim, you're doing a bloody good job. Thank you.' Both of them know that it's what people want, but that's the one thing they'll never give them. I believe that they fear that once you praise someone, that person will stop trying. I don't think it's a management technique that they have learned – although I wouldn't be surprised to find that Maurice has read books on reinforcement strategy – but I think it's just an instinct, in their nature.

I also think that, at some level, they resented the level of contact I was having with Number 10. My dealings in politics were, it has to be said, taking on a life of their own. However, I didn't want to switch into a full-time job in that field: I couldn't bear the idea of trying to climb up that very slippery pole. But nor did I want to stay part of the Saatchi acquisition machine trying to merge agencies in Mexico or the Seychelles or wherever: the kind of stuff that sounds glamorous but is actually incredibly dull. Anyway, Martin Sorrell had control over that side of the business, and was becoming more and more involved in negotiations and acquisitions. Although they gave him a bad time too: he had some ferocious rows with Charles, which made him take it out on everyone else.

I'm not sure that Maurice was too happy either. Maurice was building a giant corporation, and he had to make things happen, which required him to get people to do things they didn't want to do or agree with – and he would openly admit that he often didn't agree with his brother either. But nevertheless, his brother had told him to do it, so it had to be done.

Sometime in 1982, the brothers had bought Compton USA. I had no role at all in the negotiations and planning of that. And, as part of this, they installed their chief executive, Milton Gossett (his first name was actually Oscar), as the chairman and chief executive of the combined group. One day, Charles called me in and said, 'Gossett's got that job – but not really, because it'll only be temporary. Don't worry about it. We'll get rid of him soon. Then you can take it over.' They said that I was head of 'Worldwide', but that term meant everything except USA and UK, which was like making me head of the peas and carrots but not the steak and kidney. Even at that stage, it was pretty obvious I was being edged out.

The fact that I was going to be reporting to Gossett was not meant to be a reward for great service. He was a perfectly reasonable American, who was an engineer by training, with a noticeable red scar on his forehead, which everybody used to say was caused by a Cherokee arrow that had been fired at him when he was younger. He brought with him an entourage of well-meaning Americans – it was my first experience of those ghastly people who run inter-national networks – who didn't actually seem to do anything real, just went around the place having meetings about meetings. My job was to accommodate them and 'Saatchify' them – the most unachievable task I've ever been given.

None of this gave me sleepless nights – I wasn't doing much sleep to start with. My life was a sprint, running so quickly that I never had any time to pause and reflect – to sit down and think whether I was doing the right thing or living the right life. London was a 24-hour fluorescent playground, buzzing with new money, new-found confidence, and new experiences. In those days, you just got on with it, both good behaviour and not so good. It was a roller-coaster lifestyle – and only in hindsight can you see that it eventually takes its toll on you. The body is fantastically resilient and I have always had enormous stamina, but I was moving at an unsustainable speed. I was often taking only one or two hours of sleep a night; eating at inconsistent times, in different ways, sometimes not at all, living on the electricity of the moment. Many aspects of my life were not what you would call sensible, but this is not a confessional, and I don't want to dredge up the details of some of the unacceptable things that I was doing. I certainly didn't stop to reflect much.

As this went on, my attitude to work changed. There was a sort of feeling that the more difficult you made it to do something, the more rewarding it might be. That was the weird thing that I noticed about drink – that you would get intoxicated before a meeting (which I sometimes did) as a kind of challenge to yourself. If you were drunk, you had to be much more in control of yourself to overcome the fact that you were drunk – which is, of course, a very convoluted, and ultimately destructive, logic, but all part of that mindset, and why it happens in high-powered professions, I fear. You were impelled to make things as difficult as possible for yourself to make the result as rewarding as possible. We'd be finishing the presentation literally seconds before doing the pitch; we'd go without eating anything and be starving hungry; we'd go missing until minutes before key meetings; we'd ignore client calls; it was all like a gigantic self-imposed challenge – damage yourself, recover yourself.

The one advantage of all this – if you can call it that – was that I was able to understand the fast people around me and their lifestyle, because I was doing some of the same things that they were doing. I was one of them. I understood what motivated them in a way that Charles and Maurice couldn't – or wouldn't. The brothers were actually quite horrified by the whole idea of not being in control of themselves. This made them very harsh on, and intolerant of, people who showed any kind of human frailty or weakness or who needed to find solace in drink, drugs, sex – whatever it was. And this incomprehension and intolerance was *their* weakness.

My life was my work. I didn't have any social life or private life that wasn't connected to the business or to politics. But my conversations with business associates were evolving; no longer exclusively about advertising, but now involving the wider picture brought by my experience in politics – wealth creation, business efficiency and profitability, how you could pump more money back into society, achieve lower taxes and reduce public expenditure and all those kind of things. Discussions that had previously been immaturely and narrowly about a client's advertising or brand imagery would now as likely be about the politics of business – because that's what I'd been working on with Thatcher. I could talk about big topics and name-drop big names. These were the enterprise years. Britain was becoming a completely different country, in the business of creating wealth, building great corporations and creating a financial centre for the world. So I had something important to say, and to offer. And it was time to move agency.

During the miners' strike, I'd been liaising with Frank Lowe, of Lowe Howard-Spink. I'd helped get the agency onto the NCB account, much to the annoyance of Bernard Ingham and Geoff Kirk, the latter feeling that he ought to be the sole arbiter of this kind of thing. Frank was (and still is) one of the icons of advertising: a creative genius, as eccentric as they come; brilliant, incisive, pioneering, unpredictable, awkward, charming, volatile, vicious; inspiring adoration and terror in equal measure across the industry. At the time, he was top of his game. Frank knew that I was getting increasingly uncomfortable at Saatchi & Saatchi, and had started to think that it might be a good idea to team up. When Frank rang me and suggested that I work with him, it seemed the perfect opportunity.

Although I wasn't aware of it at the time, Frank had already asked Charles about my availability – they were friendly with each other, and the brothers had tried to buy Lowes at one point as well. And I'd already told Charles I was thinking about going. Indeed, Charles had been to see me at home and pretended to feel that we could still make a go of it: he said that we could do this and that and we could make it all so different. But I just replied that I'd had enough. He said, 'Don't be ridiculous. You can't leave. You can't afford to.' Of course, they were crocodile tears: he had already told the press that my future was no longer there. It allowed him to make it sound as though he had got rid of me. Charles did all he could to ensure his interpretation of events. Some time later, Margaret Patrick – the marketing writer on the *Financial Times* – told me that she had written a rather flattering eulogy of my time at Saatchi & Saatchi, which Charles found out about and told her that if it was printed he would make sure she never worked again. So my leaving Saatchi & Saatchi was a very low-profile event. I was just disinvented (as was anyone who went). Charles even leant on *Campaign* to get them to bury the story – 'Bell ends rumours by taking Lowe job' – in the middle pages.

I liked Frank. There were some striking similarities with Charles: they had both started their careers at the same agencies, so had similar creative craft-skills and approaches; they were both uncomfortable with being in the public limelight; and they both had a degree of narcissistic, reclusive egotism, which meant that they could be rude, unsympathetic bullies. But Frank was a vulnerable eccentric, where Charles isn't. They had pretty similar attitudes towards advertising and how it should work, but Frank didn't think he could take over the world. He was uncomfortable about his origins and his background and all that stuff, whereas Charles showed no vulnerability of any kind at all. Frank would get upset about things and if something didn't work, he'd get in a state. And he hated flying. You'd go on a plane with him, and he would sit there and as the plane started to take off, he'd yell, 'Oh my God, we're going to crash, what are we going to do?' You'd be up in the air, and there'd be a noise, and he'd say, 'What was that? What's that noise?' Like so many things with Frank, you never knew whether it was serious or whether it was all an act.

The package at Lowes was very attractive: I had a six-figure salary and some very attractive share options. My role was wide-ranging and significant, I could bring in all my international experience and what I'd learned at Saatchi & Saatchi about mergers and acquisitions, and – initially at least – it seemed like I was an equal partner. I was very flattered by it, especially following all the heartbreak at Saatchis. Some people had expected me to start my own agency. But I am a hero-worshipper, that's part of my nature. I work for my demi-Gods, and Charles was a demi-God, and Frank was a demi-God. It's about enjoying the people that you think are brilliant from the comforting half-light of their shadow – recycling their ideas, and helping them sell their stories. That's what I do best. It's why I'd get on well with clients.

Frank had been a huge success, but had never really been given the credit for the achievements of his previous agency, CDP. Maybe this was why he was as miserable as sin most of the time. He didn't need to be. The share price went up by a massive 49p on the day that I came through the doors at Bowater House in Knightsbridge. The agency started to win a lot of new business. Around the anniversary of my joining, in January 1986, *Campaign* did an article (accompanied by my photograph) headlined, 'Lowe. The year of the Bell', suggesting that the agency was flying and that my joining them had been a positive step for both parties. With our new title, Lowe Howard-Spink & Bell we won the prestigious Agency of the Year award. Our billings were just under £20 million and the shares had doubled in value.

But it sent Frank into a complete decline. All he could see was my name in the frame. He refused to come to work for four weeks, brooding, like a Sherlock Holmes figure, at his home, attended to by Vaughan, his butler. This ludicrous state of affairs carried on for a while, until Geoff Howard-Spink came to see me, as did his wife, and various other worried people. They asked me to go and apologise to him. I said, 'What for? I haven't done anything. I didn't write the fucking article. It had nothing to do with me. What am I supposed to be sorry for?' So the finance people came to me and talked about how the City would find out and kill the share price. They said, 'It's your duty.'

So I went round to the house in Glebe Place, and stood there, and said, 'Apparently, I've got to apologise to you. I have no idea what I'm apologising about, but whatever it is that I've done, I'm really sorry I did it, I wish I hadn't done it, and I'll never do it again.' He sat there and turned to me, and whispered in his strange low trill, 'You've got to understand Tim: I just want a little credit. I just want a little recognition of what I've done. That's all I ask for. That's all, Tim. That's all.' I said, 'Frank, everybody knows what you've done, and how marvellous you are. You're regarded as the great creative genius of the industry.' And in many respects, I did actually believe what I was saying. Then, I went back to work, without a clue as to what he was going to do. But the next day, he came in perfectly normally, and carried on as though nothing had happened.

Frank's long-suffering business partner was Geoff Howard-Spink. One night, Frank called me into his office and said, 'Could you do me a favour, Tim? Do you agree that "Spink" is a very ugly name and doesn't sound very nice, does it? Do you think you could persuade Geoff to change his name to Geoff Howard?' I told him that I'd have a go, and went to see Geoff. I said to him, 'You know, the Americans have a lot trouble with your name. They say "Howard", then they call you "Howie", because they think "Howard" is your first name. I was just wondering whether we might talk about a possible solution?' And Geoff just said, 'Have you been sent to tell me to change my name? Because you're about the 38th person that Frank has sent. He's even sent Alfredo Marcantonio.'

The honeymoon period of my joining had been maddeningly short. Frank and I had offices side-by-side in the building, but tensions grew. Before long, we were having fierce arguments – and then reconciliations as well – but it was all very unsettling for everyone. In 1988, I orchestrated a successful pitch for the British Rail business (which actually involved some superb creative material), but at the last stage, Frank decided that he did not want me there. I was beginning to get bored with his madness and his eccentricity and he was becoming ever more unpredictable and difficult. He would arrive at work in a bad mood, he'd fire people at random, he'd suddenly start to move all the chairs round the office, he'd cancel all expenses; he'd abandon important pitches on a whim, saying, 'I don't want to do it. I'm not doing it. I won't!'

He had developed a pitch technique that was to lower his voice as the presentation progressed, ending up in an inaudible whisper. I think he believed that if he whispered, people would have to listen more intently, so when the creative work was finally revealed, the client audience would be distracted by trying to hear what he was saying and wave the ads through. Originally, this was funny, eccentric and flamboyant even, but then it started to just become irritating and left you never knowing where the hell you stood. My approach to business had always been to build mutually enhancing relationships with clients; taking them into your confidence, and generating partnerships with great work as the output. Frank cared for nothing but getting a client to accept what he decided was the right ad. Nothing else mattered. It was a kind of creative fascism.

He had been persuaded by stockbrokers and corporate finance advisers to make acquisitions, as a way of leveraging the share price and creating more value. Nobody understood what any of it was really about, but he had decided to buy something, which turned out to be the Good Relations company (for around £4 million), because it was available and because everybody said it was a good idea to buy it. In typically nutty fashion, at exactly that moment, he called me in and said, 'I don't like all this public relations business. It's horrible. It's a sort of inferior work, and I don't want any of that around the place. So Tim, you look after it.' Not exactly a compelling sell. And he said it in a kind of mad, manic way, with his eyes popping out. He said, 'Tim. These PR people; they get in the way. They spoil jolly good adverts. These things get in the way. So I think what would be good is if I run the advertising side, and you run everything else. We'll call it Lowe Bell Communications and you can run that and I'll run the ad agency, and then we won't keep bumping into each other and I'll get a little bit of the recognition I'm entitled to.' He still saw me as the problem, taking the limelight. I didn't particularly want to get involved with PR, but I agreed, and in April 1987, I let go of the chief executive role (becoming group deputy chairman) to concentrate on matters non-advertising related.

In a way, I'd turned around completely, from being utterly dismissive of the PR industry to being its advocate. This wasn't a case of revisionism. The marketing and media climate was changing rapidly. I could see the potential now involved: if you brought communications strategy into public relations companies and stopped it being about sending out press releases, it could be a wider, more strategic product; it could be an impressive business practice. In the end, we started to think about going independent, and stage a buyout of Lowe Bell Communications, and after several months of negotiations, we agreed on a fee of £7.6 million. I'd struck up a strong friendship with Piers Pottinger and one or two other people from the PR side, including Tony Good, Judy Craddock and Jeff Lees, from Good Relations, and a chap called Mark Smith who did finance. There was also a guy called Alan Cornish, by that time CEO of Good Relations, and he had come along and explained how we could do it, and from where we'd get investment.

We got funding from the Barclay twins, David and Fred, who were wonderfully helpful; NatWest lent us £4 million (a year or so later, they gave us an award as one of their most successful new businesses); merchant bankers Hambros-Magan also came in. I had a 30 per cent shareholding, and Piers 20 per cent. We launched the new business in September 1989 (with Lowe Bell Financial Services, Good Relations, GR Design, and NML coming in as part of our group), and set up offices at 7 Hertford Street in Mayfair. Very quickly, we started to make some good money, and were able to pay off the debt and become profitable. We got rid of some of the stuff that wasn't working, brought in some new people – including Stephen Sherbourne, Margaret Thatcher's old political secretary – and started to carve out a niche for ourselves in the industry, with divisions for finance, public affairs, politics, advertising, design, and so on. Now, at last – in my mid-40s – I knew what I was. I was a PR man.

11

Matters Arising

I first heard about Distillers in 1968. My middle sister's earliest boyfriend had been a chap called David Mason, and his daughter Louise was affected by the drug Thalidomide, which was prescribed to pregnant women and led to some terrible disabilities and deaths. He led the people seeking a compensation settlement against its UK manufacturers, a company called Distillers Biochemicals. David was an art dealer – in fact, he bought for Andrew Lloyd Webber, who I know – so we bumped into each other in several ways. My life is full of coincidences.

The Scottish Distillers Company was both a pharmaceutical and drinks producer. In its latter guise, it owned a number of famous spirits brands, such as Johnnie Walker, Dewar's, Haig, and so on. In the late '70s and early '80s, the whisky market was enjoying a consumer boom, which, in turn, made the company seem an attractive commercial entity. With the ongoing possibility of Thalidomide claims against this particular company, it was not straightforward for anyone to make an assessment of Distillers' exact market value. But early in 1986, they became the target for take-over bids from retailing group Argyll and from the Guinness drinks company.

I knew the CEO of Guinness – one Ernest Saunders – a most sober and extremely intense sort of person. (In fact, they called him 'Deadly Ernest'.) He was aggressive and single-minded, and only ever focused on the matter in hand; there was no small talk whatsoever with him, and any conversation with him could turn, in an instant, into a fraught and difficult browbeating. Marketing was his life. He knew a lot about it, had considerable experience of it, and believed that it was the way to achieving anything that a business desired. He had both an eye and a determination to make things happen, and if he set out to do something, he would crush anything that got in his way. He believed that rules were, in most cases, an inconvenient nuisance. He was born an Austrian Jew, but his parents had come over to England as refugees during the war. He had changed his name, apparently selecting it from a telephone directory, gone to Cambridge and become a hugely successful businessman. By the early '80s, he was the top man at Guinness – which he proceeded to turn from an Irish family-run stout company into a £90 million global drinks giant.

I had first met him when he was a senior executive at Nestlé, this being shortly before he took over at Guinness. At that time, his boss at Nestlé was a Swiss-German chap called Arthur Furer, who would sit in his grand dining-room office (at the top of the glass-fronted building overlooking the lake in Vevey), gazing out over his empire. Furer ran the operation in a rather bossy and aggressive way, but he had a thick comedy-German accent (the office joke being to call him 'Herr Furer' – which I improved on by calling him 'Der Furer'). I worked with both of them on the Nestlé baby milk account, and never once did it seem like a stress-free way of making a living. Take for instance what happened to me in 1981. In the US, Senator Edward Kennedy (who needed some positive publicity after the Chappaquiddick incident in 1969 and a loss in the 1980 Democratic Party primary) instigated a Senate hearing into Nestlé's baby milk and its use in underdeveloped countries. There followed a World Health Organization investigation, culminating in a meeting at the United Nations of about 500 doctors and baby experts. Ernest was supposed to address the assembly on that occasion, and a small group of us had written his speech for him. But the night before, he did the sort of thing that Ernest did, and suddenly developed laryngitis, claiming he couldn't utter a word. So I had to take his place – speaking to this clever and sceptical medical audience on something about which I knew absolutely nothing. It was an ordeal that I'd rather not go through again, thank you.

The relationship had continued with Lowes when Guinness was acquiring the famous and successful Bell's Scotch whisky company. We had won a £1 million account to do the takeover advertising campaign – in those days, such a thing was unregulated, and we had run some seriously negative ads – which had played a significant part in the successful bid, for which I had been responsible. The thing about Ernest was that he always went for what he believed were the number one suppliers. He would ask around as to who were the best practitioners in whichever field and he would always hire them, whatever it cost. And at that time, Lowes (and Frank) had a great reputation.

So when Guinness started their new takeover bid for Distillers, he came to me again, which I guess was a good sign. Not so good – and something that I could in no way foresee – was that this new takeover plan would result in one of the biggest share-trading scandals in British corporate history; and that, within a few years, after a trial lasting 112 days and costing £7.2 million, Ernest Saunders (and several of his associates) would be serving prison sentences for serious fraud.

Gordon Reece could not have predicted this any more than I could have done. By the time I started on the Distillers' project, Gordon was already working for Ernest, being paid on a private monthly retainer. Not that it surprised me, as Gordon was supremely well connected, and advised all manner of individuals and institutions, and could crop up almost anywhere. He was my best friend, so, over the years, he and I did all sorts of things together, with clients in common. We'd often sit with each other, late into the night, chewing over the issues and problems of the current crop of accounts and projects.

It was a completely different era then, when nobody thought there was anything odd about discussing challenging commercial and political issues, no matter how confidential; about going and asking somebody a question, seeking their advice, and – ultimately – trusting people's word and their wisdom. That's how we thought back then – but which today seems naïve, given what would happen with Guinness and Distillers.

With Gordon heading the PR side of the Guinness bid, I was put in charge of the advertising, and a company called GJW was tasked with organising the lobbying. GJW was probably the very first public affairs lobbying company. It was run by Wilf Weeks (who had been Ted Heath's private secretary), Andrew Gifford (who had been David Steel's), and Jenny Jeger (Jim Callaghan's). They were the only lobbying firm in Britain with real stature and their selling proposition was that they had ties with all three main parties, without partisanship. They were very good at monitoring Parliament (in those pre-television coverage days), and looking for references to their clients' business interests. They could arrange for clients to have meetings with ministers and civil servants, and they were able to offer representation to the parliamentary machinery. Interestingly enough, Lowe Howard-Spink & Bell actually bought the GJW company – but then decided to sell it again. Anyway, there we all were – GJW, Gordon and I – handling an overall communications and media budget of some £15 million, trying to make sure that the positive side of the bid was getting traction.

One significant problem was that the press didn't like Ernest Saunders. He wouldn't talk to them for a start – which is something that journalists hate, and for which they can quite easily seek revenge. And which, in this case, they did. The newspapers promoted the view that Distillers were not asking Guinness for enough money; also, that the whole thing was rather lacking in candour and straightforwardness – which it was, of course. In those days, the City editors were hugely important and the views, in particular, of Ivan Fallon in *The Sunday Times* and Ian Watson in the *Sunday Telegraph* (who were being briefed by Saunders's ex-PR man Brian Basham, now working for the rival bidder's camp), were not favourable. Looking back, it's hard to imagine quite how powerful the City editors were. And in this case, they had set themselves against the Guinness bid, and were urging the government for a referral to the Monopolies and Mergers Commission. To add to our concerns, the Brewers Association – who might so easily have been a support – seemed incapable of making up their mind whether it was a good idea or a bad idea.

Faced with this, and in typically adversarial fashion, Ernest determined to bypass the press and appeal to the public perception. Following his brief, we developed an advertising campaign to persuade people that if they didn't let Guinness buy Distillers, it might fall into the hands of an unsympathetic foreign corporation and a great British institution would be lost forever. Our line of argument had got nothing to do with economics and everything to do with nationalism and emotion. But it was appropriate, because, at the time, people were receptive, anxious about iconic UK companies like Rolls Royce and Bentley being vulnerable.

Some of the work we did was aggressive and funny at the same time. In one ad, we took the eponymous image of Johnny Walker, from the whisky bottle, and gave him a pair of eyes that were obviously Japanese: it caused a huge amount of controversy and was seen as racist. It seems so odd now, looking back, but in that economic climate, it was becoming quite normal to witness aggressively hostile advertising campaigns in support of takeover bids, appealing to sentiment and nationalism where applicable, cajoling the shareholders to favour certain offers, and accusing rivals of non-truths. And at Lowes, we had robust experience in this area – through having worked with Hanson and Imperial Tobacco for example, and indeed from the Bell's takeover.

However, in February, the government bowed to newspaper pressure and announced a Monopolies and Mergers Commission (MMC) referral. Ernest was, of course, outraged by this – even getting Gordon to send a letter to Margaret expressing his displeasure. His tactical response was to offer to dispose of some of his other brands to Lonrho, thus lowering his anticipated share of the whisky market down below the 25 per cent cut-off mark. In all of this, the government was starting not to enjoy being between a rock and a

(Right)
A 1975 poster produced by Saatchi &
Saatchi for the Health Education Council
attempting to re-educate male attitudes
towards protected sex. 'The greatest print ad
I've ever seen.' (*Getty Images*)

(Below)
Maurice Saatchi (left) and his brother
Charles Saatchi (right), co-founders of
advertising agency Saatchi & Saatchi,
around 1978. 'I never really knew why they
employed me. Some say it was because I
happened to be taller than the other two
interviewees.' (*Campaign Magazine*)

(Above) A woman walks past the controversial poster devised for the Conservative Party during the run-up to the 1979 General Election. 'We were clever enough to let the controversy run and run.' (*Getty Images*)

(Below left) A triumphant Margaret Thatcher arrives at 10 Downing Street with her husband Denis after becoming Britain's first woman Prime Minister, 4 May 1979. 'She took a very short catnap and then began work on her Cabinet list.' (*Graham Wiltshire/Rex Features*)

(Left) Tim Bell outside Saatchi & Saatchi's Charlotte Street Offices. 'In many ways, I was running the place.' (*Keith McMillan/ Private Collection*)

(Left) US President Ronald Reagan shakes hands with Margaret Thatcher at 10 Downing Street, June, 1984. 'He immediately struck you with his conspicuous physical presence.' (*Getty Images*)

'Crisis? What Crisis?' The *Sun* criticises 'Sunny Jim' Callaghan during the Winter of Discontent, 1979. 'By that stage, I don't think that anyone was listening to him.' (*News Syndication*)

THE Sun

Thursday, January 11, 1979   7p   TODAY'S TV: PAGES 6 and 7

CRISIS? WHAT CRISIS?

Rail, lorry, jobs chaos—and Jim blames the Press

By WALTER TERRY
Political Editor

SUN - TANNED Premier Jim Callaghan breezed back into Britain yesterday and asked: Crisis? What Crisis?

As the country faced the threat of all-out rail and lorry strikes—amid renewed Arctic weather — he scoffed at calls for a State of Emergency.

He said: "There is no point — but plans are always ready."

Not even the threat of up to two million people being laid off work next week worried jaunty Jim.

He blandly blamed journalists for talking of "mounting chaos" in strike-battered Britain.

FEAR

Mr Callaghan told reporters at London's Heathrow Airport: "That's a judgment you are making.

"I don't think other people in the world would share the view there is mounting chaos."

He added: "As regards domestic affairs, I'm trying to raise your eyes a little because, believe me, there are other issues in the world as well."

It was an insensitive performance after his seven days in the Caribbean sunshine.

Tory leader Margaret Thatcher fired off a letter to the Premier, demanding a Commons statement on Monday and an emergency debate.

She said : "There comes a moment in the life of a country when a Government of whatever political complexion has an over-riding responsibility to keep essential supplies and services running."

And she made it clear that, with the crisis worsening declaration of a State of Emergency, including the use of troops, will soon be vital.

But easy going Jim, home at last after the sunshine summit on the island of Guadeloupe, would have none of it.

He ticked off reporters saying:

● As regards domestic affairs, I have kept very closely in touch with them. I probably knew about a number of developments even before you did.

Indeed, thanks to the miracle of modern communications, I was able to lift a telephone and press a button and I was through to No. 10 before you could say "Jack Robinson" and talk to Ministers and others, so I have kept in touch.

● A STATE of Emergency? "Not at the moment," he said. "We have been on the brink of it once or twice last week, but we have stepped back from it.

BRINK

"There is no point in declaring a State of Emergency. But plans for that are always ready."

● BUT what about the chaos? He said: "We have had strikes before. We have come close to the brink before."

And he had another rebuke for reporters: "Please don't run down your country by talking about chaos."

When his questioners persisted, Mr Callaghan
Continued on Page 8

BRITAIN IN TURMOIL
Page 2
FRANKLIN'S VIEW
Page 4

Please don't shoot the pianist

THE SUN is much slimmer than usual again today.

This is due to an acute shortage of newsprint arising from the lorry drivers' strike and is, of course, entirely beyond our control.

Just so that our readers and advertisers know exactly what is going on, we would like to explain one or two further consequences of the strike.

Some readers, for example, have been receiving copies with unusually wide margins.

Some have had copies made up of a number of pages of differing sizes.

Sorry

This is because, in order to continue publishing as long as we possibly can, we are taking in newsprint from wherever it can be obtained — even if it is not Sun-sized.

We are desperately sorry that the current problems have forced us to depart, in some respects, from the high standard of presentation which has helped to make The Sun Britain's best-selling daily paper.

But we felt that most of you would rather have an emergency Sun than no Sun at all.

Some readers have also written to suggest that it would be appropriate to charge less for smaller papers. W⁃ sympathise — but we cannot do it!

The fact is that smaller

★ ★ ★

papers are proportionately MORE expensive to produce.

In order to offer readers the best possible value for money, advertising content has been drastically reduced.

This is costing us in the region of £50,000 a night.

There is some saving on newsprint. But most costs, especially labour costs, remain the same.

To maintain our profit margins, which are modest, we should actually charge MORE for smaller papers. But we're not going to do that, either.

Battle

Whilst we are battling with the problems, we are grateful for your continued goodwill and tolerance.

The Number One Sun will be back, as soon as possible, with a full measure of all the sparkling news, sport and features which make it Britain's favourite newspaper.

Meanwhile, please don't shoot the pianist. He's doing his best!

In the news . .

SMACKER FROM ROD

● ROCK star Rod Stewart stunned Olivia Newton-John with a kiss—and Russian diplomats with his sexy act at a New York concert.
See Page 5

In the news . .

SEXY NURSE IS GUILTY

● NURSE Olwen Peel, who claimed she was paid £800 for sex with a wheelchair-bound patient, was yesterday found guilty at Wakefield of stealing the money.
See Page 5

In the news . .

CUP SHOCK FOR SPURS

● SPURS winger Peter Taylor saved the First Division club from humiliation in the Cup last night. His penalty gave them a 1-1 draw against non-league Altrincham.
See Back Page.

HARD LINES . . . THE PICTURE WHICH TELLS IT ALL—CENTRE PAGES

(Above) Tim Bell in his office at Saatchi & Saatchi. 'You become so involved in what you're doing that you lose track of how it fits any life plan.' (*Keith McMillan/Private Collection*)

(Below left) David Frost interviews Margaret Thatcher on the TV-am *Good Morning Britain* programme, 1985. 'He was a great human being.' (*Press Association*)

(Above right) Tim Bell and Margaret Thatcher, around 1979. 'She said, "Right … we'll get on then. Take him out, Gordon."'

(Right) Police and demonstrators clash in Trafalgar Square during protests against the introduction of the Poll Tax, March 1990. 'Some fool had left a huge building site unsecured.' (*Getty Images*)

(Right) Gordon Reece, surrounded by Saatchi & Saatchi adverts, in Conservative Central Office. 'When I met Gordon, I absolutely loved him … We were both on the same page.' (*Lionel Cherruault/Camera Press London*)

(Below) The Grand Hotel, Brighton two hours after it was bombed by the IRA on 12 October 1984. 'The middle of the hotel just disappeared … One voice then just said, "I think we'd better leave."' (*Simon Dack/Rex Features*)

(Above) Arthur Scargill, President of the National Union of Mineworkers, confronts police during the 1984–5 miners' strike. 'I only met Scargill a few times, although there was absolutely no point in talking to him.' (*Getty Images*)

(Left) Ian MacGregor, chairman of the National Coal Board, covers his face with a polythene bag to avoid the press as he steps out of his car at the Norton House hotel during the miners' strike of 1984–5. 'He was never going to look like he was the miners' friend.' (*The Scotsman Publications Ltd*)

(Left) A turbulent friendship, Tim Bell and Frank Lowe. 'The honeymoon period of my joining had been maddeningly short.' (*Private Collection*)

(Right) The end of Apartheid. Former President F. W. de Klerk and South African President Nelson Mandela in Cape Town, South Africa, 1994. '[They] didn't believe in emotionalising things.' (*MCT/Rex Features*)

(Below) An Apartheid notice on a beach near Cape Town denotes a 'whites only' area. '[As] a small child … I remember being so puzzled as to why black people were not allowed to walk on the same side of the street as whites.' (*Getty Images*)

(Above) Tim Bell, Margaret Thatcher and William Hague are among the guests at a 'Keep the Pound' dinner. 'When I first worked for Thatcher, I could never make up my mind whether it was the last throw of the Right, or the first throw of its newest incarnation.' (*Private Collection*)

(Left) Tim Bell and Rupert Murdoch. 'You are aware that you'd better not fuck up otherwise he'll cast you aside.' (*Rex Features*)

hard place. A revitalised Britain was fighting for its share of trade in the world, and the Thatcher government had positioned itself as a supporter of business. They believed in the creation of wealth and that the people best placed to create wealth were the business community. Meanwhile, the various takeover panels were nonplussed by the fuss and palaver: as far as many of them were concerned, financial transactions belonged in the City of London, and in the private rooms of brokers and bankers – certainly not anywhere near the Clapham omnibus. So they hadn't really worked out what they should say: they hadn't thought of any rules, and they were unprepared for what was, by the day, becoming an ever more controversial and ever more widely reported subject. Ernest instigated a month of fierce lobbying – of Cabinet, of Fleet Street, of anyone who might listen – all based on the premise of Britain needing a world-renowned drinks company. And by March, the government backtracked, announcing that an MMC referral was no longer needed.

Some time before this, but whilst I was already working for Ernest, he arranged for me to meet with the Distillers brothers and make a pitch to them to handle their financial public relations account. That was valuable work to take on, unquestionably, but it would put me in the rather odd situation where I was being paid by Ernest Saunders to advise him on how to win his bid and now by Distillers to advise them on how to defend themselves. He was hoping, of course, that I would be able and willing to keep him informed of what they were doing that might thwart his takeover bid. It's neither the first nor the last time in my life when I've worked on both sides of an argument.

Yet, from the start, we were at pains to try to stay legal. Frank had stood in the dock in a tax case with CDP some years earlier, and after a traumatic time, was determined never to go back. I'd had the odd uncomfortable experience too. But Frank especially was preoccupied by our being on the right side of the law, which – as things turned out – was prescient concern on Frank's part. In terms of conflict of interest, the requirement for disclosure at that time was considerably different from what it is now. But I still very much had to wear two hats.

As soon as I started visiting their offices, I saw that Distillers was a company from an entirely different era. The two brothers had inherited it from their father and were still very much hands-on. A typical day at Distillers would have you arriving at 10.30 a.m. earliest, going into the boardroom for a pink gin at 11.00 a.m., perhaps having a noon meeting whilst your head was reeling, then returning to the boardroom for sherry before lunch, with red wine and white wine and champagne if you felt like it; possibly all finished off with a fine Cognac. Then, at about 3.30 p.m., it would be back to your office for a snooze.

No one mentioned Thalidomide, of course, which would have been like mentioning the Nazis to a German – it was painful and offensive and so you didn't talk about it. I don't think they actually felt they were responsible for what had happened. They just thought that it was an awfully unfortunate scientific accident and that they had to pay due compensation as a consequence. But the emotional aspect of it was probably too awful even to contemplate.

Back at Guinness, Ernest treated the whole takeover process like an election campaign – or a military campaign, more like. He believed that his company was on the side of right because, in his view, Guinness were by far the better fit with Distillers – better than a retailing operation like Argyll. I suspect, if truth be known, that Distillers also actually wanted Guinness to win the bid, which is why they were so accepting of me, knowing my links with Saunders. I think that they believed that if Guinness won, they would be able to go on living their lives as though nothing had changed – that they would be able to carry on with their pink gins and postprandial snoozes. Some of that was said explicitly; some of it was implied.

When it came to final bids, the Argyll offer was significantly better than the Guinness one. But in the end, as everyone knows, the bid went our way. On 19 April 1986, Guinness finally acquired 50.7 per cent of the Distillers shares, and the takeover was complete. I actually watched the physical machinery of this take place – it was extraordinary. When you make a bid, you effectively merge the two companies and issue new shares for the joint company. There is something called 'Strike Day', when you announce the price, but, in those days, you didn't publish it – you simply informed your broker who rang up the magic circle who would send the five or six key brokers. These very serious and expensively suited chaps came in and Ernest sat behind his desk and they sat with their pads and pencils, and the lead broker would say, 'Right, now there's £400 million (or whatever it was) in shares; anybody want £100 million?' And one of the brokers would put his hand up and within the space of ten minutes, they would have sold the whole lot – no contracts, no written documentation, just people's word as their bond.

It was staggering to watch and it was a system that was done away with because of its ultimate inherent frailty. All this kind of thing, which was just how it was all done in those days, was then made improper or against the rules – not least, because Ernest had been so determined to win that he had taken advantage of that frailty. And he might have got away with it, had there not been a certain event that took place on the other side of the Atlantic.

Eight months after I'd been watching the brokers bidding huge amounts in Ernest's boardroom, the Department of Trade and Industry (DTI) were raiding the building, seizing material, and beginning an inquiry into the conduct of the bid. It was triggered by the case in the US of Ivan Boesky – an American stock-trader, who had amassed a fortune betting on corporate takeovers about which he had insider knowledge. (Apparently, the *Wall Street* character, Gordon Gekko, is at least in part inspired by Boesky.) During the investigation by the US Securities and Exchange Commission, Boesky made a plea-bargain, through which he revealed how Guinness had provided secret indemnities against any losses that supporters of the bid might incur, whilst artificially boosting the Guinness share price and thus the value of the bid. These details were duly passed on to the British DTI inspectorate and one of the longest-running corporate fraud dramas that the UK has ever known was up and running.

The investigation and its various appeal hearings lasted years and were ferociously expensive. Like quite a lot of people, I was interviewed by the DTI. It was not a very pleasant experience, and there was a hint of kangaroo court about the way they treated you. You were put in a grey room and, even though you were allowed representation, you had to speak for yourself. They didn't tell you what they were going to ask you about, or why they were asking you. Every question felt like it was a leading one – leading you into a minefield, likely to step on a trigger-switch at any moment. I don't think I was ever nervous or worried, because I was certain that I – and we at Lowes – had done nothing wrong. But these are serious grey men in greyer suits who earn their living sniffing for blood.

One of the most important witnesses was a French management consultant called Olivier Roux, from a company called Bain & Co. Their job had been to create a business plan for the merged Guinness–Distillers. It was classic management consultancy stuff whereby they put people into the company, and did all sorts of strange things, for which they were paid an astronomical amount of money – Ernest was clearly in their thrall. But having been Ernest's number one adviser, Olivier Roux turned witness for the Crown, thereby becoming a key adversary. There was an awful lot of personal and emotional stuff about relationships and friendships with that one.

In the end, Ernest was jailed for five years, but he served only a proportion of that, as his people claimed that he was suffering from some condition or other – although once out, he then managed a marvellous recovery from the symptoms that led to its diagnosis. Also imprisoned were Tony Parnes and Gerald Ronson. The latter got a year and was ordered to pay £5 million in fines. Jack Lyons, a financial adviser, was also found guilty, but he was ill, so suffered a £4 million fine without custodial sentence. And there were various other cases – some of which collapsed, some of which didn't. Then there was an American called Tom Ward who had been called in by Guinness to assist on takeover legislation. He basically understood how it worked in America, but regarded the rules in Britain as stupid, and a complete block on wealth creation, which led him to ignore them, and encourage everybody else to do the same. In the end, they tried to get him, but he was aquitted.

The Guinness–Distillers case had a profound effect on the public's perception of corporate dealings. In later years, scandals with MPs' expenses and the banking industry may have had a similar effect, further undermining the respect people have for institutions whose probity was once – rightly or wrongly – taken for granted. Before the '80s, some of the things of which these people were accused were being done every day in the City. Indeed, the widespread use of indemnified share-support schemes was used as a defence in the appeal hearings. Nobody had ever said this was wrong until this case. The Crown just chose this day and this case to start to interpret the ambiguous and unclear rules more literally.

To put it into a context, the City was run by a group of people who all knew each other and took a kind of view that rules were there to be broken, and let's not talk about it when they are. 'Let's not damage the reputation of the City' – that was the kind of conversation that went on. This way of operating was the result of a giant cartel of merchant bankers, stockbrokers, fund managers and people who had all been at school together – some had been each other's fags and warmed the loo seat, some were related to each other, some had a cousin here and a brother there. It was cosy, but – with the light of a looming new media age shining in – it was inevitably doomed. But Ernest always argued that he was made the scapegoat, and that the DTI had been politically motivated in wanting a high-profile City prosecution.

His PA, Margaret McGrath, was also featured in the prosecution. She was accused of destroying evidence and perverting the course of justice. I guess no one knows for certain what actually went through the shredder, but one interesting thing about Ernest Saunders was that he was a compulsive list-maker. We used to make a joke about how he was never listless. He always carried a writing-pad with him, and whilst you were having a conversation, he'd make lists of things. There were always lots of lists all over his desk.

I went to lunch, one Sunday in January 1987, with a girl called Jenny Hopkirk who had been Bob Gross's secretary at Geers Gross when I worked there. She was married to Paddy Hopkirk, the famous Monte-Carlo-winning rally driver. They lived in Beaconsfield and, as it happened, next door to Ernest Saunders. It was after the DTI inquiry had been announced, and I hadn't seen Ernest for a while and had no idea what was happening to him. After lunch, I went round and knocked on the door. After quite a long wait and some repeat knocking, I saw a face peering out of the small vertical window at the side of the porch. Then the chains and bolts were undone and there he was. He called me in. It seemed that he had been sitting for an eternity in his drawing room, writing long lists – they were everywhere – which he carried on doing whilst I talked with him. Then things got surreal, as they often did with Ernest, because, whilst I was there, the police suddenly arrived. Worse, they just took him away. I'm not sure whether it was an arrest or not, but off they all went, leaving me in his house surrounded by all these lists, wondering what I should do or whom I should call.

The Guinness affair was a nuisance as far as Margaret Thatcher was concerned, damaging the reputation of wealth creation. She believed that business was a vital part of the British economy and that it should be encouraged and motivated, that it should be worked with to try to get rid of bad trade-union practices, improve productivity, and to do everything possible to make business life easier. So she opened the doors of Downing Street to business and informed her policy heads that they were to consult with business when they were introducing a new piece of legislation.

In the first term, there was a clear indication that the climate had changed, as evinced by a constant stream of businessmen coming in, telling the policy heads what the problems were in their business lives, how difficult it was to do things, the difficulties of getting paid, of doing international transactions, and so on. In marked contrast to the previous administration, the new government held the view that business could influence the thinking that went into the creation of public policy. Business wouldn't control public policy – to the extent of getting this or that clause cancelled and another clause put in – but it would provide feedback to government, leading to the drafting of better regulation and better legislation. That general philosophy essentially carried on, as far as I can see, until Gordon Brown, who only seemed interested in talking with the banking community.

12

That Bloody Woman

Margaret always wanted a business-friendly environment in place. But as soon as we entered the New Year, in 1987, her attention was moving to the forthcoming election. And I had no idea how – if at all – I would be involved. When I had left Saatchi & Saatchi, the brothers had made me sign a retainer for £24,000 per annum, a condition of which was that I would not work on the Conservative Party account unless they sanctioned it. Of course, in the event, they didn't want me anywhere near the account. And neither did Norman Tebbit, who was Party Chairman. Norman had not been the same since the bombing – quite understandably – and was more ill and in more pain than he let on, which undoubtedly affected his mood. I still got on well with him, but he had concerns over the Left-wing press dredging up stories about any excesses in my past lifestyle, and he was determined to keep me in exile.

Margaret misunderstood what had been agreed between the brothers and myself, so at the first main election strategy meeting she expected me to be there and was puzzled by my absence. Maurice Saatchi and Jeremy Sinclair turned up from Saatchi & Saatchi. She said, 'Where's Tim? Why isn't he here? I thought he was still under contract with you?' Maurice said something about it causing morale problems with the staff, but she just said, 'I want him involved. I want to work with people I know.' Gordon Reece was still around, but becoming increasingly *hors de combat*, and beginning to suffer from the throat cancer that eventually killed him. But the Saatchis wouldn't have anything to do with me, and the key people on the business, including Michael Dobbs, were banned from speaking to me.

Tebbit was in agreement with me being kept out of the loop. By now, he was becoming quite hostile towards Margaret for reasons that have never been completely clear to me, and she was reciprocating in kind. She was angry with him for not being more supportive of her over Westland, and was suspicious of his motives. There were stories about him trying to get her ousted, and just as many stories discrediting him. From his point of view, the last thing he wanted was a Thatcher ally like me around.

Earlier in 1986, Dobbs (by then working at Central Office) and John Sharkey (the account director at Saatchi & Saatchi) had given what came to be known as the TBW presentation. TBW stands for that 'That Bloody Woman', and the research was showing that all manner of people – even Conservative MPs – were indeed using the actual phrase. They presented data that showed that, while on the attributes of 'strength', 'confidence' and 'intelligence' she scored highly, on 'forward-thinking' she was seen as weak. I think Margaret might have taken this better coming from me, but, already cross at my absence, she did not appreciate the news in the way that it was delivered. A presentation where they were basically highlighting Margaret as the main barrier to winning the next election was never going to go down well. Whether they'd got that research feedback or not, it was an extraordinarily insensitive thing to do, and showed that they understood nothing about Margaret. You could have given that presentation to her if you did it the right way, but if you just confronted her and told her that everybody hated her, you couldn't expect her to treat it as if she were being given a bunch of flowers. In fact, she was devastated by it. When we talked, I could see only too clearly that she was starting to lose confidence not only in them, but also in herself. As we came nearer to the election, she became ever more anxious over Tebbit's campaign, and whether he was too slavishly devoted to anything Saatchi & Saatchi came up with – which she didn't always like.

Following guidance from Central Office, Saatchi & Saatchi were focusing on a negative campaign, aimed at bashing Labour. (Although at one point, Maurice had suggested to her that Socialism had actually served Britain rather well at moments in the past – something that went down like cold sick.) Margaret had already said that she was keen on running a positive campaign emphasising the benefits of Conservative policy, and that the Saatchi & Saatchi approach seemed defensive and counterproductive. She said to me, 'I don't want to do that. I've been in power for eight years. I should be talking about our achievements, not what's wrong with the other side. Just because that worked in the previous two elections doesn't mean it's right for this one. But I don't get anywhere in my conversations with the chairman or with the Saatchis.' It got worse. As the scripts for the Party Political Broadcasts came in, it became clear that Saatchi & Saatchi were not planning to use her in any of them. They were following the letter of the TBW presentation, and keeping her away from the cameras. She could see what they were doing, and she was really hurt by this.

In May, David Young came to see me. He had been the Employment Secretary, but was desperate to become involved in the election campaign. I'd known him for some time and liked him, and he had a very sharp understanding of both business and advertising. Margaret knew we got on, and she moved him onto the campaign in March 1987 – making him Deputy Chairman. To a point, Tebbit trusted him as well (in fact, there was a view that Tebbit had pushed him forward for the role), but a lot of people thought that he was politically naïve. When David first came to see me after his appointment, he said that he thought that Margaret was completely demoralised and that the priority had to be to get her mojo back. 'She thinks she's going to lose', he said. Margaret was one of those people who, if those all around her said that she would lose, would start to believe it herself – even though all the opinion polls were showing that another landslide was likely. Anyway, Young said to me, 'She wants a positive campaign.'

It was then that we agreed for me to take a consistent role as Margaret's 'private' campaign adviser. It would have to be covert: I was involved with the controversial Guinness–Distillers bid; there was the Saatchi exclusion agreement; and she did not want to completely upset Tebbit. The secrecy would lead to several comedic moments, such as when I had to hide in a spare room at Chequers until Tebbit had left. I was there for Denis's 72nd birthday party, on Saturday 9 May, and – once Norman was out of the way – Margaret and I spent most of the night hatching plans. She spent the whole time making pages of notes. She seemed to come alive again. It was just like the old days.

I could deal with the secrecy thing, which was the least of my worries and, if anything, added an extra frisson to it all. The day after that, Lord Young nearly blurted it out in the presence of some of her ministers, and she had to practically kick his shin under the table, to be quiet. And once, when we were filming an election video, which I'd scripted with Antony Jay, Tebbit had to speak without finding out that I was involved – so it was a case of yet more odd behaviour, running in and out of rooms. But it was thrilling to be back in the centre of the activity, even if I spent half the time hiding there.

On 11 May, it was given out that the election was to be held on 11 June 1987. We had a 10-point lead in the polls, yet, in the first week of campaigning after the date had been announced, there was heavy internal criticism. We still had a tangible lead in the polls, but Peter Mandelson and Bryan Gould were running a sharp campaign for the Labour Party (now tacking to the centre ground) – including a film on Neil Kinnock (*Kinnock: The Movie*) by the *Chariots of Fire* director Hugh Hudson. It was all starting to look more modern and fresh than we had seen before from them, suggesting that, for this election, they would not be quite the easy target they had been previously. By contrast, our first PPB was, by any standard, a really tired affair.

To add to our problems, Margaret's campaign scheduling was turning into chaos. Gordon Reece was back for the second week of the campaign – we called ourselves 'the exiles' – but there were all manner of problems in terms of its management and coherence, and she was getting exhausted and emotional, and had a severe tooth abscess as well. There was a day (4 June) that they called 'Wobbly Thursday' when a BBC poll, then a Gallup one, had us down by several points (with the stock market going into freefall – although we suspected afterwards that one poll had been set up by someone in the City to make a quick fortune), and that really did send everyone nuts. Because she was off her game, she then put her foot in it by saying something about private health care (about the fact that it enabled her 'to go into hospital on the day I want, at the time I want …') that was seized upon by the press and caused a terrible stir. Another time before that, interviewed by John Cole, she said that she was going to go 'on and on' – which the press quoted against her for a long time afterwards. But this latest error was by far the worst, and it would draw a Labour and press onslaught. The next meeting, she really laid into Tebbit and Dobbs.

She was becoming almost hysterical. Much to the anger of Saatchi & Saatchi – who had started to suspect that I was involved and, like everyone else, had heard the rumours that Young & Rubicam were sniffing around – their ideas were being continually rejected. Margaret said that they had become too big and 'gimmicky', and she was desperate to be given an ad that was not same-old-negative and which could get some positive uplift back into the campaign. Sensing an opportunity, I took a brief to Frank and Lowes. Now Frank was all rather trendy Left-wing, but he was an ad man first and Left-wing second, so his intrigue at the idea of writing a dynamic advert trumped his chattering-class Socialism. So we set out with a determination to come up with a campaign-shifting idea. Howell James was David Young's special adviser at the time, so he acted as a middle man and got us all sorts of raw material and data, and we came up with a dozen or so instances of what the government was doing well – such as low taxation, lower inflation, that kind of thing. To these, we added the consistent line, 'Life's better with the Conservatives. Don't let Labour ruin it', which was similar to an idea I'd seen used in the 1959 Conservative election victory, which I'd always really liked.

The art director, Alan Waldie, drew them up – in what seemed like a few minutes flat – and we presented it to David Young who said, 'You know, this is exactly what she wants. But I've no idea how to introduce it.' In the end, he got a room in Number 10, and put out all the roughs, around the wall, and intercepted her as she arrived back from a meeting in the Midlands. She had to prepare for a challenging interview on *This Week*, but she took a look and immediately said. 'That's it! At last. Well done, David. Take it to Norman.'

Of course, Norman went ballistic. He said, 'Who did this?' At which point it all kicked off. We only have the story second-hand from the memoirs, but it seems that they grabbed each other and David said, 'Norman. Listen to me. We're about to lose the fucking election. You're going to go. I'm going to go. The whole thing is going to go … She has to be happy.' Young told him that it was exactly what they needed. But Tebbit said, 'Well we're not running it. Tim Bell did it. We're not doing it. This is Saatchi & Saatchi's campaign. So you can take it to Saatchis and say it's what she wants, and they can do what they like with it.' The press later said that Tebbit and Young actually had a fight. Nobody really knows what happened. I think from what they both told me that they actually just grabbed each other's lapels and shook each other a bit: handbags at dawn stuff. Saatchi & Saatchi were due to come round, and when John Sharkey and Maurice arrived, the arguments carried on. It's bad enough for an agency to be given work to adapt from another rival, but for Maurice to be handed something from me was the last straw. It ended up with everyone shouting at everyone else again, and with David screaming, 'Maurice. Do you know how little your company will be worth next week if we lose this election? Swallow your pride!' Begrudgingly, Saatchi & Saatchi took the campaign. But they changed the strapline to 'Britain's Great Again. Don't let Labour wreck it', which is a less subtle, less effective tone of voice. It's a Saatchi tone of voice – more brutal – but that's the line that ran.

After the election, everybody started to try and claim credit for everything. The press made a lot of the fact that three different agencies had been vying for the Party account, with in-fighting and jealousies dominating the communications campaign. Those three included Young & Rubicam who were also in there trying to sell their ideas. In those days, John Banks, who is a good friend, was chairman of Young & Rubicam. He had got to know Margaret's political secretary, Stephen Sherbourne, and his agency had been continually presenting possible options during the campaign (without Tebbit knowing, of course). During the last week of the campaign, he had presented a raft of ideas to Stephen, who was meant to show them to the Prime Minister, but he just put the material in his drawer and locked it and then shredded it after the election. I know this because he told me.

None of it really mattered of course – even the polls and the panics – because Margaret eventually won with a one-hundred-plus majority. However, it mattered to the Saatchis, who were spooked by the press going on about whose campaigns were and were not used. The *Daily Mail* in particular ran a story (written by Nigel Dempster) entitled 'Not Saatchi triumph after all', which, coming from a Conservative newspaper, was beyond galling, and especially as they put a photograph of Frank Lowe and me over it. BBC *Panorama* was making similar claims. Norman Tebbit was furious about the mud-raking. And Charles Saatchi wanted instant revenge on me.

So they mounted an all-out counter-attack. Press statements were issued, with various claims about the campaign material. Rumours started about my private life. And they launched what's known as a bear raid on Lowe Howard-Spink & Bell's share price, which duly crashed, with £12 million being wiped off our share price on one Wednesday alone. All of which greatly upset Frank Lowe, who actually sided with the Saatchis (Charles was his pal) and somehow blamed me. Margaret herself was getting involved, given that her election victory was being eclipsed by surreal post-election in-fighting. 'It really is unseemly', she said to Gordon Reece. 'I've just won an election by over 100 seats and all they do is bicker about who wrote which ads.'

One day shortly afterwards, Margaret rang me at home and said, 'I understand that those brothers are trying to damage your company. Tell me what I can do to help.' I said, 'Margaret, please don't. You've got a fucking country to run. I'm perfectly capable of looking after myself.' She said, 'I know. But all of us need our friends. I'll speak to James Hanson.' Of course, it was not in Hanson's interests to have this going on. He was a strong Conservative supporter, but he had both agencies that were involved in the dispute working on his brands. The next thing I knew, I was summoned to a meeting in his office, and to which Maurice and Charles were being invited, if not in person, then by phone. When we went round, we were met by Hanson's Indian butler, and brought in for the meeting. Maurice had reluctantly been persuaded to enter the discussions, but not Charles.

'Where is he?' said Hanson. Maurice replied, 'He's not going to ever speak to Tim Bell again.' At which point James said, 'Well, all I can say is that you'd better get him on the phone now or something very unpleasant is going to happen to you both.' There followed what was basically a ramble about how they hated me and how I was a disgusting person who should be got rid of. Hanson said, 'Well, I'm not really interested in any of that conversation. The fact of the matter is that Margaret's been re-elected as Prime Minister. That's all that matters. Therefore, I need this spat to be out of the way. So, I'll tell you what I'm going to do. If you don't stop your activity, I am going to mount a bear raid to destroy your share price. In the meantime, I'm going to invest a quarter of a million pounds in Lowes in order to return their share price to the correct level, and you will stop this nonsense and not do it any more. Do you understand?' He also said that we would all issue a joint statement to the press about us wanting to end the rift, and each of us congratulating the other on the great ads and great election result. To which Charles just banged the phone down, as he often did.

The next day's press release stated, 'All smiles at Lowe and Saatchi'. Our share price more or less went back to where it had been and we all got on with our lives. They will deny this ever took place, and you'll never be able to verify it. James is dead; Gordon Wright, who was also there, is dead. The Indian butler might be alive, but I don't know where he is, or whether he had the faintest idea what the hell we were all banging on about. However, it was not long before Norman resigned to look after his wife, and with that, the brothers lost a key ally at Central Office. Within three months, they had resigned the account, and so ended one of the most famous of political advertising relationships.

The day after the Hanson meeting, Margaret asked me around for a drink at Downing Street. She did like a Scotch, but when you get asked round for a drink at Number 10, you don't usually get a drink. What you do is go round and sit and natter and maybe you get a cup of tea. Unless Denis was there, in which case you would get a drink forced on you. She said, 'I believe James has sorted it out.' I said, 'Yes, it's absolutely fine.' She said, 'Those people are not the kind you can do business with. I understand they want to buy the Midland Bank.' Indeed, the brothers had, at that time, been floating the idea of making a bid for the bank, on some spurious piece of logic that said a bank was a service operation rather like an advertising agency and, therefore, that they were absolutely the right people to be running it – a mad idea, of course. She continued, 'Well, I've spoken to the Governor and they won't.' And sure enough, the bid was killed. The Governor spoke to their bankers who were told to curtail their interest.

13

Ambivalence

I regard myself as a moral person. I know the difference between right and wrong. But just because I do, does not mean that I should sit in hasty judgement of every client that comes through the door. I am sometimes asked if there is anyone for whom I wouldn't work – the mischief in the question being that I have worked, and do work, with clients who, to a greater or lesser extent, have a public image that has drawn criticism. That is often why they need our help in the first place. But you shouldn't jump to conclusions about whether that image is deserved or not. Indeed, from the moment I meet a client, I try to challenge every assumption, made by public or press or in the back of my own mind. One of those assumptions might be that the company involved is a bad company run by a bad person – but I don't accept that just on its face value. I meet the person and I ask questions and do the research. It is sometimes claimed that, based on this standard, I would have accepted Adolf Hitler as a client. Well, clearly not, because it would have been obvious from the research that he'd just annexed half of Europe and was in the process of exterminating the Jews, and there would have been no justification at all in trying to turn that into a positive message. But many projects are not clear-cut, even in – especially in – moral terms. And in the 1980s and 1990s, I met with many such controversial individuals and situations.

One such figure was the Egyptian businessman, Mohamed Al-Fayed, who entered my world in the mid-'80s, before he became quite so well known in the public eye. And one of the more bizarre moments involving him came between the end of 1984 and the spring of 1985, when the UK pound sterling was at its lowest-ever price against the dollar, very nearly reaching parity at one point. This was one of the worst crises in this country's economic history and, right in the midst of it, the Sultan of Brunei announced that he was transferring something in the region of £5 billion of his investment money out of the London currency market into New York.

Gordon Reece already knew Al-Fayed – Gordon seemed to know everyone
– and was aware that he had been acting as the financial adviser to the Sultan
of Brunei. Al-Fayed had been holding Power of Attorney that had allowed him
to use the Sultan's money to buy assets like the Dorchester Hotel. So we bit the
bullet and went and asked him if he knew what was going on between the Sultan
and the markets. We weren't sure whether Al-Fayed would tell us or not, but we
knew that he liked to try and impress you with his inside knowledge, so, if he
did know something, we thought we had a good chance of finding out.

Al-Fayed specialised in going round arranging things for the rich, famous,
and powerful – including the Sultan – generating his own huge wealth in
the process. He was especially well known in his 'fixer' role in London and
the Middle East, and surreally in Haiti, where, in the space of a few months,
he'd notoriously wangled rather a large amount of money out of Papa Doc's
government.

Gordon and I went round to see him at his place at 60 Park Lane, and he told
us the story: 'The foreign office recently issued the Sultan with his new passport,
because the old one had expired. He had a diplomatic passport, and they made
it out to HRH the Sultan of Brunei. But that's an error, because he is HM Sultan
of Brunei. He's a king; he's not "His Royal Highness"; he's "His Majesty", and he's
absolutely furious. So he's moving his money because you obviously don't have
proper respect for him.' Al-Fayed was always on the lookout for an opportunity
to 'fix' and Gordon knew how to appeal to this. He said, 'You know it would be
a great thing if the Sultan reversed his decision.' And Al-Fayed replied, 'Well,
you see, it's very simple what you need to do. If the Prime Minister would ask
the Sultan for tea, he will attend, and she can then deal with the problem and
I'm sure something can be done.'

We immediately rang Margaret, who called in Charles Powell to look into
the matter, and it was true; they'd made a stupid little slip-up, which was going
to completely kill sterling. So she invited the Sultan to tea at Downing Street.
On 29 January 1985, we met Al-Fayed at the Embassy and he came with us. We
all got in the back of a gigantic black Mercedes, part of the Sultan of Brunei's
entourage, which comprised about 20 such black bullet-proof limousines,
numbered in sequence, BRU 1, BRU 2, and so on. Then we all swept into
Downing Street, and the police sergeant on the door of Number 10 let us all
troop in behind the Sultan. Everybody swept up the stairs, and into the study.
The Prime Minister said, 'Lovely to see you, Your Majesty, and it's wonderful of
you to visit.' Then she added, 'I have a gift for you. I have your new passport.'

At which point, she handed over a new passport made out to 'His Majesty, the Sultan of Brunei'. Followed by tea.

We all left them to it. And the next day he moved about £5 billion's worth out of the New York Stock Exchange into the London Stock Exchange, and the pound began a very slow recovery. Al-Fayed had expected that, as a result of his assistance in the matter, he would be granted a British passport, for which he'd been applying for years. But he was involved in the DTI investigation into the Harrods takeover, so they didn't oblige, and he was furious. In that respect, I think Gordon might have been a bit guilty of over-promising, but that was Gordon. However, there were no hard feelings on our side, and Gordon Reece was still working with the Al-Fayed brothers (out of a flat in Park Lane that they'd supplied) when they bid for House of Fraser (and Harrods) in 1985.

During the 1970s, the wealthy businessman Tiny Rowland and the Lonrho conglomerate had been accused of sanctions-busting in Rhodesia, which had embarrassed Ted Heath and the Conservatives. Then they had made a bid for Harrods, and Norman Tebbit and the government had no idea what to do, so they referred the deal to the MMC. It was then that Al-Fayed came along. Having already helped the government with the Sultan and the sterling crisis, and being fairly well known as an Anglophile, he seemed, from the government's perspective, to be a better bet than the company being bought by Americans or some other insensitive overseas predator. With the government disinterested, Al-Fayed persuaded Rowland to sell him Lonrho's shareholding (based on the ruse that they could take it back in due course when the MMC had cleared any objections), the latter not realising that Al-Fayed had use of a gigantic pile of cash (which the DTI found was probably – although never proven to be – the Sultan's) to allow him to get a loan to buy the whole company. Neither the press nor the government nor the City foresaw this; they just allowed themselves to believe that Al-Fayed had a shipping and cotton fortune. Once he had won the bid, Al-Fayed put in place the second half of his stratagem, using his new House of Fraser shares as a guarantee to pay back the original loan. So he got it all without even using his own cash. This was the kind of manoeuvring of which he and his brothers were just so capable, and so willing to try.

In France, he had bought the Résidence Windsor in Paris, where the Duke and Duchess of Windsor lived in the Bois de Boulogne. And he'd also bought the Ritz Hotel. The property now extends out underneath the Place Vendôme, to the point where almost the whole square is actually part of the Ritz Hotel (where, of course, his son Dodi and the Princess of Wales would stay). As a result of all his dealings in Paris – and given he had quite an admiration for PR experts – Al-Fayed came to me and said that he would pay our fees if we could help Chirac in his second bid for the Presidency in 1988 as leader of the relatively Right-wing RPR (Rassemblement pour la République) Party.

When he had run for the presidency the first time, Chirac had lost to Mitterrand. Then, when it came to the second time around, in 1988, Al-Fayed thought that he needed a change from the American guy he had been using. So we went to see Chirac. His English was very good, but he was a difficult individual. I'd already met him once, briefly, in Downing Street. He was a tall, elegant and charming Frenchman, and – despite what people sometimes said about the antipathy – Margaret was completely overwhelmed by the French charm and voice and everything. He had a begrudging admiration for her too.

I remember that when he had first visited Downing Street, the normally well-oiled welcoming protocol was having a bad day. Chirac gave Margaret a beautiful vintage book on the history of Paris, at which point she realised that no one had thought to get a gift for him. So in the panic, she turned to Stephen Sherbourne, her political secretary. The coffee in Downing Street was absolute crap, and Stephen had always said that he couldn't drink it, so he'd bought himself an espresso machine. When Margaret realised she hadn't got anything to give Chirac, the only thing she could think of was to tell Stephen to go and make him a special cup of his fancy Continental coffee. 'They drink a lot of that, don't they?' she said. Stephen replied, 'But it's Italian, not French.' Margaret said, 'He won't know the difference. Just do it.' So off went Stephen and brought back this cup of espresso that they presented to Chirac as a kind of reciprocal gesture for the beautiful book. It was surreal. Then it got worse, because she had to go and attend to some Cabinet crisis. So they dragged in Ronnie Grierson (one of their business advisers, who wasn't far away in London) whose French was fluent. They just said to him, 'Do you know Jacques Chirac? We've got him here. Get down here and keep him occupied whilst Margaret is holding this other meeting.' So Ronnie and Chirac sat there for about half an hour, with Ronnie talking in French, even though Chirac's English was excellent, with Stephen Sherbourne bringing in one espresso after another, hoping he'd be impressed.

Sometime in 1988, I went to discuss Chirac's election strategy at the Hôtel de Ville, which is actually the City Hall and the residence of the Mayor. It is a huge and grand place, where de Gaulle had appeared at the main window to proclaim the Liberation of Paris after the war. During Chirac's time there, they would spend breathtaking sums on their entertaining – with scandals and outrages never far away. We stood in what's called the Colbert room – because it has a bust of Jean-Baptiste Colbert on the mantelpiece; in the other corner there is a huge tapestry that was a present from our Queen. He just said, 'Yes? What's your advice?'

In due course, I told him to do three things: 'First,' I said, 'whatever you do, *don't* go and meet the people from the Rainbow Warrior [who were being released from New Zealand] – because the majority of people see them as terrorists and it will look terrible if you go to the station to meet them. Much better that you just let them come back. Secondly, you talk too much economic rubbish; nobody understands what you're talking about; you sound like a boring technocrat. By contrast, Mitterrand comes over as an avuncular, lovely, jolly nice bloke who you'd like to host your wedding. And thirdly, whatever you do, don't go on television and debate with Mitterrand, because he'll eat you alive.'

But Chirac's American adviser suggested the opposite. So Chirac went and met the Rainbow Warriors and gave them all the freedom of Paris and God knows what else; he continued to speak non-stop about GDPs and so on; and he did this on television with Mitterrand. In one debate, Chirac spent ages babbling on about GDP and credit ratings and inflation and everything else, all backed up by endless figures. And then it moved to Mitterrand, who just said, 'Liberté, Egalité, Fraternité. Vive la France.' That's what happened. And, in the spring election, Mitterrand walked it and Chirac lost again. But at least we got our fees.

That was a year after Margaret's third election victory, which had already boosted my reputation again – whether I deserved this or not, and about which different people had very different views. But possibly as a consequence, I was invited to Chile, which was again controversial.

The idea came from a group of extremely rich aristocratic families that effectively owned most of Chile and were sponsoring the moderately Right-wing Democracy and Progress Party in the country's first election for two decades. The long-standing dictator Augusto Pinochet (whose reputation for torture and oppression was a nasty one) had just stood down. Margaret had never met him, but she had controversially supported his slow transition to democracy. In addition, the Chileans had given us clandestine, but invaluable, support during the Falklands campaign. In sole power since 1973, Pinochet had suddenly decided to hold a presidential referendum asking the question, 'Do you want five more years of me as your president or not?' – and the 'Or not' won.

The Centre-Right party knew of my role with the UK Conservatives, and made a request for us to come over and advise those of them running their side. Although any involvement with Chile was always going to be a thorny issue, my support at the time was for the principle of holding an election, which had to be a good thing, and for the side that I believed would serve the country's best interests. In fact, I knew the people who had done the anti-Pinochet 'No' campaign – they were led by Mark (Lord) Malloch Brown, who later became a minister in the Labour government. He went on to become the UN Deputy Secretary-General in 2006. But originally, he worked in a political lobbying company that was run by a Mexican called Sergio Zyman, who had once helped launch Diet Coke. Following his referendum defeat, Pinochet had moved out of the public eye. Contrary to all the speculation, I'd only met him once, for about five minutes – and he didn't speak any English, so I never really said anything of significance to him. But my view was a pragmatic one. He was a tyrant; but Chile was moving in the right direction.

So we at Lowe Bell were invited to fly over there and help them with their campaign. They held a dinner for us in Santiago. Bertie Way (who was our new business director) and I went. In effect, they told us, 'We want you to handle his campaign and get our side elected because we don't want the Socialists coming in, destroying all our businesses and taxing the living daylights out of every-thing.' They were sponsoring a man called Hernán Büchi as their candidate, for an election that was to be held in December 1989. For the previous four years, he had been Minister of the Treasury under Pinochet (having actually worked for Pinochet for about 15 years in total) – so he was an economics expert – and his previous involvement with Pinochet was inevitably likely to make any work I undertook controversial. My argument was that, as in all of these things, nothing is straightforward, and I genuinely believed that the Centre-Right would make the better future government for a country in transition. The rival was a Christian Democrat-led coalition headed by Patricio Aylwin Azócar, a law professor, who was always the favourite.

These Chilean aristocrats all lived in an extraordinary compound in the middle of Santiago – in beautiful houses, but with machine-gun nests and anti-bomb defences at the gated entrances. They all used to live in each other's pockets, driving around in huge limos with armoured car escorts. It was absolutely mad. Though when you look at what rich people do in Russia and the West these days, maybe it's actually not that different.

I met Büchi at a hotel in Santiago. It was about 5 o'clock in the afternoon, with the sun setting. I don't think that I've ever met a politician less like the people that he's trying to represent. He was well over 6 feet tall, in a country where the average height of a Chilean is 5 foot 1. He was divorced, in a country which is 98 per cent Catholic. He was a vegetarian, where the main product is beef. And he rode a bike, because he just didn't approve of gas-guzzlers (during a period when every single Chilean male wanted a gas-guzzler more than they wanted a place to live).

I said, 'Well, we're going to have to work on how you present yourself', and he said, 'What for? Why can't we have the Swiss system?' I asked what on earth he meant by that, and he said, 'Well, nobody knows who is the President of Switzerland. He doesn't have to appear in public. So no one cares about his image.' I saw what he meant, but said, 'It's not Switzerland, so you're going to have to appear in public. You're going to have to hold rallies and you're going to have to persuade the people to vote for you and what you're like. They won't do it just because of a vague principle.' He said, 'Oh, I don't really want to do that. I don't like to mix with all the people, trying to explain what's going on. I'm not very good with ordinary people. I'm better off with economists.'

I was trying to think of how to reply to that, when the light changed and suddenly I saw him in profile. I said very loudly, 'Fuck. Do you know who you look like? … Clint Eastwood. You look exactly like Clint Eastwood.' He replied, 'Who's Clint Eastwood?' Anyway, against the backdrop of this amazing sunset, he looked the spitting image of the guy in *A Fistful of Dollars* (and, for that reason, in the actual election he would poll much better amongst the female audience). So in the next few days, we took him out on to the top of a hill, put a poncho on him, and blew wind at him from a large fan – and got the most astonishing picture of him looking like Clint Eastwood. Then on the poster, we wrote, 'Büchi es el hombre' – Büchi is the man – and stuck it up absolutely every-where. His popularity rating went from 26 per cent to 54 per cent in a fortnight.

But then, when he held his first public rally, he addressed this vast crowd in a way that was not at all like Clint Eastwood. After which, he immediately went back to 26 per cent, showing that his belief that he could only talk to economists might have had some truth in it. Then we tried, 'Büchi es diferente'– Büchi is different. Well, he was certainly different from the people. But, as a member of the political class, he was not really different at all. It goes to demonstrate one of the most important points in any kind of PR communication: you can't pretend to be somebody that you're not. He lost the election – obviously.

Only tenuously related to this was an incident that occurred back in London, sometime during 1988, when Virginia and I were invited to dinner one night at our neighbours in Belgravia. The host was Maria St Just, an actress from

Petrograd, who had married Peter Grenfell (of the Morgan Grenfell Bank), the second Lord St Just. They had two daughters, called Natasha (who used to go out with Mick Jagger) and Katya. Lady St Just was the literary executrix of Tennessee Williams – she was known in the theatre trade as 'the cat' (as in 'on a hot tin roof'). Of the other guests at this gathering, I seem to remember the American writer and activist Gore Vidal, Lady Antonia Fraser, Harold Pinter, Lord Goodman, and the Old Etonian antiques dealer Robin Hurlstone (who was Joan Collins's partner).

Gore Vidal started going on and on about Chile and Pinochet. Eventually, I joined in by saying, fairly innocuously, 'Well, he's at least a bit more democratic that Allende.' I'd forgotten that Vidal and Pinter were deeply involved in the anti-Pinochet movement and had organised demonstrations all over Chile. But I carried on about how President Allende had burned the electoral roll, making the point that there can't be anything much more undemocratic than setting light to the basis on which everyone gets a vote. But he was a Marxist, so that was all right, wasn't it? Vidal was furious at this unexpected challenge, and he turned on me. With a seriously nasty snarl, he said, 'What on earth do *you* know about Chile? How can you know anything?' So I said, 'Well, actually, I know Jack Henderson, who was CIA Director of Operations in Santiago. I know him very well.' This stopped Vidal in his tracks, and he started to bluster, 'Oh, you knew Jack Henderson did you? What do you know about him?' To which I replied, in the manner of delivering a punch line: 'Well, I know that I just made him up, so you can't have known him that well, can you?'

This was, as you'd expect, the last straw for Vidal. His buddy Pinter started swearing and shouting at me and calling me the c-word. Vidal said, 'You must stand up at the table and apologise immediately.' So I stood up and said, 'I am very sorry, Mr Pinter, but will you take your hand off my wife's leg?' At which point Antonia Fraser couldn't take any more and ran out to the bathroom. But then she came back a few minutes later, rather sheepishly, and said, 'I'm terribly sorry, Maria, but I've just broken your loo seat.' And at that point, we all got up and went home.

That incident confirmed for me just how much people would hold forth on topics long before they have experienced the practicalities of what people and politicians on the ground have to deal with. It's easy to pontificate – until you actually have to make things work.

14

Major Difficulties

I once saw – in the most visual of demonstrations – how power shifts. I saw it physically cross a room. It was the day when John Major took over the role of Prime Minister. We were all gathered around Margaret, with most of the Cabinet and some other MPs. Major hadn't yet arrived. Everyone was chattering away, telling her what a good job she'd done, and how it had been the greatest leadership ever. Then, suddenly, Major walked in. And like a huge swarm of bees, the entire group moved, as one, in a single instantaneous surge, across the floor to surround him. In a second, it had left only Gordon Reece and me standing in the middle of a newly vacated large space talking to Margaret. It was hurtful, embarrassing, shocking, terrifying ... grotesque. Gordon and I looked at each other, hoping, beyond any reasonable hope, that she hadn't noticed. We had witnessed the power move, literally.

Over a year earlier, as we entered 1989, I had been working in British politics for well over a decade. All of that time had been for Margaret Thatcher, at first in opposition, then in government. In terms of this country, she was the only leader that I had known. But that was about to change. Fortunately, the arguments over responsibilities and who was doing what had diminished, and I had a fairly established role – which would give me a ringside seat at one of the most talked-about moments in British political history.

Saatchi & Saatchi were now off the Conservative Party account, Norman Tebbit was no longer Chairman (he needed to look after his wife, but he'd not been happy with the way the Party was going either), and we had a new Director of Communications at Central Office in a chap called Brendan Bruce, who I had helped put in place. In these favourable circumstances, I was back to my old level of largely unhindered involvement, with direct access to Margaret and a wide brief on what I could and could not advise. That was the good news. The bad was that, almost immediately after the election victory, the government was floundering, and Margaret was behaving in a different way from that which had seen her so successful in previous terms. Now she was more autocratic and more opinionated, the hubris had increased, and her judgement was slipping – all of which meant more enemies and a lot more trouble. She was now at her most ambitious – and most vulnerable. She was hurtful and rude to ministers she thought were weak. In return, the continual criticism throughout this term would be that she had stopped listening. And although I still got on really well with her, I myself saw some of the truth in that, especially when the crunch of the leadership challenge came.

It wasn't too long into the new term before the Party was tearing itself apart because of the conflicting views on how we should best approach the issue of Europe. (Nothing changes does it?) As we entered the campaigning for the European Parliamentary Elections, there were the twin problems of disagreement within the Party about how to campaign, and a British public who remained stubbornly indifferent to why they should even bother to vote. This worried us, given that a particularly low turnout would almost certainly favour our opponents.

In an attempt to try to stir up a bit of public jeopardy, we ran an ad with the line, 'Stay at home on 15 June, and you'll live on a diet of Brussels.' But straight away, people like Leon Brittan – who was very pro-Europe – and Nigel Lawson took great umbrage, and started going on about how this was a flippant or tawdry attitude to Europe and our European partners. I think that was a complete over-reaction and served only to pour fuel on the sense of division and uncertainty leaking out to the public at large. And the public always punish a divided party.

When the election results came they were appalling. This was the first time since 1974 that Labour had beaten us in an election of any kind. For many a year, Labour had been wondering whether they would ever win an election again. We'd been so successful in winning them and they at losing them. Even with Mandelson on the case. They'd thought, for a brief interlude, that they were going to win in 1987, when they produced what they considered was their best ever campaign – but it never happened. Margaret had been too powerful and too secure, with her huge majority. Now, our advantage was crumbling. It wasn't a general election, but Labour had turned a corner, and there was panic in our ranks. Momentum is important in politics for all sorts of reasons – public perception, press opinion, internal confidence, the markets and the economy, and so on – and as soon as you start a slide, everyone starts to worry. With just cause: by April next year, Labour would have moved to 25 per cent up in the polls, and Margaret would have dropped to an all-time low in personal popularity versus Kinnock.

It's human nature to sweat an anxiety into a reality. That sometimes happens in life and it particularly happens in politics. After the European results came the recriminations, and I took as much flak as anyone. Margaret had to do something, and one response was to bring in Kenneth Baker to replace Peter Brooke as Party Chairman (who has the job of making sure that the internal Party machinery operates effectively). Ken was an amiable enough man, with a permanently genial look on his face, but he wanted for neither cunning nor political steel. Early in the term, he threatened Margaret with his resignation over the National Curriculum – and he was very good at playing both sides of any issue (telling one person one thing, and telling another another). Although deep down he held a mainly Thatcherite view of the world, there were occasions when he went and pretended that he was something else – as he did many years later when he shared the pro-European platform with Blair. But he and I got on well: he was keen that I stay as adviser, and actually requested that my involvement be increased.

As the summer passed, one problem that was occupying ever more of our attention – and many of the discussions with Margaret at this time – was the issue of her 'unassailable' Chancellor, Nigel Lawson. The pair of them never saw eye-to-eye over Britain joining the ERM, which he strongly favoured, and which she would adamantly not sanction (disliking the idea of our interest rates passing out of our direct control). It amounted to a festering tension between them, which could not last without something giving.

Lawson was clever and knew that he was. He had a brooding, secretive and non-collegiate style (maybe it's something to do with Chancellors of the Exchequer), always feeling that he should be allowed to run the economy in his way, and his way alone, doing anything that he saw fit, without having to explain his wishes to anyone or wait for approval. When he couldn't get his own way, he would still try to do what he wanted – even if it meant going against Margaret's wishes, such as when he was shadowing the Deutschmark by using the interest rate. The irony in all of this was that once John Major (as Chancellor) had taken us into the ERM in 1990, within two years, we would then have to get back out of it – on Black Wednesday.

In 1989, inflation was going up, which always puts pressure on a Chancellor – and Margaret felt that he ought to shoulder responsibility for it, given that he wanted to take responsibility for everything else. Then, in October, Margaret brought in another economic adviser from the American Enterprise Institute (although he was British) called Alan Walters, who was anti-ERM. It was bound to send Lawson crackers. I'm not quite sure whether she did it to annoy him, or because she was so preoccupied that she didn't anticipate that it would – it was a strange thing to do, either way. And you can imagine what Lawson thought of it. John Smith, the Shadow Chancellor, started talking the piss out of him in the Commons, talking about two Chancellors and singing the theme tune to *Neighbours,* and that kind of thing. Lawson had a sizeable ego, and having all that happen was the final straw, so he walked out (with Walters following him, bizarrely – which fed, even more, the perception of a madhouse).

Lawson's going wasn't a surprise to anyone. Margaret had been complaining to me for ages that she thought he was a disloyal bastard: she felt that she had got him to where he was, only to find that he was now trying to bring her down – and that, at some level, he had actually wanted an excuse to make a point anyway. Now he was gone, she thought that it would end there, but it didn't.

That weekend, she had a shocker of an interview with Brian Walden on ITV, and he wouldn't let the subject drop. Brian Walden was like that. His Sunday lunchtime show was an hour long, often with just the one guest, so it was a long, long grilling. He's what I call a pinhead interviewer: he'd sit there and ask whether it was the third word that was the most important or the fourth word, and so on, and the audience would just sort of glaze over and wonder where the hell it was all going. He was like that in normal conversation, until he got drunk, when he told you a hell of a lot of things that you weren't supposed to know about. He had that in common with Frosty, who liked his drink shall we say, and yet could do these extraordinary interviews whilst off his head to varying degrees. People just used to say that Frosty looked a bit overtired, and nobody ever said he was pissed. But after *Breakfast with Frost* they'd all go and have breakfast in the BBC canteen and he used to sit there with his giant cigar and drink a bottle of white wine.

They rarely do this level of detailed interview any more, unless it's tucked away on some digital channel somewhere – not on prime-time television. But the format allowed Walden, on the day he was interviewing Thatcher, to take his time, like a prosecutor, marshalling his words and cross-examination carefully, and slowly but surely building to the big question. For a while he gave her quite an easy ride – all rather fawning and sycophantic – until she was tired, then he hit her with the Walters–Lawson stuff, at which point she more or less fell to bits.

Instead of the attention being on Lawson's autocratic style, wherever you looked, Margaret was being accused of his kind of unwillingness to listen and talk. That, in turn, made her behave all the more erratically and defensively. The media – and in particular, the BBC – had now started to discover that they could get away with insulting her without anybody doing anything about it: which they hadn't been able to do for the previous 12 years. And now, even some of the Right-wing papers started to wobble. The Labour people were cranking up their attempts to befriend the *Daily Mail* and even the *Sun*, which were staying broadly loyal for the time being. But you could just tell that the tide was turning. Too many in the Party started running around and squabbling like headless chickens, and stories about Michael Heseltine – as the darling of the pro-Europeans – were increasing exponentially. All the talk was about running the Party, not running the country. This really was trouble, and it was going to be hard to turn it around. I could see that.

To replace Lawson, she brought in John Major, as Chancellor. I'd first met Major at a cocktail party at Chequers, and hadn't thought too much of him from the very start. But she liked him, and it was possible to see why: he appeared firmly Thatcherite in his philosophy; he was a Eurosceptic at heart; he came, like Margaret, from a fairly unprivileged background; and he was good at talking with people – and with women especially (which was certainly not a universally held skill amongst the Cabinet), to which Margaret always responded well. The *Financial Times* had been the worst culprit in siding with Lawson during her dispute with him, so we suggested that Major's first interview should be with them. It seemed to go down well.

The new session of Parliament opened in November 1989, and it brought with it a stalking-horse challenge. Tony Meyer was staunchly Right-wing, but he was also a committed Europhile, and believed that as soon as he put his name forward the pro-European big cheeses, Michael Heseltine and Ian Gilmour, would take over the race. They didn't – which showed that he was naïve and they were cowards – but Meyer kept going. He was a rather weird candidate, and no one took him seriously: they nicknamed him the 'stalking donkey'. But in the vote, taking into account spoiled papers and the like, 60 Tory MPs failed to support Margaret. It represented a small flesh wound, but a major turning point. Kenneth Baker and I had thought from the start that it was far more dangerous than it seemed, and than she acknowledged: it was the first time anybody had dared to suggest that she should leave office. The word 'maybe' was no longer embargoed. When a party starts to talk in this way, it doesn't matter whether there's much substance or not; it just starts the idea and it gives permission for all those people who didn't like her to find others who share a similar view and head as a gathering mob ever closer to the tipping point.

More people in her own party started to whisper against her; people in her own Cabinet started speaking against her behind their hand; people started to just look at her differently or say, 'Good morning' with a different intonation; and one or two of the crises that had happened in the past were spun again, like Westland. It's subtle, but tangible; it's how a politician is brought down: not by a full-frontal battle – they're just insidiously pricked and stabbed and picked at until they bleed out. Death by coyote bite. In almost exactly one year, she would be gone.

As we entered 1990, it was the Berlin Wall that was going first, and with it the Cold War, so colossal world events were where Margaret's attention was. She liked the big-picture tasks as much as she hated the internal pettifoggery, but then, on 30 March, we were hit by a domestic issue that blew up: the Poll Tax – Margaret's self-proclaimed 'flagship' policy – which had been threatening trouble from the start of the new Parliament.

That sunny Saturday, the day before it was due to be introduced, a very large part of Central London was given over to anti-Poll Tax demonstrations, that then became riots – starting in Trafalgar Square (where some fool had left a huge building site unsecured, with the result that any anarchist lunatic so minded could go in and help himself to bricks and planks of wood and stuff). The cameras filmed every smash and bang and airborne policeman's helmet (plus the rather dramatic cameo of a scaffolding pole, courtesy of the building site, going straight through a police car window) – and the press, of course, used it as a metaphor for the government's chaos.

With the Falklands, and even during the miners' strike, there had been a sense that Margaret was fighting from the moral high ground, where her single-mindedness was an asset; here, despite public shock at anarchy on London streets, the view was that she had brought this on herself with an unjust tax policy, where that single-mindedness was a failing. The Tories were not supposed to be the party of tax, yet here they were incurring riots for it.

To make matters worse, the first bills had just gone out in the mail, so MPs were going home to their constituencies, only to be met by remonstrations from their own angry voters demanding to know what the hell they had been sent. Margaret had never been told, or had never fully appreciated, the full truth about what it was going to cost individuals, and – all-importantly – how people would be hit with a figure in a buff envelope that would take them by surprise.

Some people, who'd never had a rates payment to make in their lives, were now getting bills for thousands of pounds, without understanding why or what it was instead of. She had never anticipated what the effect would be.

One reason why Margaret had agreed to the Poll Tax idea in the first place (back in 1985) was her dislike of local council profligacy and domestic rates. However, one of the first, and most important, lessons that I learned in politics was not to try to save the public from something about which they aren't complaining. If people haven't noticed something that is unpleasant or unattractive, don't, for heaven's sake, bring it to their attention. Somebody convinced Margaret that the new system would be a lot fairer than the rates and that we should spend a huge amount of political energy and goodwill on trying to improve the system. But she agreed too quickly, without thinking through the pros and cons as she usually did. Lawson had disagreed with it, which meant that she saw it as a trial of strength against him. It was one of those subjects where, even when I tried to talk to her about it, she didn't want to hear.

It was full of flaws, both conceptually and strategically. The only way you could establish who was in the 'community' was to look on the electoral roll, hence the term 'Poll Tax', and even the 'vote tax'. No one called it the 'Community Charge'; everyone called it the 'Poll Tax', which became a poisoned word, spoken with venom. Kenneth Baker and I knew full well the damage that the Poll Tax was doing – long before the riot. The stock phrase, used all the time by Labour, was that 'the Duke and the dustman of the Duke all get asked for the same amount of money': that was how everybody talked about it.

Ken and I worked out what we would have to do to make it palatable: in other words, who we would need to exclude from having to pay this tax, and how much would have to be injected into it (around £3 billion) to fund the inevitable compensatory payments to the people who, having paid their Poll Tax, would then qualify for some kind of benefit or rebate because of their circumstances. We went to see Margaret at Chequers one weekend and gave a presentation about what was needed. We asked for another million or so as a communications budget, to try to turn around public opinion. But she lost her temper and decided that we were being disloyal to her, and started shouting at us. All she would say was that it wouldn't matter once it was up and running and that people could make their payments in instalments to ameliorate the impact of the bill – which we could never have suggested as a sop to angry punters. She was getting herself into quite a state. I think that this was the occasion when Denis leant across to her, put his hand on her knee and said, 'Steady, Pet – friends.'

After that, she went back to Cabinet and asked John Major, as Chancellor of the Exchequer, to find those sums of money – but he refused. He would have none of it. It was like Lawson all over again. And this was the moment when Ken and I got an inkling that Major – whom Margaret had essentially invented – was now as ready as any of the others to stab her in the back. The added irony was that, once he became Prime Minister, it was the same sum of money that he put into the scheme when he turned it into the Council Tax. Major always looked the quiet, grey man, but he was actually a very calculating individual. Later, during her leadership battle, when Margaret wanted him to support her (along with Douglas Hurd), he had prevaricated – albeit when he was recovering from his wisdom tooth operation. He always argued that she asked him in a typically peremptory fashion and that he didn't want to be rushed without thinking about it. Some may call it being considered; others may think that he was a calculating character. But he had a very different persona from his public one, which meant that people were surprised when he was caught in a scandal or when he started calling people 'bastards' and all that kind of thing: the quiet ones are always the worst.

Too early in the term, Margaret was becoming very unpopular personally. To both the public, in presentational terms, and her MPs, in a managerial sense, she seemed to be changing, becoming more hubristic, more rude, more supercilious, more dismissive – and her appeal was crashing. The facile explanation was that power had corrupted her. It hadn't. But she was suffering the fate of many senior politicians, quarantined within Westminster, once momentum starts building against them. The more unpopular a leader gets, the more both ministers and backbenchers start thinking about their own futures. It is where politics starts and ends: the love they once had for you when you got them their seats turns to hate for you for jeopardising those seats. She was floundering, and it might all have been avoided had a lot of them been able to see the wood for the trees. Instead, ones like Geoffrey Howe – emboldened by Lawson – would see an opportunity to push the process further in the wrong direction.

Margaret had a very ordered mind, and this was another area where erstwhile strength was present weakness. Once she had defeated Meyer, she felt that the process was over (as had been her experience with Lawson) – done and dusted. We all knew, however, that actually, matters were getting worse with each event. Heseltine was permanently on manoeuvres, prowling about everywhere, cropping up when and where you never expected him, flanked by his ever-present wingmen, Hampson and Mates. The only saving grace was that an awful lot of people would rather have lost a kidney than have had him their leader. But all Margaret would say was that if the government is so successful, and Britain is doing so well, with everybody so very much better off, 'Why would they bring me down?' Well, the polls were showing that the electorate were developing a mind to. Her 65th birthday party that year, at Chequers, was not a good evening for any of us. Kenneth was there, as was Gordon and the Archers, but she was exhausted (she nearly nodded off during dinner) and not at all herself. And later that week, she had more cause for concern when we lost Eastbourne to the Liberals.

Within the month, Howe was on his feet. Margaret had been to the EU Summit in October, and that had prompted her famous 'No! No! No!' speech. It humiliated Geoffrey – yet again – and he could take it no longer. I'm always surprised at the level and duration of humiliation and hurt to which people – especially in politics and business – are willing to subject themselves, if they think that there is a vague possibility of an even vaguer reward at the end of it. Why bother? Why put up with every day being a bad day? Obviously, Geoffrey finally reached that conclusion, and on 13 November 1990, early in the parliamentary session of that day, he made his famous resignation speech. Its impact came both from what he actually said and from its totally unexpected nature – including the way he finished, calling for others to follow in his footsteps. Nobody thought that he would say much at all, let alone say what he did.

Obviously, Margaret and Geoffrey had not the slightest respect for each other. I don't want to be too rude about the Howes, because both Geoffrey and Elspeth were always nice to me. But Margaret disliked him in what I can only describe as a metabolic manner. She didn't just dislike him; she physically loathed him being in the same room. Of course, she had been rude to him all the time – but he had the kind of personality that invited it. He was grey and mumbled and shuffled and she despised all those things. She would bully him, and humiliate him around the Cabinet table, and say things like, 'Speak up, Geoffrey. If you've got something to say, say it out loud.' And when she took him out of the Foreign Office and installed John Major there (a move which, incidentally, led to Major being in a position to eventually win the leadership), it really was too much for Geoffrey. So, as everyone now knows, there was an inevitability that, when he had the chance, he would serve his revenge below room temperature.

Plus, there was a problem between Margaret and Elspeth Howe, his wife, for whom Margaret had no respect. Elspeth was fantastically and aristocratically grand, wanting to do good, and with her heart in exactly the right place. But none of it impressed Margaret – do-gooders never did, and I'm not sure she ever quite understood charity (a bit like the merchant banker in the Monty Python sketch, when a flag-seller arrives). For whatever reason, Margaret was just down on Geoffrey, so that made her equally cynical about Elspeth. I remember how, in those days, the milkman used to arrive at the end of Downing Street and walk through 10, 11, and 12, and so on, putting the bottles down outside all the flats on the second- and third-floor corridors. And Margaret would say, 'How much milk has Elspeth had? What on earth does she do with it all? She must give it to that milksop, Geoffrey.'

When Geoffrey gave his resignation speech (I heard it whilst I was driving somewhere), it had a seismic effect all right. To be honest, I didn't think that it was as impressive – in itself – as is sometimes made out. Neither did Margaret. But the fact that he did it took her aback somewhat, as Ken (who sat next to her on the front bench to hear it) told me later. However, in the final analysis, we all just thought that it was a piece of utterly disloyal back-stabbing, and only served to confirm our poor impression of Geoffrey as someone who had not dared to say what he thought to her face. Actually, some people said that Elspeth had written it for him, because he wouldn't have been so daring. But its timing and the surprise element were devastating.

One problem with Margaret was that, by now, she had completely lost interest in the machinations of the Party, which seemed trivial and irrelevant to the bigger global picture she had of a world outside of the Westminster Tory bubble. The apparatus by which the Conservative Party gets rid of, and chooses, its leaders, is a dusty catacomb of arcane procedure and arbitrary rules. Indeed, it was only about this time that I myself started to learn about how it worked – at that time, with the rules that we had then, which have all been changed numerous times since. And I discovered that absolutely nobody in the Party knew what all the rules were or how they work anyway.

In Ken Baker, she had a loyal chairman, and she had a few loyal ministers. But there were an awful lot of people who wanted to bring her down: who were interested in their careers developing, and who thought that – for whatever reason – those careers would never develop whilst she was PM. Most politicians are eventually stabbed to death, usually in the back, but occasionally somebody is brave and plunges the knife in the front. But I've always said that it hurts just as much from the front as in the back, so what's the point of making any difference? There is the old joke about the MP who goes to Parliament, sits on the benches, and remarks how he can see the enemy in front of him.

And someone replies, 'No. That's the Opposition. The enemy is on the benches behind you.' That is the essential truth of politics. It is testimony to her success that she stayed the course for all those years. However, the runaway train could now be heard coming down the track.

It was not a matter of months or days – it was minutes. I was still travelling at the time, but I know that, as soon as Howe had made the speech and the MPs could get out of the Chamber, the Party went into psychic meltdown. People were running round not knowing where they were running to; an actual physical fight broke out in the tearooms; groups were gathering within groups. All eyes were on one man with a lot of hair, and within a few hours, he had announced his leadership bid. This was not Anthony Meyer. This was a big beast of a lion: the Tarzan who had been plotting for almost half a decade for this moment. Michael Heseltine issued his leadership challenge.

Ken and I had a list on the wall of all our MPs and we'd put a cross against all the ones who'd been passed over, fired, or insulted, plus those who had ever voted against her. Doing this exercise made you realise that the majority of the Party had a reason, given a following wind, not to support her. Ken then produced a more detailed schedule of all the MPs who, in a ballot, would vote against her and everyone who would vote for her (which, in the end, he got 100 per cent correct), and we took it to Margaret. We discussed with her how to act; to pre-empt matters with some goodwill-generation, talking to those who'd asked to see her, and internal campaigning – at least to offset Heseltine's manoeuvres. But she had gone into ostrich mode. She refused to give any interviews or do any canvassing – which she seemed to think was unnecessary and beneath her ('my MPs know me and my beliefs') – other than a very rare trip to the tearooms. Having been the UK's international standard-bearer for three terms, it was next to impossible now for her to turn her mindset from the coruscations of the changing global village to the bare-knuckle street-fighting of the Westminster one.

She chose Peter Morrison to be her campaign manager. It was not a good move, and he was no Airey Neave. Peter Morrison would walk into the tearoom, and go up to an MP and say, 'The Prime Minister would like to have a word with you. Would you mind?' He was a terrible old woof, Peter Morrison, near-legless most the time, with a bright red face giving off the whiff of gin. Margaret's euphemism, which she had always used to describe Ronnie Miller, was that 'he's very sensitive'. There was one day when he simply wouldn't let Gordon and me in to see her. We'd managed to get a copy leaked to us of the proposals that

Heseltine would make in his draft manifesto. It was explosive stuff, including the way he would call a review of the Poll Tax. But all Morrison would say was that he didn't want any media chicanery brought to bear on an internal Party matter. It was a breathtaking illustration of his complacency and lack of nous. He just kept telling her she was wonderful, that everybody loved her, and that it would all be fine – which was palpable nonsense, but I'm not sure Peter was aware of anything different. His figures were based simply on what the MPs had told him. I said to him, 'Peter. They're politicians. They lie all the time.'

Gordon and Kenneth and I were busy pushing and cajoling her, telling her that she had to get out and take the initiative, go through some leadership motions, and talk to people through the press. In the 24 hours after the challenge was called, Heseltine had completed over 50 media interviews. Eventually she succumbed. But somehow, Morrison then got her to give the one interview to Simon Jenkins, editor of *The Times* – without telling us, her media people – and Jenkins was the last person on earth you'd choose for a moment like that.

But she had already listened to far too many of the wrong people. It's a weakness everybody has, even a great person like her. It is human nature that if somebody tells you something you want to hear, you choose to believe it over the thing that you don't want to hear. Thus it was that she had no doubt that Kenneth and I wanted her to win by a mile – but she just couldn't hear us warning her that it was never going to work and she was heading for the rocks. I'd say, 'Heseltine's going to fucking well win, Margaret', and she would reply, 'No, no, no, no, you're exaggerating terribly, Tim. You people just aren't in touch. You don't understand.'

On the first ballot, held on Tuesday 20 November 1990, she took 204 votes, against Heseltine's 152. However, the rules dictated that she needed a majority of 56, and in the event, she was an agonising four votes short. It is perhaps worth remembering – although no consolation – that she never lost. And Heseltine never won. An awful lot of people never trusted him at all. He was vain and volatile, and his campaigning had been excessive, where Margaret's had been recessive. Norman Lamont said that Heseltine had been pouncing on MPs like a 'child molester'.

Heseltine was temporarily halted, but Margaret had not won. Blame was put on the fact that she was on a Paris trip (including a stay at the Elysée Palace) when the ballot took place, which is rubbish. That was just people wanting to manufacture a 'Palace coup' headline. On the actual day, hardly anyone had even spotted that she'd gone to Paris. But if she had pulled out of that summit (it was the crucial Conference on Security and Co-operation in Europe), they would have known, and assumed she was 'frit', to use her expression. But in hindsight, people started asking why she had even bothered to go. Well, actually, she was only meeting with Bush and Gorbachev and ending the Cold War. Not as important as meeting a few backbenchers in the tearooms, obviously. However, it did mean that her proposers were not around to help with the election day canvassing: Douglas Hurd had to be with her in Paris, and John Major was having an operation on a wisdom tooth.

On that evening, with the result announced, she said (in the insane early-evening mid-news interview with John Sergeant outside the British Embassy), 'It is my intention to let my name go forward for the second ballot.' Cecil Parkinson always said that she was trying to sound thoughtful at that precise moment, but, alas, she sounded a bit manic. She had promised Ken not to make an impromptu speech before she spoke to him, but she probably didn't even remember that.

The people who did view it as a 'coup' were people like Bush, Gorbachev, and Mitterrand in Paris, who were dumbfounded about what was going on, and how a few rogue members of her Party were causing such mayhem. Douglas Hurd, who was there, described the scene as that of a 'wounded eagle ... unable to soar again'. Crawfie sat up all night with her, drinking Scotch. My guess is that it was the moment when she realised that her time might be up – even though, when she first got back to London, she kept saying, 'I fight on. I fight to win.' All Denis would say was, 'Don't go on, love.'

Back in London, she asked Tristan Garel-Jones and Richard Ryder to be her campaign managers for the next round – given the disaster that Morrison had been – but they both refused. Garel-Jones had the previous day hosted a meeting of ministers at his home in Catherine Place, trying to figure out who they wanted to replace her, so, tragically, she approached one of the least suitable people she could have done. Most people had decided that it was now a *fait accompli*. Richard was husband to Margaret's secretary, so that was a vicious blow as well.

At the Commons, she called each member of the Cabinet in, one by one. Ken Clarke went in first. He was one of the few who wasn't really scared of her: in fact, he never seemed to be bothered about anything much – you could tell that from his shoes – although he did like jazz, which I guess is something. He said that he thought that she could not win the second ballot, as did Rifkind and Patten. It had been Morrison's idea that she interview them separately. Had she asked them collectively, I'm not sure that anybody there would have had the guts to stand up and tell her to go, because I just don't think they had it in them. Most of them were scared stiff of her, and they knew that the only reason they wanted her out was to make life easier for themselves, and possibly to avoid Heseltine getting in by default. Clarke might have resigned had she stayed, given that he was so pro-Europe, and that might have given some of the others the courage of their convictions. But whatever had happened, we all probably knew that her time had come. Cranley Onslow and the 1922 Committee then asked for a wider choice of candidates, which is what they say when they want you to fall on your sword.

One has to understand the mind of a politician – which, in the main, is a place of icy darkness. They're not nice people. They start off being nice, and some genuinely want to get into public service and help their electorate and the nation. But the machinery turns them into zombies: unfeeling, but deadly. She had always had a group of loyal friends, but they were never in the Cabinet. There was only really Tebbit with whom she had a meeting of minds, and he was a great supporter now – but even he had turned on her from time to time in the past.

The next two or three days were chaotic. In the end, I never found out who talked her out of carrying on – probably Denis. I don't know, and I never will know. It could have been anybody, or maybe she came to her own conclusion. But we kept telling her to fight on. On the Wednesday, at around about 11.00 p.m., I got a phone call asking for Gordon Reece and me to get to Downing Street immediately. We'd all been out to dinner at the time, and there were journalists as guests, which made everything difficult. Nick Lloyd, the Editor of the *Daily Express*, asked us, 'Where have you got to go? What's happening?' I stayed schtum, but I think he knew full well what was happening.

Once at Downing Street, we sat down with her until the early hours. We said, 'You've got to fight on. We will fight and stand with you. We'll go down fighting with you. We'll die with you. We'll jump off tall buildings; we'll do anything ...' Portillo pleaded with her to stay and fight. She was in tears, and then she said, 'I'm sorry. I'm going to have to let you down. I'm going.' And at that, we all hugged and hugged. The room was a strange mixture of despair and togetherness.

And then, in the midst of all that, her private secretary started worrying about who needed to be told: Bank of England, Bush, the Queen, Secret Service – that kind of thing. That's how the Civil Service works; why they're there. Within seconds, I'd seen incredible emotion, and the utter coldness of government operations.

Thursday came, and we knew it was the *fin de siècle*. She issued her resignation to the Cabinet at 9.33 a.m. Ken Baker told her that she had acted selflessly. It was an extraordinary moment. A morning of tears, many of them – but not all – Margaret's. Obviously, I wasn't in there, but tears and guilt were vying for airspace. In the afternoon, she gave a sublime speech at PMQs (which she'd worked on all night with Norman Tebbit, John Gummer and John Whittingdale), which was everything that Howe's speech had not been, and which united the Party (for an hour or so) behind her. Now the mutterers and plotters of the previous day's tearooms had turned into her greatest admirers. It was the personification of hypocrisy. And before too long, there would be more mutterings of 'What have we done?' As her friends and advisers of many years, we stupidly thought that she had so changed the Conservative Party that it would eventually elect another leader cast in the same mould and would win the next few elections and carry on the radical transformation of Britain. Little did we know what would be coming in time.

Denis was ambivalent about the day. I think, on the one hand, that he thought that it was a tragic way to treat such a great figure; at the same time, he was relieved that the pain was over. Margaret, meanwhile, just kept saying to me, 'But I haven't finished. I haven't finished.' She was in shock. I've always wanted to tell everybody that they were her last words before she died. Unfortunately they weren't – but if this were an epic novel, they would be. I'm almost tempted to write that in this book as if that did happen, and try to modify history – but now I've told too many people what really happened, I'm stuck with the truth.

After the last day at Downing Street, I didn't see her again until Christmas Day – which I'd spent at Chequers most of the previous dozen years. Alistair McAlpine threw a party for her at the Dorchester (where, by the way, he was born, during the war – because his family had owned it). Alistair was a wonderful man – 'tubby and eccentric' was how Charles Moore described him – and his recent death was a tragedy, especially after he had been so viciously smeared. He was one of Margaret's most important and devoted advisers, and a master at fund-raising and literally 'selling' Thatcherite Conservatism. He had the quirkiest of hobbies, collecting things like dinosaur eggs and exotic hens for a coop he had in his garden – until a very rich Middle Eastern potentate gave him a couple of eagle owls, which were delivered when I was there with him one day. He wasn't sure what to do with them, so he rather naïvely put them in the same coop as the hens, thinking that, all being birds, they'd all get along swimmingly. Of course, when we came back, the two owls were all that were left, along with a lot of feathers and carnage.

Normally, Alistair's parties were the most enjoyable of occasions. But this Christmas Day one – the first Christmas out of power and not at Chequers – was horrible; an absolutely cold, ghastly, artificial event, with us all knowing where we would rather be and what we'd like to be doing. We all knew it was all over, and yet there we were, celebrating what? Nothing.

After her exit from Downing Street, I kept in touch with Margaret and she would often be ringing up on trivial matters, for example to get people's addresses or their telephone numbers. Sometimes she had to ask how to go about quite mundane tasks. You forget how completely shielded you are as a leader – until you're not. She once rang Charles Powell on a Sunday morning to ask how to find a plumber. The problem was that, even though she had lost most of her governmental privileges, she was still regarded as a prime terrorist target, so the police didn't like her going out, even to get a pint of milk.

Then there were the tens of thousands of letters that were not stopping coming. She needed a team to help her with this, and with sorting out the ones that were from important dignitaries and the ones from the stray lunatics (although sometimes you might be half-pressed to see much difference). It's not quite as easy as it seems to delegate that kind of task, and we needed her to be involved in the process at some level. But the task could be quite upsetting for her, and she was all over the place with it. She would, for example, write pages and pages to a random citizen who admired her policies, whilst postponing doing something about a reply to an important foreign minister.

Indeed, she was acting like a retired office worker who gets told that he must come back and see people, and does just that, ad infinitum, until people start giving each other funny looks. She found it hard not to think it was still her job. She would talk about how she still could not stop expecting her car to turn into Downing Street, and, of course, it always carried on. It is impossible to get anywhere near what it feels like when you are at the highest point of political power and then, suddenly, you're not. It must be like this – worse, no doubt – when they finally take the nuclear codes back from the President. She suffered; how could she not?

They had a house in Dulwich already, which was great for Denis's golf, but little else. In fact, they hated it – especially as it seemed like being in another world to a throbbing Westminster village. In what I think was an impressively short space of time, we set her up in Chester Square, Belgravia, organised the staff for the Thatcher Foundation, and worked out the publishing contract for her book (which in the end worked out at about £3 million, from HarperCollins, which was not bad going, even for a best-selling memoir). It was all about fathoming what a decent retirement might entail.

Unfortunately, she wasn't really focusing on any of it. She was in a state of utter grief. She was bereft, and would possibly never get over it. Neither, I think, would the Conservative Party.

15

African Adventures

Of the challenges that came to me from abroad, there could be no question as to the most complex. That was South Africa in the early '90s, and the transition to multiracial democracy from the evils of apartheid. I was working there with one man in particular who would seem an anachronism today – namely, F. W. de Klerk. I saw him again at Margaret Thatcher's funeral recently. He repeated to me what he had so often said of her: that she had appreciated the complexity of South African politics far better than most world leaders. In the circumstances, that was a great compliment.

Racial discrimination, and an ugly system of apartheid that favoured the white population over the black and coloured, had been a formal part of the South African administration since the end of the war. Black opposition parties, such as the ANC (African National Congress), had been banned, and its leaders exiled or imprisoned – most notoriously, the black rights lawyer and revolutionary, Nelson Mandela. However, as we entered the 1990s – after years of international pressure, and a realisation that the system was unsustainable – the government began a move to full democracy, and in February 1990, in his speech to the opening of Parliament, new President de Klerk announced that the ANC would be unbanned and be allowed to campaign for office, and that Mandela would be released.

From the moment we first met, F. W. de Klerk struck me as such a calm, restrained individual – which, in the tense, transitional environment, was a rare and most appropriate and useful quality. Even with earth-shattering events going on all around him, he maintained the same unexcitable tone and disposition. Of course, he held some firm opinions, as any politician would, but was never prone to lecture or patronise people – he would just express his point of view and then sit and listen. He was the right man for the moment, and, in my opinion, had the right personal approach to it.

It meant, however, that he was not always the easiest of conversationalists. One common characteristic between de Klerk and Thatcher was that they had no interest in small talk, no time for anything other than the big political picture. Everything was part of that process, and the people who distracted either of them from it tended to irritate or bore them. F. W. (one would call him F. W., which was pronounced 'Eff Ear' in Afrikaans) was clever and smart and he could argue the hind legs off a donkey, but he didn't believe in emotionalising things (which, by the way, Mandela never did either, despite all that he had witnessed and been through personally).

South Africa has always played a significant part in my life, and I have a fondness for the place. I was a small child when my father left home and moved there, but I went to see him a couple of times when I was still young. It had been on these occasions that I had witnessed apartheid for the first time, and I remember being so puzzled as to why the black people were not allowed to walk on the same side of the street as the whites or why they would go on separate buses, and not speak to each other, and all that stuff. No doubt it had been the same in parts of the US. Even though I was an uncomprehending child, it was disturbing to see it – and to see that it was, for many, the normal behaviour.

As well as my father, my uncle had spent a lot of time there – and sadly, turned native racist. It led to an odd situation when he was travelling in Australia, when he took umbrage at a black guy walking along trying to share the same part of the pavement and – ludicrously – shoved him out of the way. Unfortunately, the black Aussie guy was a professional boxer and took umbrage back – punching my uncle so hard that it broke his jaw. I think the principle of a black guy actually retaliating was more traumatic than the fractured bone. And so it was with the switch from apartheid in South Africa: the most difficult aspect was the sheer sense of shock to the national white psyche – and possibly to that of the black as well. As regards these great historical shifts – as with the fall of the Berlin Wall, for example – it can be easier to live a life wishing for something to happen than one where it actually does, and where you then have to fathom out what to do next.

During the '80s, mainstream opinion in Britain had been in agreement that apartheid was an evil way to run a society, but this did not prevent interminable argument (with its attendant protests and disruptions) over how best to end it and whether sanctions might be effective in encouraging a solution. Margaret was not convinced, and just thought that sanctions would hurt the entire population in equal measure, whilst strengthening the far-Right adherents to apartheid. I think she was correct, and I do not believe that the transition came about primarily because we had banned the country from international sport or through a few trade restrictions. (And how ridiculous it thus is that some Tories have subsequently apologised for her view on this.) The change came about for the simple reason that most people in South Africa realised that their heinous system had got to be abolished in the interests of basic human decency.

I actually remember the day we read in the papers that de Klerk was going to release Mandela and hold a proper general election (to be held in 1994). It had been coming for a while, but it was no less a world-shattering event when it was officially announced. And I remember immediately thinking that I could – and would like to – get involved in what was about to take place in that great country.

So I made the ultimate cold-call. I kid you not – this is exactly how it went. First, I got hold of the direct presidential telephone number. I can't remember from whom, but obviously, it helped that I had the right contacts. I picked what I thought would be a good time of day, and dialled Cape Town – and heard a secretary say 'President de Klerk's office.' I said, 'Would it be possible to speak to the President?' She said, 'Who's calling?' So I replied, 'My name's Tim Bell and I'm ringing on behalf of the British Prime Minister, Margaret Thatcher', which was at least 10 per cent true. There was a long, long interval, and then, suddenly, came a deep and distinctive South African voice saying, 'Hello?'

By that time, I had met a lot of very famous people and was used to it. Nonetheless, it was very unnerving to do a call like that: and especially when I actually got through. F. W. de Klerk was quite polite, even though I'd called up out of the blue – but you could tell he was really wondering what the hell I wanted. It was all very surreal. I burbled on about how he was obviously going to need specialist communications advice in the transition from apartheid and that it was not going to be easy preventing the election turning into a civil war – and that I had a track-record in election campaign strategy and communication. 'So,' I said, rather feebly, 'I wonder if I could come and help you?' The first, and rather odd thing he said was, 'Have you got the fare?' I said that I had, and he replied, 'Well, get on a plane and come down and we'll see what you can offer.' And that was that. I flew to Cape Town, stayed for six months, off and on, and handled the National Party's election campaign. An American pollster called Stan Greenberg – he was Bill Clinton's man – was my near equivalent, advising the ANC.

There were two presidential headquarters in South Africa – one in Pretoria, and the one in Cape Town, where I went first. I was picked up from my hotel by somebody who drove me there in a rather rapid and aggressive manner, and I was shown into the Cabinet room by an official who walked and talked in a similarly rapid and aggressive manner. It was a big room, painted in pale blue. Centre stage was a large circular table with places for each of the Cabinet Ministers – at each one, microphone, glass, cup holder, pad and a pencil – and de Klerk was sitting there in the President's chair that was three times the size of everybody else's. He was smoking. At the time, he was an 80–100 per day man (he's given up since then), which meant that, from the start, we had something in common. I sat down in someone's smaller seat, next to him in his bigger seat, the pair of us occupying one tiny segment of this huge polished mahogany circle at the end of this big room.

We got on quite well, quite quickly: certainly it wasn't as awkward as it might have been. In fact it was not long before he became quite affable – something you often find with South Africans. He asked me what I did and what I had to do with Thatcher and so on – although he'd obviously already rung her up to ask who the fuck I was. People had often criticised him as being a bit diffident, especially when he was in unfamiliar political situations, but I never saw very much of that side of him. In fact, the more I got to know him, the more I came to like him and respect him as a truly extraordinary character – clever and charming in equal proportions, with an impressive understanding of history, economics, and politics, yet with a clear feel for human dignity. And he's a very dear friend.

Probably the most important element of de Klerk's character was his open-mindedness – unusual for a politician in his position at that time – and he took a very pragmatic view of his country's history and politics. On the one hand, he knew the significance of Verwoerd's founding principles of apartheid, and the intellectual underpinning of the system: that, in part, the black people actually didn't want to integrate with the whites and the whites didn't want to integrate with the blacks – that each wanted to have separate development. As a tentative defence of it – if that can be considered for a moment – Verwoerd's apartheid policy had been produced as a way of enabling two groups of people who hated each other to coexist in the same place. (Indeed, there are some similarities here with what's going on in Palestine.) And anyone climbing up the National Party's hierarchy, as he successfully had, could not fail to have an appreciation of this rationale.

The problem, which de Klerk also acknowledged, was that, with a segregated structure, one side would invariably do a lot better than the other, causing increasingly pent-up anger and hatred and acting as a block to growth and prosperity. He had long held a belief that for South Africa to realise its greatness, all its people – not just the whites – had to be in a position to reap (and be in a position to be incentivised by the possibility of reaping) its benefits. And the only way to achieve that was through transition from the current system to universal franchise.

But for a long time, change had not been a very popular thing to be even hinting at within the Party. Even in the top job as State President, de Klerk could only achieve it if he brought the Party and white population with him – which threw up unprecedented challenges. Not surprisingly, he didn't get on at all well with his predecessor, P. W. Botha (otherwise called 'the Big Crocodile'), who had hoped to be succeeded by his nominee, Barend du Plessis. Now, however, there was momentum for change, and more and more people in the country were contemplating a shift to full democracy. The country knew it had to, and de Klerk knew it. But it would be traumatic for blacks, coloureds and whites alike: it meant overturning an entire way of life and challenging some extraordinary shibboleths.

When I first came to South Africa as an adult, I was prepared for the prejudices, but there were several aspects of the entrenched racism that were absolutely mind-numbing. Even as we approached the elections, it was quite common to hear the unchallenged assumption among some whites that the blacks were mentally deficient, that their brains were physically smaller, that they cannibalised their relatives, and so on. The problem for the National Party – and about to become my problem too – was that after half a century of this stuff, these self-same non-whites were being told that a non-white vote was suddenly important and respected, and wanted by the very party that had been governing with that system of apartheid.

Sitting there in the Cabinet room, de Klerk and I had a good and long chat about all this. I knew the country well, both through my father's life there, and because I'd been there working for several clients already. I told de Klerk an anecdote about Michael Caine, who I knew. I'd met him shortly before I'd flown out, and he'd told me a story about filming *Zulu*, on location in South Africa in the 1950s. Apparently, one of the film-unit guys had been sleeping with a few of the black locals. The police got wind of this and came to threaten everyone, explain the principle of segregation, and get an arrest. The police chief threatened them all, saying: 'We have been watching you, and anyone having intercourse with a black woman gets at least six lashes and probably a few years of hard labour.' So Stanley Baker put his hand up, claimed to be in charge, and asked, 'Can one have the six lashes whilst one is having the intercourse?' I don't know if that story is true, but I told it to de Klerk and he was in stiches.

There was, however, one claim to fame that I had which probably trumped all others. When my father left home in England, he went to work for Pan American Airways, eventually as Managing Director of the SE African region, based in Johannesburg. At the same time, he began hosting various programmes on Springbok Radio, and was very successful at it. So successful, in fact, that, within a few years, he became South Africa's most popular radio compere and chat-show host – known as Uncle Paddy. He had a sponsored children's hour called the Clipper Club, and his catch phrase, delivered at the end of the show, was 'Goodnight children, everywhere'. The kids listening would all burst out crying because it was the end of the show. And an awful lot of the politicians who I would potentially be advising – including de Klerk – had grown up on a diet of the iconic Uncle Paddy, my long-deceased father.

So, with all these political and non-political things to talk about, our meeting went really well, and we seemed to get along. Things looked promising. As we were finishing the conversation, however, I had a rather troubling thought. I realised that never for a moment had it occurred to de Klerk that we might want to be paid for our work. He actually thought that I was volunteering: here I am, and I've come out of love and good nature to help you sort out your country's future. It struck me that I was going to have to be both subtle and quick – 'Er … by the way, there's a fee …'

In due course we put together a team, and I set up in temporary residence there, running the National Party strategy and communication, as we slowly but surely headed to the first election of the new era. After years of bickering, the NP, ANC and Inkatha had reached something of an agreement (named CODESA) – to seek a fair and peaceful transition with a multiracial national government, and without a lurch from one racially dominated administration to another. They had agreed to certain standards, which made things complicated, but there was a very clear sense of objective, to get to a peaceful new government. Mandela was always adamant about this. Everything was geared to making sure that neither side did anything that would cause some kind of violent flare-up or civil war. We used to meet one day every week with the ANC side to discuss our respective campaigns – what ads we'd be running, what we were planning, etc. – and we got some excellent advice from Helen Suzman, the white liberal activist, who was working with the Independent Electoral Commission. On the

ANC side, all Clinton's people thought that they were so very smart with their campaigning, so they were happy to meet and talk, thinking that we would be a push-over and that they would have an easy victory.

But it had not been easy and was never going to be easy. One problem was that the grass-roots nationalists – particularly the ANC breakaway movement, the Pan-Africanist Congress – were distributing leaflets to the non-whites that said things like 'On Monday, *you* will move into his big house and *he* will move into your shack.' So there was a huge expectation being created among the black population: not of an integrated society; more like a society where the people with the big cars and those with the small cars were going to be swapping their vehicles – and everything else they owned. Obviously, this got the non-whites excited, but it also particularly agitated the far-Right – such as the AWR (the Afrikaner Weerstandsbeweging), who were incredibly violent. Their flag was like the Nazi swastika. Some of them seriously believed that black people should have their sexual organs removed at birth so that they would die out. They were completely mad. (They were led by a white supremacist ex-policeman, Eugene Terreblanche, who was eventually thrown out for allegedly having an affair with a British journalist. He was a very strange character indeed. Louis Theroux did a documentary about him. He met a terrible end – stripped naked and hacked to death – which perhaps wasn't altogether surprising.) But people like this could easily have started a full-blown civil war.

This is what we had to deal with – all being played out against the background of a very politically illiterate electorate, many people never having participated in any kind of election before. Many were illiterate in all other ways too, because they had never been to school. So it is hard to overstate how difficult was the task, just of generating a sensible discussion about future public policy.

Meanwhile, the police – who had to administrate the whole thing – were also finding the new climate very challenging. Until this point, they had been used to taking the sjambok to anybody with dark skin, as soon as they as much as looked in the wrong direction. I had a cousin who was a regional commander, and he was just about the most violent person I have ever met in my life. Given half a chance, he'd have shot anybody who wasn't white (in fact, he probably did), and assumed that it was God's will. Suddenly, all these law-enforcement officials were told that they couldn't beat anybody any more, yet they were still expected to maintain perfect order – so they were troubled and confused, and no less eager to give a good thrashing to people they didn't like the look of.

One of the first things that I said to de Klerk was that he had to have a black person in the hierarchy of the National Party. Otherwise, the black and coloured vote would be non-existent. There had to be a piece of iconoclastic symbolism, no matter how crude it now sounds. So we found a black vicar in Soweto – I can't remember or find his name – who came and joined us.

It is easy to get the impression that all white people were in favour of apartheid, but my experience was that only a minority were convinced about it – the lunatics, the entrenched Right, and a few very hard-faced Afrikaners in government (who faced losing their jobs). Certainly, most of the business community wanted the end of apartheid, and, in the final analysis, they often count for more than the morality or the politics of it all. And as time went by, more and more ordinary folk supported de Klerk in wanting to get rid of it – providing the circumstances were equitable. In this respect, there was a genius of a man – a South African Supreme Court Judge called Richard Goldstone – who was in charge of the commission dealing with outbreaks of violence during the election and who probably did more than any other person to keep it all on track. The *New York Times* once called him 'the most trusted man ... in South Africa'.

However, in running the NP campaign, we became increasingly concerned over the attitude of the core vote. Many of the whites held the view that the non-whites would automatically vote to keep the whites as the majority party in power. They believed that because they'd been the government for so long and they'd built all these roads and run the country reasonably efficiently, the blacks would take the same view, and automatically vote us back in. Of course, they were deluding themselves.

Clearly, it was an election the result of which was inevitable, in the sense that Mandela and the ANC would win. Our primary task was to boost the vote sufficiently to stand the Party in good stead for the subsequent period of running the country. We all knew that if South Africa was run entirely by the ANC, they would be able to change the constitution, Communism would gain an easy foothold, and South African share prices would collapse. The market doesn't pay any attention to political philosophy. It pays attention to stability, sustainability of supply, and price in the marketplace, and people know that. The balance was needed to hold it all together. If we could get a million non-white votes, we would achieve that aim. On the calculation of numbers, even if the NP got all the white people that we expected and all the coloured people, we still also needed that million or so non-white votes to prevent an ANC outright victory. We had to make it possible for at least some significant numbers of the non-white people to vote for the National Party. Which was a very tall order indeed.

I gave a speech to the caucus of the National Party – all their MPs and the big dignitaries. It became known as the 'steamroller speech'. I said something like this: 'You're all sitting here, thinking that this election is going to give you a few ANC people and maybe a black President, but that it doesn't matter because you'll still have your white Deputy President and he'll really run the country. But what you don't realise is that this may well not be what happens. Because there's an enormous steamroller coming at you that will flatten every single thing that you hold dear to your heart. Every single one of your values is going to be turned on its head. Because it may well be the case that you will be totally obliterated. You're all standing there thinking that they'll give you a white man to run the economy, and a white man for education, and a white man for all the clever posts. But has it occurred to you that a black President-Elect might not quite share your views?' I had to shake them out of their easy-going complacency.

Our first NP campaign rally was in an enormous hall in Wolverhampton, on the outskirts of Johannesburg. The whole of the centre section was made up of white people, whilst the coloureds sat on both sides, and the upstairs area was all Zulu (that is, mainly Inkatha), who always dress up in their national costume with the spears. They all stand in these huge groups, stamping and thumping at the ground and shouting 'Viva' at the top of their voices – which, if you've ever heard it, is a very frightening noise.

The vicar from Soweto came out and starting pumping up the crowd into a frenzy. He was saying things like, 'Who released Nelson Mandela from prison?' and they'd all shout back, 'F. W. de Klerk', because they'd all been briefed to do that. 'Who released all the political parties to be free to campaign?' and they all shouted out, 'F. W. de Klerk'. And so he did this over and over again, building up the tension, with each question mattering less and less, so the last question could easily have been 'Who won the 100 metre final at the last Olympics?', and as they all screamed 'F. W. de Klerk!' the curtains swept aside and out he walked – to be immediately swept up into the air by a group of pre-placed heavyweights on the stage who started carrying him into the crowd and around the hall. He's the only man I know who I've seen remain paralysed in a sitting position whilst being carried by the outstretched arms of a rugby scrum. It was as though he had been taken off a chair, but stayed frozen rigid. He told me later that he was utterly petrified – not just physically but also in mind, because every time they said 'F. W. de Klerk,' all the Zulus stomped and boomed 'Viva! Viva!' and he had no idea what they might do next.

The plan was that he would make a speech, but they had then decided they would begin with two national anthems. The first was 'Die Stem van Suid-Afrika,' which is the Afrikaans national anthem (meaning 'the Call of South Africa'). All the whites knew the words, but nobody else did – so they had a big screen with a bouncing ball over the lyrics. Then they sang the African national anthem, which is called 'Nkosi Sikelel' iAfrika' ('Lord bless Africa') with the same bouncing ball. But as that was all in Swahili, none of the whites could get even near to the right sound.

The entire experience was utterly weird. I was the smallest man there. Most of the white men were huge farmers whose red necks were the same diameter as their heads. They were all married to the Queen Mother – every wife had a floral hat and white gloves. The coloureds were all wearing T-shirts and jeans – because that's what they always wore – and most of the stomping Zulus were in ceremonial dress, as though they were getting ready to attack Stanley Baker's small group of British redcoats.

Pik Botha was present as the foreign minister. He was MP for Durban and was going to bring the Zulu vote to the National Party. In the end, he didn't, but it was the plan. He'd had a mild stroke and came in a wheelchair, but there was nothing wrong with him. He just thought that if he were in a wheelchair, they'd probably treat him better. He was a very strange man, but, to be fair, he was also instrumental in the process of ending apartheid. The rally was one of the most extraordinary events in which I have ever been involved. It was a far cry from Brighton, Bournemouth, or Blackpool. And in the end, it got terrific media coverage, everybody noticed it, and – all-importantly – our black vicar was leading it.

Another absolutely memorable day came from a combined event with Mandela, once he was released, and the ANC in Soweto, at a football stadium, where a gigantic crowd gathered. I was once advised that the locals just loved any event with a famous person there, be it a film star or singer or whatever, so they were going to go delirious here, with Mandela centre stage. I could never understand a word the man said, but it didn't matter. He stood at the microphone, started speaking, and the crowd went berserk. He could have read out the telephone directory – it didn't matter. Then de Klerk spoke – in sort of very heavy Afrikaans, so I couldn't understand a word he said either. But everyone cheered just the same. No one said anything at all about what they were going to do when it came to policy, and none of the audience seemed remotely interested in the content of anything anyway. It was theatre, start to finish.

Then we did one rally where we had a piano player on the stage who was going to play 'Nkosi Sikelel' but, half an hour before it started, somebody lifted the lid off the piano and found a fucking great bomb sitting there. It was a very salutary reminder that these were acutely dangerous times for everyone involved. All the security people went nuts, and that made it quite difficult for us to do any subsequent rallies.

Meanwhile, there were other aspects of our campaigning where we tried to address the non-white vote directly. For example, we ran ads in all sorts of different tribal dialects, we did radio commercials in dialect, and – impressively, in my view – we set up the first-ever Presidential debate with no ground rules. In fact, we did two televised debates. There was an invited audience, divided between NP supporters and ANC. It was not at all like a US Presidential debate: the audience had rattles and trumpets and vuvuzelas and God knows what, and were allowed to shout and yell and sing and do all the rest of it. But, in the event, the pressure was too great and Mandela and de Klerk both played safe and dull – they were terrified by the pressure of the moment and of the history.

F. W. always spoke about how impressive he thought Mandela was in the flesh – surprisingly tall (which you don't get a sense of on television) and 'ramrod straight' – so, as with all these things, you had to be very careful how you orchestrated the pair of them coming together. I personally only met Mandela briefly, with Cyril Ramaphosa at one of the constitutional meetings. But as the campaign went on, de Klerk used to speak to him all the time. They were political rivals, but they also had the same objective, which was to avoid a bloodbath. However, on the first public meeting, we knew that Stan Greenberg's lot would try it on. We feared that they would get Mandela to reach out first, making de Klerk look defensive. So we had to prep F. W. to walk up with an outstretched hand, and – given the height differences – not get so close that Mandela would start peering down at him.

The second debate made for much better entertainment. It was between Pik Botha and Thabo Mbeki (who, years later, did become President). The interviewing panel was bloated, to say the least. They had to have two joint chairmen of the debate, one black, one white; they had four journalists, two black, two white; one South African black, one not South African black (an African-American). Then there were the BBC correspondents: two white ones, one South African, one not. All they seemed worried about was scrupulous equalising of the colour. On one side, in front of Mbeki, it was all ANC; and in front of Botha were the National Party supporters.

Mbeki was a tribal chief and was not used to being questioned – because tribal chiefs are never ever questioned. In fact, tribal chiefs don't really speak – they listen. It was the first thing I noticed about the Chief's Council: they sit in a circle in order of precedence, hierarchy, status and knowledge, with the chief and the elders at the head. One by one, they each get up and they say what they think. Nobody comments or argues. They go around the table like this, and then, at the end, the chief sums up and makes a ruling – and that's that. Nobody argues. And then they all go and get on with it. In a curious way, that sums up just about everything that our current politics and media *don't* allow.

So, in this debate, Mbeki was a bit thrown by all these impertinent journalists asking him pointed questions. Quite understandably, he came across as uncomfortable and grumpy (I'd always found him rather unfriendly anyway). Botha meanwhile was a huge personality and very quick-witted. At the end, one of the chairmen said, 'I think I'd now like to ask the two contenders to say their own form of "Goodnight".' Pik Botha said something like, 'To all those people here and at home who are intending to vote for the National Party, I say this: Drive home carefully. And to all those people who are *not* going to vote for the National Party, I say: Who am I to tell you how to drive?' And the place fell about laughing. Even Mbeki was laughing. It was absolutely fabulous as a piece of television. But, at the end, everybody had to claim that it was a draw between the two of them.

On several occasions, Margaret sent me notes saying good luck, and she rang de Klerk all the time. Anyway, the first-ever South African election where all citizens of all races could vote took place on 27 April 1994, and the turnout was almost 20 million people. We did way better than expected, with just under 4 million votes, and over 20 per cent share (where we had been widely predicted in polls to do around 16 per cent), which deprived the ANC of a majority, and gave us 82 seats.

Did we make a difference? I think we did. I like big radical change. That's why I enjoyed Thatcher – it felt a significant change from what we'd been going through – and it's why I enjoyed all this. These things are not on the margins of life; they are fundamental. You can actually do things that are going to change lives, and change nations; maybe change the world. So I was not only fascinated by the direct election work with de Klerk, but also by the constitutional debates which were conducted by Roelf Meyer on behalf of the National Party and Cyril Ramaphosa on behalf of ANC. After the election, I did more work as part of this process. In the end, we were all fantastically proud of what we did in that first election. Because, above all, we got through it with relatively little violence. The first three years were as good as we could have expected. The whites were there in government, Mandela went from strength to strength, and – despite some inevitable differences – de Klerk kept his side of it all together and organised. It had been one of my most proud and enjoyable experiences.

16

We're All Right

My son Harry came along in 1992. Before that, in 1988, daughter Daisy was born – on the 11th of the 11th, which is Armistice Day. We decided that she would be called either Poppy or Daisy, and in the end Daisy won. Some people said that it was a form of 'Margaret' and have made an inference there, but that's rubbish. I didn't even know that about the name at the time. During this phase, an increasing amount of my time and attention was, rightly, going to the children, and that was mirrored by a slowly decreasing involvement with the Tory Party. My commitment had been to working with Margaret Thatcher and her brand of conviction Conservatism. As soon as she was gone, I knew that the Party's direction (and sense of it) would change and that my own sympathies would fade. I also anticipated that, whoever took over, my role would quickly and unceremoniously be reduced – and so it was.

The second ballot of the leadership election was between Heseltine, Hurd and Major, and, to be honest, I didn't see any as leadership material: Hurd and Major were 'wet' Tories who didn't really believe in anything; Heseltine was far too pro-European and had far too much crazed ambition, so no one was going to dare let him loose on the top job anyway. And I found it hard to put aside my own belief that getting rid of Thatcher had been a bad move – although I understood only too well why it had happened, and was not so blindly devoted to think that she bore no responsibility for her own demise. But I still thought that she should have stayed on, and that, without her, it would all come unstuck. Once she had gone, for a brief moment, the Party was demob happy – but that moment lasted barely a few minutes until some MPs started to worry about what they had wished for. Kinnock, meanwhile, was baying for an immediate general election.

As we moved into the week of the new ballot, Gordon Reece took on the role of advising John Major on his media strategy, and succeeded in getting the *Daily Mail* behind him, which in those days was of considerable significance.

In the end, on 27 November 1990, Major took almost 50 per cent of the second ballot, and – with the other two quickly withdrawing – was declared victor and became the new Conservative Prime Minister. But to me, it all seemed hollow and artificial. No one was jumping up and down.

Major now set about a 'reconciliation' process, which, to my mind, was a euphemism for having a bit of everything and not a lot of anything. I am staunchly on the Right of the Party with my views, so I dislike 'wet' Conservatism. But what I dislike more is the lack of a clear sense of vision: that is what a leader needs in order to be great. And now we were a party without anyone who fitted that description. Without conviction, you convince no one.

So I had not been involved in the second ballot of leadership election and, once Major was confirmed leader, it was clear very quickly – even from my first meeting with him – that I would have limited value to him. He asked me to go and see him in the flat in Downing Street. When Margaret was there it was a frightfully proper place, and everything was neat and ordered. All her belongings had long been unceremoniously thrown out, which was to be expected, but what struck me now was that on the coffee table was a huge bowl full of Mars Bars and Snickers and Toblerones taking centre stage as though they had significance. Major was wary of me – not least because he (mistakenly) thought that I had been responsible for Margaret saying, 'Now I'll have to do some backseat driving' (a comment that she had blurted out to the Conservative workers on the day she was leaving). But he was civil, and seemed willing to listen.

He asked me for my opinion about several things, including possible strategies for the next general election, but I learned afterwards that he had asked about 85 other people the same questions. I couldn't shake off the sense of an anodyne, neutral individual – some of which was probably the effect of his bank-manager appearance (and people were already calling him 'grey'); I got no sense, being in his presence, of a vision burning through. Here was the country's Prime Minister in the seat of the nation's power, yet he reminded me of a newly installed company chairman, who in four years' time would judge it a success if he could leave with the business intact. Of course, I'd been working for 15 years for a fiercely driven individual whom I had idolised. However harsh it sounds, now, I was in front of a figure of supremely contrasting ordinariness, with whom the only thing I had in common was that we both liked cricket.

As part of his 'reconciliation' strategy, Major brought Heseltine back into Cabinet, and appointed Chris Patten as Chairman of the Party – with the plan to give him responsibility for running the election campaign in around a year's time. Given that Patten hated me, I suspected that, from now on, I wouldn't be allowed near the building.

Patten had been the minister in charge of the Poll Tax – although, many years later, with razor-sharp hindsight, he was able to say that he'd never liked the idea after all. I've never met anybody so self-important. I don't know what made him like that. I found him charming and attractive, but we never got on. He probably thinks exactly the same – that he's never met anyone as self-important as me. Anyway, he visibly disliked me, opposed me whenever he could, and would never let me penetrate his self-importance. Maurice Saatchi, on the other hand, practically crawled up his trouser leg, and pretended to like the same music and read books that Patten liked, so I was not at all surprised when the brothers were re-hired the following spring.

In fairness, it didn't quite unravel as quickly as I'd thought it might. Major actually started to get praise for this new style of consensual Cabinet decision-making; there was a degree of public support for the first Gulf War, and even when he signed the Maastricht Treaty, he was praised for sidestepping the Social Chapter, not to mention the single currency. Nor did things go as badly as people expected when the next election arrived in 1992. My feeling there, however, was that, regardless of whoever had become the new Tory leader, they would not be truly tested in the first poll that they faced – for the simple reason that the Labour leader, Neil Kinnock, was completely unelectable.

I'd met Kinnock, but never got to know him. The first time I spoke to him was when we were appearing together on *Good Morning Canada*, and it didn't go well. I can't actually remember what we were talking about, but it might have been the miners' strike. The Canadian television people kept saying, 'Neil Kinnock, who's the member for Bedwellty.' To which Kinnock would say, 'No, no, no, no – Bedweth-ty, Bedweth-ty. Learn to speak Welsh!' And he went on and on about the pronunciation of the *ll* in 'Bedwellty', which didn't dazzle the Canadians a great deal. I can't remember exactly what I said, but I think I called him a 'Welsh git' during the conversation. I have to admit that he gave me a deep prejudice against Welsh people.

Whilst campaigning was taking place, the 1992 election seemed like a fairly close-fought contest, but many were predicting a Labour success, and there were times when I wondered if it would happen. The UK was in recession, homeowners were experiencing widespread negative equity, Major was still a bit of an unknown quantity, and Kinnock had been ahead in the polls throughout the campaign. No one imagined that it would be a large majority for Labour, but they were the favourites to win. And on the Wednesday week before polling day, their lead in the polls had hardened. That was when they held the Sheffield Rally. We were all gathered round watching it on a television at Conservative Party Headquarters, wondering what the hell was going on.

Philip Gould was a nice man – the Labour strategist and pollster under Mandelson. He had been planning this event for well over a year, and it would cost them a vast sum of money. They put 11,000 delegates in the hall, and rigged it all up like a rock concert with coloured lighting and opera and rock music warm-up acts. On cue, they introduced the 'Cabinet in Waiting', and then, finally, a helicopter landed, bringing the leader and wife Glenys hand-in-hand. It was all modelled on the style of American presidential conventions. But Sheffield is not Philadelphia. Kinnock didn't quite realise this, and no sooner was the microphone in his hand than he adopted an insane American accent and started shouting 'We're aw'right ...' The climax of the night was flesh-creepingly horrendous.

For a while, the received wisdom was that this piece of premature self-indulgent euphoria might have cost Labour the election. But I never thought that. In fact, I doubt that anyone but a few political fanatics, minds made up, took much notice of it at all. The event only became well known – and popular comedic viewing – *after* the result, when the market research people were looking for a single explanation for a result that they hadn't seen coming. It was interesting, however, because it showed how careful you need to be with this kind of thing, especially if you are dealing with someone like Kinnock, who was always a bit of an unpredictable PR liability.

Major was the opposite of this; safe but mundane. You were never going to find him falling over on the beach or yelling his head off. Whilst Kinnock was doing his cod-American convention act, Major was behaving like a street-trader selling apples. Some idiot adviser had taken literally the idea of getting on your soapbox, so the Prime Minister of the United Kingdom was to be found on Luton High Street, squeaking at shoppers through a loud-hailer perched on a crate 12 inches above the ground. The semiology was just as ludicrous as Kinnock's – and fortunately, it was just as irrelevant and unnoticed. Again, the psephological folklore suggests that the soapbox contributed to the win, when it did nothing of the sort.

I was not responsible for any of this, thank goodness. We at Lowe Bell still had Stephen Sherbourne working in Downing Street, and I would still feed in a few ideas, but they had a visceral terror of anything being seen to come from me, given my link with Thatcher – and Patten definitely didn't want to know. Their next wheeze was to do a dour film of Major going around Brixton looking for his old house and buying tomatoes and kippers. Even Major himself thought it would be cheesy, but Patten insisted. Everything that they were doing just made Major seem even greyer than he was. For me, it was incredibly frustrating watching them trying to lose the election. When polling night arrived, I went over to Alistair McAlpine's house with Gordon and Nicholas Ridley, and watched it all from there. It was a sign of just how much of an outsider I had become, and in such a short time. That's how it works.

Remarkably, the Tories defied the predictions. Or maybe it was not so remarkable. I think the result was eminently understandable because, in the end, the voters were scared to death of Labour taxing the living daylights out of them (which John Smith's Shadow Budget had threatened to do) and the unions coming back. It was as simple as that.

The *Sun* claimed credit by virtue of their pre-polling line, 'Will the last person to leave Britain turn out the lights.' Afterwards, they came up with the unflattering headline, "It's the *Sun* wot won it' – which Rupert Murdoch was not at all happy about. The fact that the *Sun* was audacious enough to even make that claim – and that, by implication, Major had not had much to do with winning it – said a lot about where the new PM now found himself, even in victory. It was a very vulnerable majority (a record-breaking share of the popular vote not translating into numbers of seats), which would be badly eroded with defections and by-election defeats and the like: long before the next election, the government would be in a minority. The truth is that, despite a very brief honeymoon period, Major would never find a way to address the entrenched difficulties of the Party that had already seen off a more formidable predecessor.

We were now in a truly awful period for the Conservative Party, fighting amongst itself, riven by rumours and scandals, conflicted over Europe, and with nobody able to take it by the scruff of the neck and stop it undoing all its successes. It was often claimed that Thatcher had been a divisive presence. With her hands now off the levers of power and the fingerprints that were left slowly being rubbed out, the Party had even less holding it together. I found it hard to know which was worse: not being allowed to try to help (which was more or less my situation), or having to try to solve the mess (which fortunately was no longer my problem).

One thing I did do for Major was to employ John Taylor. The son of a Jamaican cricketer, Taylor would become famous, then notorious. He had started out as a lawyer in Birmingham, before getting involved in local Conservative politics. Major saw this as a chance to demonstrate that the Party was no longer entirely made up of old white males, so the plan was to fast-track him into a seat as an MP. They needed a way to fund his position, so we at Lowe Bell employed him: we paid him a weekly salary and that's how he managed to run his office. He never did any work for us; he just got paid. I set it up. I was running the company by then, so I didn't have to ask anybody. Then they picked him to run for the safe Cheltenham seat, which was fairly ridiculous: presumably they thought that Cheltenham liked cricket or was a bit near Birmingham; but it's very middle-class and, at that time, not, shall we say, well known for its open-mindedness to diversity. In fact, his campaign turned rather ugly and racist, and he lost to the LibDems. But it got him a lot of publicity and a role with the BBC (he even tried to become its Chairman), and then in 1996, Major made him the first black Conservative peer. Unfortunately, it ended badly, because he was convicted for expenses fraud, and sentenced to 12 months' imprisonment.

It was a sign, however, of how I was now working more with individuals, as well as global companies and political parties. During the 1980s, not surprisingly, I'd met a lot of politicians and got to know many of them. I was thought of as something of a media expert, so when one of them would get into trouble with the media, he or she might ring me up and ask if I could help. There were other times when I'd see somebody in trouble and, because I liked whoever it was, or felt I'd like to help, I'd ring them up and offer assistance. The important thing that I'd spotted was that MPs cannot use their existing press officers, or the press officers in their departments, funded by the tax-payer, to deal with their personal issues. So they were usually grateful to find help from an external source.

When a crisis comes – whether it's from an indiscreet one-night stand that affects a handful of people, or an oil spill that affects a handful of nations – it quickly develops a life of its own: you can't control it; you have to manage it and deal with it day by day, week by week. You should never imagine that there is one single remedy that you can deploy and then it all vanishes. It's a process and it will almost inevitably cause damage of some sort. So the best you can achieve is to limit the damage. More tangible effects are often felt some time later – the loss of a job, the loss of an election, whatever it might be. But the point is that you're in a bad situation; the challenge is to keep it from getting worse.

The first, most obvious thing about what to do when a crisis hits is not to panic. That, of course, is easy to say, and hard to follow, because your head is swimming and people are probably shouting at you, whilst the phone will be ringing and people may be outside your door with cameras. I am yet again minded of Kipling's 'If': 'If you can keep your head when all about you are losing theirs ...' The second rule is about 'acceptance'. Don't waste any time saying, 'If only'. Get over the recriminations – of others, and yourself – because the time for reflection and lesson-learning comes after the storm has passed. You are where you are and now you have to deal with it. The best example of what to do in a crisis and what not to do is the contrast between the Chilean mining disaster and the BP drilling disaster in 2010.

In April of that year, BP's Deepwater Horizon rig suffered an explosion and then sank in the Gulf of Mexico, leaving a sea-floor leak which they could not seal for 87 days. A fortnight earlier, in Copiapo, Chile, 33 miners were trapped in an underground collapse, some 700 metres underneath the desert floor, for 69 days. As well as the timing, there were numerous similarities between these two disasters: lives and livelihoods were at stake, national emotions ran high, technically complex and heroic deep-level rescue solutions were needed, the media took great interest, serious mistakes had been made beforehand, and blame was there to be attributed, with huge damages subsequently sought. But if you look at the way they were both managed, in PR terms, one was pitch-perfect, while the other was the opposite.

Early in the proceedings, BP seemed at pains to say that it was not their fault. That's not a good line to be taking when 11 people have just lost their lives. That immediately alienated a big part of the US audience, turning the situation, from the start, into a crisis of trust between BP and the American people. And in that situation, people will look to apportion blame on the foreign company. That gave the President – with an anti-business and blame-diversion agenda – an opportunity to scapegoat them (hence his repeated use of the uncommon phrase 'British' Petroleum). BP's spokesperson, CEO Tony Haywood, was simply not up to the job, saying the wrong things, sounding evasive, disclaiming any responsibility and being seen going sailing when he should have been facing the press. Americans do not need any encouragement in seeking moral retribution, but BP's PR efforts gave them just that.

BP attracted foes, whereas, in Chile, the government made friends. They immediately took over the rescue (from the mining company). President Piñera, unlike Obama, went straight to the emergency zone, and was there for much of the crisis, turning a national disaster into a focus for national pride, whilst bringing in top advisers from all over the globe. Even Pope Benedict XVI and NASA got involved. They called it Operation St Lorenzo after the patron saint of miners. Never did they talk about blame for the accident, only responsibility for its resolution. Piñera was an ex-media owner, and knew how it all works. Along with his media director, Reinaldo Sepulveda, they seemed forever at the forefront of the heroics, and gave press conferences in English, supplied the media agencies with undoctored information and imagery, and exuded a tone of calm authority. And the gamble paid off when the men were rescued. They turned the miners – and their foreman, Luis Urzula – into folk heroes, and the whole nation, from top to bottom, bathed in the reflected glory and good feeling. It was a superbly effective communications effort, which put everyone on the same side, with the same desired objective.

The one PR response was the mirror image of the other, and the comparison shows how to manage a crisis. First, don't panic. Second, work out a plan. Third, avoid blame, but take responsibility. Fourth, accept help, but never lose ultimate control yourself. Fifth, manage expectations (about what is and isn't possible). Sixth, be there, and be available. Seventh, be as transparent as possible, and play it straight with the media (helping them with their job). And eighth, understand your media and audience. A lot of these are common sense. Yet it is amazing, when a crisis hits, how many of them can be forgotten.

The same principles apply to personal crises, a memorable example of which was the David Mellor episode. The 1992 election was barely over before this particular story broke. Mellor was the 43-year-old MP for Putney, as well as being recently appointed Secretary of State for National Heritage. He was a clever and cultured intellectual, so that post suited him. But he had made enemies with the press by calling for curbs, and when that happens, they will always be looking for a chance for revenge. The trouble started when he was introduced by a journalist friend to a Spanish 'actress' called Antonia de Sancha – an exotic creature who had been trained at RADA, and, surreally, had been in a film called *The Pieman*, where she played a one-legged prostitute who gets off with the pizza-man. Indeed.

Mellor and de Sancha began a less-than-discreet affair, and, before the MP knew it, the newspapers were all over it. At the time, it was the scalp-hunting season among the press, and bagging a top, newly promoted minister meant a big trophy on the wall. In this case, the *News of the World* and the *People* began their own battle between themselves to run the scoop. The actress was paid and her flat in Earl's Court was bugged. He wasn't exactly an oil-painting, whilst she looked the femme fatale, so there was an added 'beauty-and-beast' element to the imagery. And on Sunday 19 July, the *People* became the tabloid to splash the story – pages and lurid pages of it. And so began the end of his political career.

In the long run, it would probably make him a happier person, because he was smart enough to bounce back and pursue various media and business ventures. He's a complicated man: sensitive over some things and utterly brutal over others. But above all, he was someone who couldn't keep his dick in his trousers and paid the penalty. People often do not realise – or don't anticipate, until it is too late – how terrible the things they do will look when the press come looking.

Mellor couldn't use the government media machine to deal with the situation and speak for him, so I offered. And that would be a mistake on my part, for several reasons. Mellor was on the 'wet' side of the Party – a Major acolyte and not at all Thatcherite in political orientation – so he and I did not have an obvious shared world view. Moreover, he was a very arrogant man and didn't bend the knee to anybody. So there was a cocky part of him that thought it was just funny or something to brag about: he liked to play this side of himself up, rather than tone it down. But people didn't admire him for being the lad; they just thought that he was an idiot who had been set up like a stooge.

I came to regret taking him on. Indeed, I probably knew as soon as we started that it would all end in tears – especially as he wouldn't do what I told him to do, and he avoided telling the truth when I advised him to. People remember the deeply awkward family shot – his wife, her parents (who were furious with him, obviously), their sons, all at the gate of the house. I'd actually told him not to do it. But he wanted to, and given that he was my client, I did what he asked and tipped off the newspapers that he would be there.

Had he been more open about what he had done and less adversarial with the press, the story might have faded more quickly. But the opposite happened. By September, the *Sun* was serialising de Sancha's story (with Max Clifford acting for her), with all the lurid stuff about his use of literary quotations, toe-sucking and the wearing of his Chelsea strip during sex – a story that had been completely made up to add a bit of comedy to it all (and possibly to bring him down a peg or two). But at this stage in the game, they can make up practically anything and you can do nothing about it. It was open season on him, and my line of counter-argument was there was a limit to what the press ought to be making up about a minister. Major was standing by him – on the grounds that there was no threat to government business (this was not a Profumo) – so, as time went by, it was just possible we might have got him through.

But then they found out that he'd been given a free family holiday in Marbella courtesy of Mona Bauwens, daughter of the Treasurer to the Palestine Liberation Organisation – a day before the Iraq invasion of Kuwait. With timing like that, his resignation was inevitable. It had not been a happy time for Mellor (then he lost his seat at the next election), but it had not been the most satisfying challenge for me either.

These days, the basis of scandal has changed. Many things that were once guaranteed to wreck your career have become acceptable or even normalised: divorce, extramarital affairs, children out of wedlock, eccentric sex, maybe even drugs in some professions – they're all run-of-the-mill now. Indeed, there's a good chance that saying something that is non-PC will cause the most ructions. Along with money: that remains the one thing most likely to bring you down. These days, there's an absence of common sense about it. If they find you using First Class on the railways or travelling Business Class on a flight or taking a posh holiday, you're likely to be pilloried on the front pages. That is a consequence of years of systemic expenses over-claiming and fraud – but now, in some respects, it has swung too far the other way and there is a more obsessive, prurient interest over money than over most other things.

Twenty years before the *Daily Telegraph* revealed the scandal of the MPs' expenses, we were already entering an era where people started not to trust their politicians and to feel that their representatives were hypocrites, happy to follow double standards. It was partly triggered by John Major's 'back to basics' speech at Blackpool in 1993, which was really about the taking of responsibility for action. But the press deliberately misconstrued it as a statement of moral purity – which then gave them a reason to look for salacious betrayals of it (including going after the PM's cook) and generate a moral panic. In fairness to them, the media were probably just reflecting the public's increasing annoyance with the political class, seeing them as lacking definition, empathy, experience, becoming out of touch, unconnected, not understanding, whatever you want to call it: the rot was beginning. I think the cards were on the table: the result of the 1992 election was so close; the majority the government had was so small; people were tired of the incumbent government, which in turn looked tired; and a new, young, fresh opposition could be heard in the wings.

In 1994, against this background of the press looking for muck and murk, and the public anticipating it, came the Neil Hamilton saga. I'd known Hamilton for donkey's years, and I actually liked him. He was a 'proper' Right-wing conviction Tory (he had been one of those wanting Thatcher to stay on), who, along with MP Gerald Howard, had successfully sued the BBC for libel in a *Panorama* programme. The problem with this kind of thing is that it inspires the Left-wing media to come back looking for ways of taking revenge – and in 1994, that's just what happened.

Make no mistake about it, the BBC is an intrinsically Left-wing organisation (and I say this, having done work for them in the mid-'80s). It doesn't admit that, of course, because it's bound by a code of impartiality, and pays lip service to neutrality – hence the iniquity. It has been operating like this for decades. Indeed, I'm not sure half the people there can see their own inbuilt bias, so obviously correct do they regard their socially progressive world view (and so obviously heinous do they regard anyone supporting its antithesis) – which is why they cry foul when they are accused of being partial. But there is, without any doubt, a metropolitan, politically correct, *bien pensant*, Liberal-Left-leaning bias that forms the consensus from top to bottom. For example, they will rarely have anything said against state spending, the NHS, state education, social welfare, immigration, the EU, minority rights, or environmentalism; and, in the same breath, they are generally anti-privatisation, anti-defence, anti-Israel, anti-Atlanticist, anti-Irish Unionism, and anti-Monarchy, and sneer at British history and British mainstream Christian values. Left-wing think tanks are quoted as self-evidently true without qualification, while Right-wing ones are labelled 'Right-leaning' as a kind of health warning; views that do not conform to the BBC ideology are self-righteously deemed racist or fascist or sexist or some other bad-ist or just insane, as if no one in their right mind could consider Conservatism as a valid intellectual position. Producers routinely use the *Guardian* as the go-to source of what line to take on a story. Some of it is subtle – sometimes the bias is reflected in what they leave out as much as what they put in – and some of it is very unsubtle, such as the unrelenting torrent of Leftist comedy shows they broadcast. You have only to listen to the *Today* programme on the radio in the morning or view *Question Time* to appreciate how the process works.

Of course, parts of the public have a vague nostalgia for 'Auntie', see it as 'free', and regard attacks on the corporation as being rather mean-spirited. So Right-wing politicians are reluctant to fight back. Hamilton was an exception, and he became a temporary folk hero of the Right because he'd done this and actually won the *Panorama* case. But that – and his Thatcherite inclinations –made him a juicy target for the Left, who would look for revenge, which they duly got.

Hamilton was of a generation of politicians who took advantage of their position. And his wife Christine had for years been advising all sorts of people off the back of being Neil Hamilton's wife. In principle, I don't have a problem with that. If someone is getting a consultancy fee for advising on how the government works – and providing you're within the rules – I don't see anything wrong with it. But his enemies started to argue – rightly or wrongly – that the Hamiltons were well outside of the rules. He was a flawed individual – aren't we all? – so target he became.

But he amused me, and, when more trouble hit in 1994, he asked me for help and I offered to do what I could. John Major was not going to support him – as he pointedly had done with Mellor – because Hamilton had been a staunch Thatcherite. The case was full of claims and counter-claims, and allegations of corruption and conspiracies, on all sides. At times, the whole thing was impenetrable, but I just tried to get him through what would be years spent in courtrooms. It started with the *Guardian* alleging that he had taken cash from Mohamed Al-Fayed in return for asking questions in the Commons. Eventually, they settled this issue out of court, but the famous 'Cash for Questions' parliamentary enquiry subsequently took place, which found against Hamilton – who denied its conclusions. Hamilton then brought a court action against Al-Fayed that he lost, leading to an appeal, which he again lost. All of which led to the Hamiltons becoming bankrupt. Later, bizarrely, the couple were falsely accused of rape, by a woman who was subsequently charged with perverting the course of justice.

It took some doing for the pair of them to get through all this. To give them credit, they have completely reinvented themselves as kind of professional media interviewees – behaving eccentrically, wearing strange clothing, allowing themselves to be humiliated, and doing other peculiar over-the-top stuff. He calls himself an 'object of professional curiosity' (he went on to do some work with UKIP which, you may argue, proves the point) and it's a bit undignified at times, but, to their credit, they live perfectly well on it.

At the end of the day, I really enjoyed working with people like them. But the downside was that I often became a target by association as well, on the receiving end of attacks, lies and innuendo. It's par for the course, and you have to be prepared to take the rough with the smooth. Contrary to the public's opinion, many of these people are not awash with cash. Often, they could not afford any kind of PR help, and so I rarely got paid a fee, but I didn't mind. I had enough money. And I regarded it as a worthwhile way of building relationships;

it was a way of developing business contacts, and I learned an awful lot about how to crisis-manage into the bargain. Meanwhile, there were plenty of others with whom I was working who were happy to pay what it took, and for whom money was not something over which they were usually troubled.

17

Old and New

At first, when Major arrived at Downing Street, any informal role I had became even more informal, until I barely had a role at all. Lowe Bell was thriving and occupying my energies – with ever-increasing numbers of new clients in other countries – and I was working with a semi-retired Margaret Thatcher, helping her with new projects and life after Downing Street. That I was seen as Thatcher's man meant, by definition, that I was not Major's man.

That might have been the end of it, had it not been for the fact that I had also started talking to Maurice Saatchi again. Things move on and time changes how we feel about those things. The 1990s had not been a good time for the brothers, and on a couple of occasions they even asked me to go back. But then Maurice resigned. A group of the Saatchi & Saatchi shareholders, led by the American David Herro, moved against him, and the whole place descended into uproar and back-biting. Together with Charles (and David Kershaw, Bill Muirhead, Jeremy Sinclair and other resignees), a plan developed to launch a new 'Saatchi' agency.

As we entered 1995, Maurice asked me if I would take on a role with them as PR adviser, and I accepted. Our challenge was to get across the idea that this was not just an alternative Saatchi & Saatchi: it was a qualitatively superior reincarnation, harnessing the experience and wisdom of earlier years. I wanted to emphasise that the new agency was building on a success story, not making an escape from jail. And, in the main, the media accepted this idea. The new founders decided on the name of M&C Saatchi and had almost instant fame, which encouraged several very big-ticket clients to move to the new entity – BA, Qantas, Gallaher, Mirror Group, Mars and Dixons all came over. It was the most successful new UK start-up ever, with first year's billings of over £100 million. And then, to cap it all, the agency won back the Conservative Party advertising account as well. That really did make it feel like things were going back to their natural order.

During all the years building up to this, even when I was not working directly with the Tories, I had kept many friends and contacts in the Party, and I'd maintained connections with people in Downing Street and Central Office. I knew Jonathan Hill, who was Major's political secretary until 1994, and who then came back to us at Bell Pottinger, before going off to found his own consultancy. And Howell James, who took over Hill's role, was a very good friend. Howell was an intriguing character. He was from humble origins, openly gay – they once named him the 14th most important homosexual in politics – and was much liked by Margaret Thatcher, but also a great friend of Peter Mandelson. He was involved in the launch of TV-am and later became Director of Corporate Affairs at the BBC.

I'd have many a conversation with people like this, without my having any official involvement. But then, against expectations, in the middle of the 1990s – and in concert with the Saatchis reinventing themselves and becoming more involved again with the Tories – I found that more and more people in the Party started ringing me up again. Maybe there had now occurred a safe interlude since Margaret's resignation; maybe people were forgetting. However, even if some things felt familiar, there were other things that were not the same at all. Labour being one of them.

One year before M&C regained the account, Labour leader John Smith had a heart attack and died, and on 21 July 1994, a certain Anthony Charles Lynton Blair took over (beating John Prescott and Margaret Beckett for the role – can you imagine how different history would have looked if either of those two had won?). Blair immediately started making waves with his modernisation programme – saying he didn't like the word 'Socialism' and talking about good capitalism and business-friendly Labour policies. He took over at a very strange moment, because the Tories, at the time, were polling much lower than Labour on economic competence, no doubt as a result of the Black Wednesday fiasco, despite a recovery now taking place. And by August, with the 'sleaze' stories not going away, the polls were going ever further against the Tories. Panic was in the air yet again.

Major was taking fire from every quarter, and on 22 June 1995, with all the papers talking about a Portillo–Heseltine 'dream-ticket', he finally got so fed up that he actually resigned. The Party squabbling over Europe, in particular, had become such a distraction – and such a draw on resource – that he thought he needed to try to put a stop to it once and for all, by instigating a leadership contest in which he would compete. Everybody thought that Michael Portillo would stand because he had the backing and half a mind to (they started buying multiple telephone lines for his offices, which *Newsnight* caught on film), but in the event, he stayed out of the early skirmishes, as did Michael Heseltine.

The only other challenger, in fact, was John Redwood, the Welsh Secretary (not that he was particularly fond of Wales), who ran on a Eurosceptic ticket, with the line, 'No change, no chance.' Redwood regarded himself as a serious leadership candidate (this was no 'stalking horse' situation), and he refused to agree with Portillo that, in the event of a victory, he would stand aside. But he was never really taken seriously by the press (who called him the 'Vulcan' as he had a slight elongated likeness to Mr Spock – if you squeezed your eyes together), until Thatcher suddenly made it official that she gave him her support. Then the press changed its tune. Nonetheless, I rang Major and asked him if he needed any help. Immediately, we sent Jonathan Hill back over to join his team which, strangely, put me in the anti-Thatcherite camp, although it never really seemed like that to me. And that might have been a turning point, looking back.

Of course, Major won reasonably easily with around 66 per cent of the ballot (although 89 MPs voted against him, which was a blow). It gave him a tiny bit of breathing space, before the squabbling would start all over again. Brian Mawhinney came in as Chairman and he put Danny Finkelstein in as a sort of assistant, with Andrew Cooper as the Head of Research. Central Office then put in a team of Peter Gummer, Maurice Saatchi and me as the election advisers for the 1997 election. Maurice didn't really want me around, but we got on with each other and Mawhinney was quite happy about it.

What I found salutary about the 1997 campaign was that, although almost everyone thought that we were going to lose, you've got to keep telling everybody – you even try to convince yourself at times – that you're going to win. I really feel for MPs in this situation – those in impossible seats. (I certainly felt for Robin Wight, of the ad agency WCRS, trying to become MP for Bishop Auckland in 1987. 'Yes it's true. Wight can be blue' was his line. It was a safe Labour seat, and he never had a hope in hell. How do you keep up the pretence?) You have to keep standing up and saying, 'I'm going to win', and, in doing so, you look ridiculous; but there is no alternative, I guess.

Our new strategy for 1997 was based on the idea (and line), 'New Labour, New Danger', inspired by something Clare Short had blurted out, as only Clare Short could blurt out, about the 'dark forces' behind Tony Blair. M&C devised a press ad featuring a crazed-looking Blair, but with the page torn to reveal two red, demonic eyes behind the mask. We managed to get it approved, and put it out – although Major was not keen. We had one version with the line, 'What LIES behind the smile', but that never ran. It cost around £125,000 but the resulting coverage was huge, and, as with 'Labour isn't working', must have generated millions in free publicity. The Labour Party, as you would expect, went ballistic. But then there was an enormous furore over it. The Advertising Standards Authority, under pressure (including one complaint from a clergyman), ruled against us and ordered it to be withdrawn. But, by then, it had probably done a good job, and indeed, it later took *Campaign*'s annual best ad award.

In tandem with this, M&C had come up with a truly superb PPB – possibly the best PPB I've ever seen. They had an actor portraying Tony Blair and sitting in what looked like the Labour Party Headquarters in Transport House. The look-alike actor was sitting there in a slightly darkened room, doing all Blair's gestures, and he says, 'Do you know, I think we could win? ... But I'm a bit worried about the economy, because we're going to have to put the taxes up.' Then a sinister voice in the background whispers in his ear: 'Tell them you're not going to.' The viewer can quickly figure out that this is Peter Mandelson – always seen only as a shadowy presence in the background, who repeatedly encourages the Blair character to lie. Finally, he says, 'Tell them you're going to be tough on crime and the causes of crime.' Blair says, 'But then I'll sound like a Tory.' And Mandelson replies, 'Exactly!' The idea was both inspired and marvellously well executed. Mawhinney, of course, was spooked, especially by the title – which was *Faust* – and then, when Maurice showed it to Major, he refused point-blank, despite Robert Cranbourne and Howell James both pleading with him to take the chance.

Maurice and Peter were never going to get on with Mawhinney, who was a blunt, Belfast Protestant, like my father – which meant that I had an understanding of where he was coming from, even when I didn't agree with his decisions. Mawhinney himself was in the continually impossible position of telling the Prime Minister that he was going to win, which he knew perfectly well would never happen.

The truth was probably that no advertising campaign or PPB could have done anything for us. For too long, the Party had been without any kind of clear positioning strategy. By that time, no one understood what we stood for, and even if they had done, it would have caused an internal row between one faction and another. In this situation, when MPs know that they will lose, it becomes open season, with them either saying exactly what they think in not very quiet voices, or doing anything that will save them locally in their seats. As they near an inevitable election defeat, people working at the centre are faced with trying to do what's best for the Party in the longer term. Mawhinney had to veto all manner of campaigning ideas: not so much because they were wrong or too controversial, but more because he wanted to preserve the budget – why throw all your money onto an inevitably losing ticket?

You could smell the death wish in the air around Conservatives. Everybody thought it was ghastly and that everything that could go wrong had gone wrong. A perfect storm of threats and weaknesses was approaching. By 1997, the overall mood in the country had completely changed. The unions were no longer the threat that they had been – in fact, many people had completely forgotten the bad old days of the strikes and the Winter of Discontent. In addition, the Conservatives had been in power for so long that people were bored and fancied a change; the Party seemed disorganised and split, and there were scandals and stories coming out of every orifice; the press had, in the main, taken against us and were excited by the prospect of a new, vibrant character in Blair, who felt more like a media star than a typical politician.

In contrast to Kinnock, Major had looked safe; in contrast to Blair, and after four years of internal attrition, he looked a rather diminished, slightly sad, grey character. Thatcher was loved and hated, but she always looked magisterial in a way that Major could never have looked. Blair looked something else entirely: most of the public thought he was the new Messiah – and how he knew to play to that!

Given what had happened in 1992, and starved of power for so long, Labour had become voracious. They were willing to do whatever was necessary to secure victory, and any notion of gentlemanly conduct disappeared. Blair was – is – a very clever man. In opposition he crafted an entirely new party, even appropriating the 'New' word itself, that everybody in marketing knows is magic. He attracted the intelligentsia and business, and unceremoniously ditched all the old Labour crap. Suddenly, he made Left-wing politics palatable to the middle ground. Like Obama, he knew just what to do, and what he could do, in opposition. But like all leaders, his time would come and go – the craven, faceless ones would eventually appear from the shadows, keen to make him bleed, as they had been for Thatcher and then Major.

I'd met him several times and, straight away, he came across as young in spirit, ambitious, in a hurry and, above all, breathtakingly self-confident. Where Major sometimes seemed devoid of conviction, Blair, by contrast, gave the impression of knowing *exactly* what he wanted – both for himself, and for the country. Unlike Major, I think he was a great leader – it's just that I profoundly disagreed with the direction in which he wanted to go, and some of the things he did once in power.

He would do anything that would make his image palatable to people. He had no principles that could not be compromised in the interests of expediency; no standards that could not be amended; no promise he would not make to someone, regardless of the likelihood of it being delivered. He wore make-up much of the time – in case he was filmed I guess – and I think that symbolised his modus operandi.

When you're trying to come to power you tell lies. You're not supposed to – whether you are in power or in opposition. But in opposition, people forgive you for the hyperbole, exaggeration and distortion that, in office, is subject to more scrutiny and scepticism. And because he got people to like him so much, Blair had, for a while, the luxury afforded by being an attractive and forgivable character. He became one of those people who could say anything and people would nod in agreement because it was Tony. You can see why he sent Gordon Brown nuts with jealousy and bitterness. Starting with Blair, all party leaders put as their priority the need to say things that pleased people, which then, they hoped, would give them the vote. Much of what they actually do to govern is seen as a sideshow, or even an irrelevance. All they care about is appealing to a population who they think could not possibly grasp the issues and problems inside government. Election cycles are such that you are barely in power before you have to start thinking about the next election, which then inhibits any unpopular actions that might be for the country's good. Let alone having to satisfy a Coalition partner. (Look at how difficult it was for the Coalition to implement any deficit reduction.) And, of course, politicians will often see, as part of this, the need to hide as much as possible from the scrutiny and mischief of 24-hour internet-centred news; to go on television or radio, but say as little as possible once there. And as an adviser, if you tell them to say something that somebody might not like, they won't.

Blair shared with Thatcher the important benefit to his Party of getting them into power and keeping them there for a useful length of time. It's like getting promoted into the Premiership, but knowing that you will not be relegated at the end of the season – you play better football. The majority and the extended honeymoon period gave Labour time to do what they needed to do – or at least some of it.

Labour realised that the best way to keep winning elections was to make as much of the population as possible dependent on the state, through some or other form of implicit or explicit welfare, coupled with a vast increase in the number of jobs provided in servicing that welfare. Increasing the dependent population through an active immigration policy was part of the grand plan, and in many ways they succeeded, because there is now a vast body of opinion that has a vested self-interest in the Labour client state. Along with the boundary changes, this makes it very difficult for the Conservatives to achieve a majority. And the BBC have always been complicit in this.

The lengthiest conversation I had with Blair was before he became Prime Minister, at a Rupert Murdoch cocktail party. It was a key part of Blair's ambitions to get the Murdoch titles behind him, and he foresaw the opportunity created as the papers increasingly lost faith with the Conservative Party. Rupert was suspicious of Blair, but – in later years – became ever more intrigued as well, when he saw that Blair's policies might deliver a less hostile business environment than would ever be likely from the more unreconstructed Left. Blair was Labour – but he could have been a lot worse Labour. In fact they eventually became friends, and Blair is godfather to one of the Murdoch daughters. Blair and I were in a small group, and we got talking. He said to me, 'Have you got any advice?' To which I said, 'Yeah. Don't peak too soon.' Some time later, after his victory, I happened to see him in Parliament and he said, 'Is this too soon?' And so I said, 'Obviously not.'

He had that ability that all the great leaders have (Clinton was incredible at it) of remembering who you are – remembering what you've said, and remembering just enough to make you think they actually know and care. When I was ill with cancer, Blair knew about it and very sweetly sent me his best wishes. Ever since then, for the past 20-odd years, every time I see him, he says, 'Are you all right now? Have you got over it all?'

Part of Blair's ongoing success came from him getting all the right people in the right places, and in doing so, he rebuilt the stature of the Labour Party, after all the years when it had been hopelessly undermined by Kinnock, Healey, Foot, Wedgwood-Benn, and all the union leaders and the Looney Left – people who the public just couldn't understand. He had a very sharp team around him. Mandelson, Gould, Anji Hunter, and, of course, Campbell from the *Mirror*, as his Press Officer. I think it's wrong to overstate the role of advisers, but it was a time when the strategists, key public relations people, market research pollsters and communication specialists were starting to get a profile. It had been there to a very small degree with Gordon Reece and Bernard Ingham and myself and the Saatchis under Thatcher, but now, suddenly, everybody seemed to be writing about Blair's sofa team.

I know Alastair Campbell very well. He's a very nice bloke, but he likes to tell everybody that he is and, amazingly enough, they believe it. I do. I like him a lot. I don't agree with any of the Labour people on the issue of their politics, but it's a bit like football managers. When you get into this world, you will fight your opponents and want to beat them, but with many of them you also have a relationship and can shake hands and have a good conversation.

There have been two times when this has struck me quite acutely. The first was during the first-ever Prime Ministerial Debate between Clegg, Cameron and Brown, when all the advisers were getting drunk and having a great time together in the back. Then, once it had finished, everyone suddenly returned to their tribes and started preparing responses and criticisms of each other. The other time was in South Africa, working on de Klerk's campaign, when we all used to meet and talk to each other – because our first priority was to avoid a civil war. You can always admire what the competition is doing, even if you disagree with their philosophy. By contrast, one of the reasons that I always found it so difficult to work with Charles Saatchi was because he was incapable of admiring anything that anyone else had done.

So, in 1997, in came New Labour. Any role I had at Downing Street would now, most definitely, be done. Britain was out on the streets celebrating. Inside our offices, we had changed our name to Bell Pottinger, after Frank Lowe had kicked up an almighty fuss about his name being appropriated. He'd sued me for passing off – I think he served about 13 writs one Christmas Eve – saying that I had stolen his name, and that I was using it in such a way that his reputation was being damaged. So we changed the name of the company from Lowe Bell to Bell Pottinger and made it into an event by having a name-change party. We even invited Frank – but he didn't come. My relationship with Frank has always been perfectly amicable. He gets bees in his bonnet and behaves in the most peculiar manner, and then comes and apologises to you – before he starts it all again.

Anyway, Bell Pottinger was servicing a lot of very good clients and doing a lot of very good work – making some serious money as well. For me, I felt that it was about time that I did. Although I had made an enormous contribution to Saatchi & Saatchi, I had certainly not become stratospherically rich on it, contrary to what some people wrote about me. The brothers probably ended up with about £50 million each and, when I had left, I had ended up with

£9 million, of which I gave £6 million to HMRC. Tax at that time was 60 per cent and I did it, tragically, six months before Margaret lowered the tax rates – which just goes to show that I didn't actually know what was going on. I got £9 million and wrote a cheque for £6 million in tax. It's a rare breed that gets rich from politics. I needed to do something different.

18

Demons

It was in the early 1990s – a few years after the Lowe Bell buyout – that my health started to deteriorate. I was told that I had cancer of the colon. And at almost exactly the same time, Piers was diagnosed with liver cancer, although his growth was eventually found to be benign as opposed to malign; mine was the wrong one of those. We tossed a coin as to who would take time off first, and I won (or lost, depending on your perspective). I had colon resection surgery and convalesced for a couple of months – then came back to work. During that interlude, it dawned on me that all I owned was the house in which I lived, and some shares in a private company that had no value unless one gave it some by floating it. Piers was in the same situation. So flotation it was. I think the company was worth about £25 million or something like that: most of us sold off half our shares, taking the money, and keeping the other half to remain as equity partners. I'm not sure I linked my health and the fate of the company, but you do reach a point where, suddenly, you realise your time is a very finite thing, and there comes a need to get some coherence into one's affairs.

I would have thought that the presence of cancer would change my attitude to life more than, in the event, it actually did. After a few months, I'd gone back to essentially the same lifestyle that I had just immediately before the illness – although obviously, nothing like my earlier years, which had been quite irresponsible. I was about 50 when the cancer diagnosis arrived on the scene. As it happens, I had given up smoking, so probably that first operation was far less damaging than it might have been. But then I started smoking again in 1994, after I'd got myself fantastically depressed about things and decided to enjoy myself. It was also because I'd sat for nearly two months with F. W. de Klerk in South Africa and he smoked about 80 cigarettes a day, so I took the view that I might as well have been smoking myself given what I inhaled by just being in the room with him. When I gave up, it was because of the pressure imposed by our society on people who smoke, so I was sick of feeling guilty every time I lit up a cigarette. I gave up by reading Allen Carr's book – *The Easy Way to Stop Smoking* – and that worked, coupled with a hefty slice of willpower. But I've never had the inclination to do it again since and now I don't have any desire to. Given the amount I now smoke, I've certainly made up for the intermission.

My physician at the time was Brian Gazzard (now Professor, a leading gastroenterologist and HIV expert too). I had gone to him because I was also diagnosed as being type-2 diabetic at the same time. I'd started getting stomach pains and other worrying symptoms, and my GP, Robert Lefever (I only choose doctors with apposite names) had indeed thought it was probably some form of cancer – without saying as much to me. But he'd made me go through all the tests, including the one where they force liquid up your bottom.

Brian called me into his surgery and said, 'There are three things I must tell you. First, you have cancer. Second, it's a colon cancer. And third, the good news, you won't need a colostomy bag because it's sufficiently high up.' I had no idea what he was talking about. I hadn't the faintest idea what a colostomy bag was, nor why having the cancer high was better than low, wherever high and low actually were. Then he said, 'I should tell you that seven out of 10 people diagnosed with your cancer live at least another five years.' I heard the words 'five years' and thought that it sounded like a medium-term death sentence. What he meant was that if you last five years after this kind of cancer operation and then die, the odds are that the death will be caused by something else, not from the cancer. But it all still sounded crap.

That afternoon, I went to my daughter Daisy's birthday, but I was extremely emotional as you can imagine. I hadn't told Virginia, my wife, anything about this. In fact, I hadn't told anybody. I was in a sort of traumatised depression. My PA, Wendy, who came to help run the party, started shouting at me for been so bad-tempered and miserable – so she was the first person that I had to tell, in order to explain why I was so miserable. When I had received the results of the biopsy, they said that I had something called Dukes' B. In those days, they used four stages in their classification of colon cancer, called Dukes' A, B, C and D (named after the British pathologist who invented it), with D being not good at all. My oncologist, who was called Adrian Timothy, had told me that I'd got B, which meant that the tumour had gone through the wall of the bowel – so it may have spread, but there was a reasonable chance that it might not have.

I had no idea what to make of all this, but the fact that it had gone through the wall of the colon sounded a bit – a lot – unpleasant. That evening, I had been invited out to a supper by a South African businessman, Johann Rupert. No one around the table knew about my cancer, but when we got talking, one chap said to me, 'I'm in a bit of a gloomy mood tonight.' 'Why's that?' I said. He replied, 'Because my best friend has just died of pancreatic cancer. It started in the colon and went through the wall of the bowel ...' That put paid to my appetite, but the very next night, I had to go out to dinner with David Mellor, who was then the Health Minister. When I told him about it, he said, 'Well, it doesn't matter so long as it hasn't gone through the wall of the colon.' So within as many days, two people had confirmed my death sentence.

I visited a fabulous consultant surgeon called Nick Theodorou, who examined me and said he wanted to operate fairly quickly and get rid of it. So within a week or so, I checked into the Cromwell Hospital. My life is peppered with instances where, one minute, I'm in trouble and, in the next, I get lucky – and this was no exception. The Cromwell was owned by Sheikh Zayed bin Sultan Al-Nahyan, founding president of the UAE and emir of Abu Dhabi. At that time, we were working for his lawyers on the BCCI scandal via an intermediary called David Youngman, who is sadly now dead. David was the Sheikh's personal accountant, and held a top position at the Cromwell Hospital. So he came and saw me and I got put in Sheikh Zayed's suite – which was enormous. It had two separate bathrooms and you could have got about 16 beds in there. I even had a proper matron checking on me – she looked and dressed like Hattie Jacques – who was a devoted fan of Margaret Thatcher. And thus, when Margaret came to visit me, the matron made all of the staff dress up in their full uniform and line up in a row for the PM to shake hands and review the parade.

Anyway, they did the operation, removed a huge lump, resectioned my colon, and gave me the news that they thought that the tumour hadn't spread. I then got what they called 'bib and braces' treatment – which is radiotherapy and chemotherapy for a few months. The chemotherapy was fairly mild, so my hair didn't fall out, but you have a device on your belt that injects poison into your body all day long, killing off the diseased cells plus half the non-diseased cells as well – so you have to check your white blood cell count, and you want to throw up all the time.

When I was first diagnosed, one of the worst things was the experience of telling people. Most people were unbelievably sympathetic – but that can be a mixed blessing. In fact, I tended to elicit one of three reactions: some people wanted to ask when I was going to die, but never dared quite come out with that (so they would say things like, 'Will you be going on holiday next year?' or 'What about your pension?'); others were extremely interested in the symptoms, because they wanted to know whether they'd got it too; and finally, some actually wondered if it was contagious, so they would rather un-coolly avoid shaking hands, or stood back just a bit too far for normal.

A story about me appeared in the *Telegraph* diary, and I got letters from people – in the main, really nice letters, which surprised me too. Alec Reed (of Reed Executive) sent me a letter saying that he'd had the condition and recovered completely. You see, anybody who tells you that they've had it and are now fine is a fantastic boost to your own sense of hope and self-confidence. Lord King, the chairman of British Airways, rang me and said to me, 'Colon cancer! That's nothing. I had that in 1960. It had no effect on me whatsoever. Come out to lunch when you're recovered.' Those were the people who helped the most – the ones who were just reassuringly phlegmatic and kept on talking to me as though I was still the same person that I'd been before it struck.

As a result of all this, I became involved with a charity called Cancer Backup, which was run by a brilliant South African oncologist called Maurice Slevin at St Bartholomew's. He is still practising, and is one of the top people in his field. The organisation eventually merged into Macmillan Cancer, but its approach then was a pioneering one: namely giving patients as much information as possible, so that they could make informed decisions and work out what is best to do for themselves. It operated via a network of cancer nurses on telephones, who, if you got a pain, would talk to you. The lady that had looked after me when I was in the hospital was a Cancer Backup nurse, who worked during the day in the hospital and, in the evening, sat on the end of a telephone and talked to people. In those pre-internet days, doctors wouldn't tell you much, and they weren't required to share their diagnosis with you, so, most of the time, you didn't have the faintest idea what was going on.

So I helped Cancer Backup raise money. I did one of my fundraising things and helped them produce a book on prostate cancer. That was inspired by a very close friend in Australia called Andrew Richardson, who was very, very rich, but who, one day, got the dreaded news. He had decided that he'd blow some of his cash on flying himself round Australia, for which he'd need to train for his pilot's licence and when he sat for the medical, they discovered signs of prostate cancer. His doctor suggested that they remove his prostate, which would result in an inability to produce semen and limit him to dry orgasms. He said, 'But that's impossible. All I'm interested in is going out with girls. I can't start telling them I can't ejaculate any more.' As you do when this kind of thing happens, he started to do his own research into the disease, and came across a professor at Beijing University, who was researching why many more Caucasian males contract prostate cancer than Oriental males. Andrew flew across to see this professor who told him that, in China, they don't usually cut out your prostate. 'Instead,' he told Andrew, 'we get you to stop smoking, change your diet, do relaxation and meditation', and so on. Being very rich, Andrew hired himself an Indian guru (I have no idea why it wasn't a Chinese guru), who lived with him for about four years, coaching him on an alternative lifestyle. And Andrew is, to this day, living a life of happy non-dry endings, having conceived two healthy children. After my own surgery, I had lunch with him, and he said to me, 'If they're going to cut your cancer out, don't let them.' I said, 'It's a bit late to tell me now for fuck's sake. They've already done it.' Of course, no one knows whether any approach is better than another – but there are always alternatives with which to chance your luck.

When Gordon Reece got throat cancer, he was sent to Denver in the US. The cancer was at the bottom of his tongue and their first inclination was to remove the entire organ. Gordon felt that being unable to talk to people would give him a life not worth living, so he'd accepted a very aggressive chemotherapy instead. He kept his tongue, but it was still horrendous what the chemo did to him.

On the anniversary of her tenth year in power, Margaret invited a group of her closest friends and advisers for a party – although her mood at the time was fairly low. When she noticed that Gordon was missing, she insisted that I call him up on the telephone. When I got through to his room, there was this tiny little voice on the other end; he sounded awful. He whispered, 'Hello, who is it?' I said, 'It's Tim. How are you?' He replied, 'I'm feeling terrible.' But when I said that Margaret wanted to speak to him, he cheered up no end. When he was discharged from hospital, he and I were invited to Chequers for dinner with Margaret and Denis – a fairly boozy affair, it has to be said. This was just at the time Michael Heseltine was making a bid for power. Whilst she was out of the room, a slightly worse-for-wear Denis said to Gordon, 'Do you know, I think it might be time for the old girl to go. Whilst she's still ahead. And Gordon, you're the man to suggest it to her.' Gordon was appalled at the very idea, and said to Denis, 'I can't tell her that. I love her too much.' To which Denis replied, 'Steady on, old chap. You're referring to my wife.'

Gordon lasted another three years, but he could hardly speak during that time anyway. He had to drink water every few seconds to keep his throat lubricated, and he had to give up cigars and give up champagne. As he was a devout Catholic, they eventually got the Nuns to come and provide palliative care for him. He wrote a heart-breaking private diary about his times with Margaret, which he gave to her just before he died. He let me see a bit of it once. It has never been published and almost certainly will never see the light of day. He was an extraordinary man and wrote in the most extraordinary manner. After he died, Gordon's funeral was a full high mass, with a very eminent monsignor of some kind, with genuflecting and huge candles and the full rigmarole; I think it might even have been in Latin, but can't be sure. None of us knew how you were meant to behave. Margaret was there, as were many of the astonishing array of famous people that he'd got to know in his life. There was a lot of incense being waved, and we laughed at this, saying that it was really his cigar smoke. It was appropriate for Gordon: he would have liked all the ceremony.

It's odd, but once you have the disease, you join the club of cancer people, of which no one wants membership; but once you're in there, you have a unique affinity with its fellows. There was a fantastic guy called Gordon Greig who was the political editor of the *Daily Mail*. In his lifetime, he had made some extraordinary scoops, being first to know about the Profumo affair in 1963 and first with the news that Margaret was going to challenge Heath in the leadership election. He had been diagnosed a Stage IV or Dukes' D or whatever awful upper level there was, so he knew that he was going to die. I remember going out to lunch with him and trying to do what people had done for me, by telling him he would be fine and he would recover from it. He said, 'Yes, Tim, they're wonderful stories, but I'm going to die in about the next three months, whatever you say.' I said, 'Well, you mustn't give up hope. It's terribly important that you stay psychologically positive.' But, of course, he did die as he'd predicted, which was a tragedy.

Another thing that surprised me, but shouldn't have, was the number of people who, as a result of my conversations with them, rushed off to their doctors. I became a kind of cod-authority on colonic cancer and colonoscopies – because when these things hit, you become preoccupied. Of course, I read everything about the disease, and learned that it can be genetic: it wasn't in my case, but I did have my kids tested. Nobody tells you this stuff. Like the fact that one of the frequent outcomes of the colon treatment is that your gall bladder stops working – and this duly happened to me.

I was on a holiday in Tuscany and suddenly got this insane pain. It was breathtakingly bad – literally. I was (again literally) banging my head on the wall, on the floor, on anything solid; I was getting in and out of a hot bath and then a cold bath to try and stop the pain. Eventually, they managed to get me an emergency surgeon at Florence Hospital, who was more interested in combing his jet-black hair than my diagnosis, but he worked out that my gall bladder had, apparently, swollen up to the size of a grapefruit. An emergency procedure was needed, ideally back in the UK so that I could convalesce without travelling. So they sent out a plane with an anaesthetist on board who pumped me full of morphine and home I flew – in more ways than one. The aircraft was actually owned by Peter Scott, founding partner of the WCRS advertising agency and who later formed various other giant media groups. In those days, he was a sort of flamboyant polo player in his spare time, and the pilot nattered away to me about his boss's exploits, although I was so drugged up, I hadn't a clue what he was actually talking about.

We landed at Heathrow in the private aircraft zone, and an ambulance drew up with a driver smoking a hand-rolled fag, dangling from the corner of his mouth. He said, 'Right, mate. Let's get you in the back. We're off to the Cromwell.' He wanted to talk politics and he said – in these exact words – 'You'll never guess who I had in the back last week. That there Michael Heseltine bloke. He'd had a heart attack in Venice.' So back to the Cromwell I went; back to the suite and the matron. And the gall bladder went the way of the lump of colon they'd taken. Over the years, I've lost all sorts of bits and pieces, but I think I stay the same person – apart from being a few pounds lighter.

19

Big People

I have been extremely fortunate in my life to have met some of the most famous people of modern times – and even more fortunate to have liked some of them and got on with them. I often find myself drawn to the people who have an abnormally high level of drive and conviction, and, contrary to what the public may often think, there are many famous and great people who are workaholic and are also often only secondarily occupied by status and reputation. Fame and wealth can easily distort your judgement and make you do all sorts of irrational or downright terrible things. So when you reach a point where you can afford any of the things that most 'normal' people are motivated towards – the car, the house, the holidays, the fame – then something has to fill the gap, or boredom and disillusionment set in. That's why many of the great political and business leaders are relentlessly driven by wanting to keep *doing* things (at a ferocious pace), not by just wanting to *have* or even *be* something (which is often reversed, in the most unattractive fashion, by some people in the modern popular cultural spotlight).

I like people who are comfortable in their own skin, and who don't take themselves too seriously – Reagan, for example, was very much of this order – and have that particular type of calm charisma that you experience when you're with them. In this respect, Nixon was the polar opposite of Reagan (and Brown contrasted with Blair in the same way). I like people who don't show anxiety or fear (emotions that, in politics, can be very catching, and can create mayhem); I like people whose self-interest is appealingly low (and it is both frightening and sad how few modern politicians one can say that about). Such people go into conversations interested in the conversation, not how they look or whether they will win the argument. Often, they are charming, polite and courteous. They care about protocols and they care about making other people feel comfortable. One such person is the Sultan of Brunei, Hassanal Bolkiah.

After Brunei's independence in 1984, Lord (Alun) Chalfont had been asked by the Foreign Office to work on the draft of a new constitution for the country. For whatever reason, it hadn't gone very well and Lowe Bell were approached to help out. The Sultan was, at the time, the richest man in the world, and because this was regarded as being a distraction to the more serious aspects of the newly independent country, part of our brief was to try to stop people focusing on that. The very first time I met him, I said, 'Your Majesty. There's a very simple solution to this.' He said, 'What's that?' And I said, 'Give me all your money, which would then make *me* the richest man in the world.' It's not that funny, but he laughed.

The first time we met was in London. He had a house in Kensington Palace Gardens as well as one in Chiswick – the latter, because it was usefully near to Heathrow Airport. The Sultan was being advised by a man called Christopher Hanbury, an army major who had been the Commanding Officer of the Green Jackets, alongside Field Marshal Lord Bramall, under whatever regiment was left behind at the time of Brunei's independence in 1984 – the remaining link to the British government. Hanbury was an army officer, who loved polo – frightfully, terribly, terribly, posh … and I always quite get on with people like that. He was our link to the Sultan, and our job became to look after Brunei's image in Britain (and that of the Sultan) because they were great friends of our country.

Unfortunately, the British press kept on writing unpleasant things about him. Most of what they alleged had actually been done by his younger brother, who led a very flamboyant lifestyle (he had his own private 747, and a yacht called *Tits*, with its engine outlets marked *Nipple One* and *Nipple Two*). But the British press – whose attention to detail can be a bit casual – hadn't worked out the difference between Prince Jefri and the Sultan. So when, for example, 75 very upmarket call-girls from Rome were shipped over to Asia for a party, the press got hold of the story, and mistakenly named the Sultan, who'd had nothing to do with it all. However, we couldn't just go to the press and land the other younger brother in it, so it was a very delicate situation.

The Sultan was very good-looking – albeit quite short, so he wore big built-up shoes. He loved gossip, especially that of the Royal kind, because to his mind his peer group was other Royalty around the world, British Royalty being the most significant.

After the London introduction, I went to see him in Brunei, the idea being that I would have an audience with him once a year at alternating venues. A small team of us were flown out to his residence – the Istana Nurul Iman palace – that sits on the Brunei River and has almost 2,000 rooms. In terms of its cost, there was not much change out of $1.4 billion, but the property came with a garage that could hold over a hundred cars (mostly custom-built Bentleys, Rolls Royces, Bugattis, Ferraris, Lamborghinis, and a few helicopters), stables for 200 polo ponies, and some of the biggest rooms I've ever seen, like decorated aircraft hangars with sofas in them; and rather a lot of it is covered in gold.

I went down with Field Marshall ('Dwin) Bramall, who was then the Chairman of the Dorchester (which the Sultan had just bought) and my great journalist pal, Rod Tyler, who was going to conduct an important first interview with the Sultan. 'Dwin was very deaf and, unfortunately, the batteries on his hearing aid had expired and he had no spares. Even in Singapore airport, in transit, we couldn't find a shop that sold them. So we were having comedy sketch conversations: 'Do you want a drink, 'Dwin? Are you thirsty?' and he'd reply, 'No, it's Friday.'

I mentioned Rod Tyler, so perhaps you will forgive me an interlude in this story to explain who he is. He had been Educational Editor of the *Daily Mail* and Features Editor of the *News of the World*. My wife was working at Capital Radio, from where I got to know a lady called Kara Noble – the daughter of Peter Noble, the showbiz writer in the *Sunday Express*. She was running a Kissogram business and one day rang me up to tell me that she was having a problem with the *News of the World*. 'They're being horrid to me', she said. 'They're going to destroy my business.' She complained that she had sent a girl to a rugby club, and that the paper was going to print a story about said young lady giving each and every rugby player there a blowjob. This, Kara informed me, was plainly nonsense, as the girl was very nice and would never do such a thing. So I said, 'All right. I'll try and do something about it.' So I looked up the Features Editor, who happened to be Rod Tyler. I said, 'You don't know me and I don't know you but it all seems very unfair.' He said, 'If you're in your office, I'll come round', which he did. He came in, sat down, and took out 15 photographs of 15 different rugby players each being given a blowjob by a very nice young lady who would never do such a thing. But he killed the story anyway.

From that day, Tyler became a great friend and a great help when dealing with the media because he could always find out what they were doing, and what they knew. He understood all the industry-speak and the coded phrases and what to do if you get this or that letter or phone call. From Rod, I learned all the techniques that journalists use and the best way to deal with things in their very brutal world.

Back in Brunei, in the capital, Bandar Seri Begawan, we waited in the hotel for the Sultan's call, sitting round the swimming pool, in thick European suits. We had to wait until all his jewellers had done with their morning's pitches to him, before we set off to the palace. Once there, we were shown up to his audience room on the seventh floor – a beautiful space decorated in green and white, with yellow marble. Outside was a row of shoes, because in Brunei you take them off in the presence of the Sultan – unless you're European, in which case you're excused the bother. Not understanding this, Rod took his shoes off, but left his socks on (something that wouldn't apply to Bruneians as they don't wear them). So when we entered, with all that slippery marble flooring, Rod just went careering across the room and practically landed in the Sultan's lap.

It got better. 'Dwin Bramall said 'Good Morning, Your Majesty' and the Sultan went 'Pardon?' and 'Dwin said 'What?' and then the Sultan said 'What?' Hanbury had briefed the Sultan about 'Dwin's battery problem, and they thought this would be a great joke. At one point, 'Dwin said, 'Your Majesty, I'm afraid the cost of refurbishing the Dorchester has gone up a bit. In fact, I need another £2 million.' To which the Sultan said, 'Now I really have gone deaf.'

One thing that stood out in the room was a series of paintings, including one on an easel, which was Van Gogh's 'Irises', which I think around that time was the most expensive painting ever sold, at around $54 million. I said to him, 'Isn't that Van Gogh's "Irises"?', and he replied 'Yes. I'm just trying to see whether it fits in with the room's colour scheme.'

The Sultan is a lovely man – sharp, intelligent, with good advisers around him. But he's in a strange environment, and has many enemies because of the oil. By that time, I was also advising Doctor Mahathir (bin Mohamad), the Prime Minister of Malaysia, so I was quite knowledgeable about the region and its cultural nuances and local difficulties. That allowed me to get on well with the Sultan – fantastically well, in fact. His full title is His Majesty Sultan Haji Hassanal Bolkiah Mu'izzaddin Waddaulah ibni Al-Marhum Sultan Haji Omar Ali Saifuddien Sa'adul Khairi Waddien, Yang Di-Pertuan of Brunei Darussalam (or something like that), and there are about 85 different roles that come with the job. I once got there and found him in the filthiest temper. I said, 'Good morning, Your Majesty … Is something bothering you, Sir?' He replied, 'It's just impossible! I run this country and I look after everybody. They get given money from cradle to grave; we've got the highest per capita income of any country in the world; and yet I'm supposed to do this and I'm supposed to that, and I'm supposed to do the other. Some days, it gets too much.' So I said, 'Yes, Sir. It's must be a burdensome task. So difficult. So many jobs: King, Prime Minister, President, and even the Messenger of God.' And he just looked back at me, shook his head, and sighed out loud.

Another extraordinary character with whom I have been fortunate to work on several occasions is Rupert Murdoch. I first met him, oddly, not through Thatcher, but through my wife's father, who was his ophthalmic surgeon. In Australia, because of the ozone layer and the light, practically every Australian seems to have an eye doctor; they're essential and important. Jack was a top surgeon in the field, and a lot of the very rich and successful went to his practice. Sydney society is not like London: it has no social structure to it, but because of that, everybody seems to know everybody. Even if they don't, they pretend they do. Yet in this case, Murdoch really was one of Jack's patients.

By that time, the world had started to talk a lot about Murdoch, so it had reached the point where I knew a lot about him, even before I was introduced to him. Sometimes, when you've read so many things about a person, when you meet them, you can be under-awed. But Murdoch was not at all a disappointing figure – and nothing like what I had expected, having read about him. Sure, he radiated power, but in the most impressive of ways: there was no one he had to impress; no one he needed to convince; no one he needed to fear or mistrust; he just was what he was. But in that, he stood for what I could understand and believe in: someone from outside of the establishment (like Margaret as well); a man who took risks and benefitted accordingly, a man who knew what he wanted; a truly global entrepreneur; a pioneer.

Murdoch was brought up in the shadow of a vicious press war between his father, Sir Keith, and Sir Frank Packer. They used to set fire to each other's lorry loads of paper and try and destroy each other – that kind of thing. Australia is a pioneer society: it's survival of the fittest, all about the bloke who gets there first – crosses the line first. Sport is everything to them, and that means that they see everything in sporting terms and in terms of victory. Murdoch was driven by money. Initially, he wanted to cast a longer shadow than his father – like many a son, actually. But now, I think he uses money as the yardstick by which he measures himself. Probably more than power – which I think he sees as the means to the end. (As opposed to money being the route to power – which is how you might expect it to be.) He's got that extraordinary entrepreneurial personality that involves taking frightening risks to achieve extraordinary ends.

Like many powerful people, he pits himself against challenges that most people would find intolerable.

Just before the first election in 1979, Murdoch rang me up and said, 'Now you have my direct number. Call me any time you think we're not putting across the right message and any time we can help you.' I think he was very quick to grasp my role. In Britain, if you're the communications adviser to the Prime Minister, you're not treated seriously. But to an Australian, you're an acceptably relevant and credible person. A few years after that, News International bought *The Times* portfolio, at which point he had a hand in both broadsheets and tabloids, and later, television. I still have his number and he still answers it.

I like him and we agree on many things. Not the monarchy, but then he's an Australian so what do you expect? He's unbelievably charming, friendly, well mannered and supportive. He can also be bad-tempered and foul-mouthed. He is – as you would expect – utterly ruthless and extremely focused. He's also quite frightening, because you are never not aware that you are in the company of one of the most powerful people on earth. Equally, you cannot help but feel privileged to be in his company, with him listening to you, and aware that you'd better not fuck up otherwise he'll cast you aside and get somebody else before you have turned to leave. He is not terribly interested in gossip – and, in that way, he shared a similarity with Margaret. In fact, he is not that interested in anything other than business and politics – in that order, the latter informing the former. He liked Reagan and he liked Thatcher, and really disliked Clinton and Major (who he thought was weak). Indeed, he hated 'wets', so there was a time when he was worried that Patten would get the Prime Minister job (he'd not forgiven Patten as Governor of Hong Kong for irritating his Chinese clients), and wanted a stop put on that possibility. And his political philosophy was straightforward enough: free-market, radical Right, Christian moral majority, with a tough stand on crime, and – obviously – not at all PC. Everything else followed from that position. He's in the mould of all my heroes. Thatcher was the same. And he actually knows the effect he has – which he uses when it suits him. But he's not a bully – which is what some people wrongly say about him. He simply doesn't need to suffer fools gladly; he doesn't like his time being wasted because he's in a rush all the time. He puts you in a box: that's your expertise and that's what he will talk to you about. Not the weather.

He's an exceptional human being. And I've been very lucky, because I've met a hell of a lot of them in my life. I love exceptional behaviour: I don't challenge it or question it or try and analyse it; I just recognise it. You can call me what you like for this, but sometimes it feels that the right thing to do is just to simply revel in the glow that comes from the talent of another individual – be it a great painter, writer, film-maker, actor, politician, entrepreneur. Why can't we just sometimes revel in the sheer joy of how talented they are, instead of envying them or criticising them or begrudging them their success? These days, admiration is in very, very short supply. And that is such a sad state of the world – and of Britain.

Murdoch played a key role in the second bitterest dispute in recent British industrial history after the miners – the print dispute. It was yet another battle that had to be faced before we shook off the legacy of the 1970s strife-torn and under-performing British industry. The truculent and immovable print unions lived in a barely legal framework – enjoying extraordinary privileges – created for them by various governments who had not wanted a protracted fight. As with the miners' strike, success against them was all about preparation before battle. To which end, Murdoch had set up a new electronic printing centre in Wapping in the East End, pretending it was all going to be for a new London paper. But when the unions went on strike in 1986, he just transferred Fleet Street production there, manned by the electricians, and was able to carry on with getting his papers out. He had also agreed before that with Margaret that, if the balloon went up, she would guarantee ample police support to keep open the Queen's Highway. When the rail unions refused to move papers, Murdoch just transferred delivery to road haulage.

The strike lasted for a year and I had a very small involvement, helping with the PR. Wapping on a Saturday night became the regular scene of riot theatre, residents watching from their flats as thousands of police and (on occasions tens of) thousands of pickets clashed – usually after the pubs had chucked out. It was vicious and bloody. But the government – and Murdoch – decided to play the long game, and simply waited until the unions ran out of steam, which they did in February 1987. Thus ended the Spanish practices that had blighted the newspaper industry, which was now transformed.

In later years, I thought that Murdoch's thinking over satellite television was fabulous. It was way ahead of its time, and anything that broke the grip of the BBC was extremely attractive to me. You have to remember how archaic and anachronistic were BBC news and BBC sport before the bomb that was Sky was placed under them. Lord Reith and his successors had sat around and told people what they could and couldn't watch on television. ITV added very little to that situation. Murdoch broke that duopoly – which is why they've always loathed him and attacked him on the spurious grounds of opposing him trying to create a monopoly. You see, one of the greatest tricks of the Left is to attack others for the things of which they themselves are most guilty. It's smart distraction tactics. They do that all the time.

I love the media; I love newspapers, I love television, I love journalists, I love journalism, I like information, I like to know what's going on. And Sky offered much more choice and I believe in choice. I think that there's an analogy here with the NHS, which is an unbelievable sacred cow in the UK. So much so that successive governments, whatever their persuasions, are terrified of saying anything remotely threatening against it. We even had an Olympic ceremony devoted to it, for Heaven's sake. The fact of the matter is that it is a bloated, inefficient service that often doesn't work and costs far too much money. Some doctors and nurses are wonderful, and – would you believe it – some are absolute rubbish. But we're not allowed to mention that. Especially if you're the BBC.

In 1990, Sam Chisholm took over as CEO of the newly merged British Sky Broadcasting and Sky TV. At the time, their losses were mind-blowing – around £10 million per week – although he had got these down to around the £1 million mark within a year or so. By 1994, following the introduction of fee-based services, they were into 3.5 million households and, then, after a stock-flotation, the debts were halved. Although he would eventually fall out with Rupert, I just got on fantastically well with Chisholm. He took to ringing me up and telling me that they had a problem to discuss. For a while, we never charged. Then it was happening more and more so one day, I asked if they'd mind paying us something. So they did.

As for Rupert, I've continued to do various tasks for him. I did talk with him about his own appearances at the Select Committee recently, but he couldn't pay me for it. Then Bell Pottinger were asked to look after Rebekah Brooks, because he couldn't get involved. In all the years I've known him he has always been absolutely careful to behave within the law. He has to. Everything he does is lawyered to death. Of course, he'll absolutely push it to the edge and see if he can find a clever way round something, but that does not mean that he condones criminal behaviour.

Regardless of the trial, Rebekah ran a good paper and was in charge of some fine campaigns, and exposed some bad people. When it comes to misdeeds by people in the public eye, Rupert's view ties in with that (famously) of Kelvin Mackenzie, that, if you don't want it written about, then don't fucking well do it. If you don't want to be photographed drunk, don't get pissed when you're out. Yet it's amazing how many people come along, after the event, and ask journalists not to write about something. Their attitude is along the lines of, 'I did do it. But I'd really rather prefer if nobody knew.' Which is stupid. David English used to say to me, 'Don't tell me a secret. It's not fair. I'm a journalist. You can't tell me a secret when my job is to pass secrets on.'

Rupert Murdoch still rings me, we go through things, we see each other, and I go to his parties. If he wants anything that we might be able to help with, he just picks the phone up – if he doesn't, he doesn't. He actually invited me to the Olympics in Los Angeles in 1984, with tickets to everything, and Cadillacs to drive you from the hotel and back. It was a wonderful trip; we went to see anything – including Zola Budd running in her bare feet.

I didn't realise at the time, but years later, I would be involved in another Olympic venue; namely that of Sydney in 2000. I'd done a small piece of work for Bronwyn Bishop, a Liberal Party Senator for New South Wales, who was inclined to the Right-wing, and was impressed by what Thatcher had achieved here in the UK. She didn't get anywhere with her leadership ambition (although these days, she's the Speaker in the House of Representatives), but meeting her brought me into contact with the head of the Sydney Olympic bid – a guy called Rod McGeoch. The tradition in the campaign is not to criticise the opposition – which sledging Australians can't grasp – so he came to me asking us at Lowe Bell to come up with a covert PR plan against the joint favourites, Beijing. They didn't dare use their own local PR agency (although they came and had meetings at our offices). The Australian government were very uneasy about all this, and in the end, we didn't do very much, although we did arrange for the tank to be parked outside the Olympic voting headquarters with a Chinese chap standing in front of it to remind them all of Tiananmen Square.

The Olympic decision day is massively exaggerated in the interests of stage-management. It's mostly decided months before the announcement date; most of it is phoney. People are bribed, either implicitly or explicitly. It's like the football World Cup: the stakes are so enormous, so they will always find a way. They're just completely contrary to everything that we now accept under the concept of transparency and openness: there's a little bloke here, a bureaucrat there, and nobody can say anything about any of it. Some of the stuff that takes place is beyond imagination.

Sydney duly won the right to host the games on 24 September 1993, and it was around this time when I first encountered Princess Diana. The Waleses had separated, but were yet to divorce. The Camillagate tapes had been published and the press were obsessed; meanwhile, she had said that she was going to withdraw from public life – which was, of course, impossible for someone in her shoes. Although he never got very far with the idea, Gordon Reece was desperate to take on her case and sounded me out about it, but I was not really interested. He was completely infatuated by her – she turned him into a puppy dog.

Her premature death immortalised her, as it had done James Dean and JFK: the Paris underpass was her Highway 466 or grassy knoll. But long before that, she had already built herself a career as a tragic figure, working at it with public relations people and journalists and sharp lawyers. When the accident happened, enter Tony Blair, with his 'People's Princess' hagiography. All in a morning's work – whilst the Queen wandered around Balmoral wondering what to make of the hysteria, here was her self-styled spokesperson and, by clever implication, the People's Prime Minister. Blair was never one to underestimate a populist opportunity.

I had never had much time for Diana, and thought those scenes following her death were absurd – a complete suspension of reality by half the British population, who had never met her but started buying flowers, weeping over their television sets, and buying Elton John CDs.

She had been offered the opportunity of becoming the Princess of Wales, and had accepted voluntarily, marrying Charles on 29 July 1981. I can't believe that she was unaware of what she was getting herself into with the lugubrious prince who wanted to marry someone else, but needed to produce an heir. She fancied the privileges but not the sacrifices and responsibilities of duty, and when it became apparent that she couldn't be a Disney-princess all the time, she behaved like a sulking brat, doing the weepy demagogue interview with Martin Bashir and destabilising various foolish married men who should have had the sense to keep their distance.

She was very tall – I remember her very long legs – and very vain. We had dinner with her, courtesy of Gordon Reece at his flat. I think it must have been after her divorce in 1996. Gordon was still desperate to be her publicist and thought he might earn brownie points if he got her to meet with the Chairman of the Press Complaints Commission – who had been John Wakeham since 1995 – and discuss how terrible the media were being towards her. Gordon had invited me because he wanted to show off as to who was coming to dinner. With both the Wakehams, it made a very peculiar group. The four of us sat around downstairs waiting until her car arrived. Alison Wakeham had got herself into such a muddle that she had put on one black shoe and one dark blue shoe, which horrified her when she noticed her footwear didn't match, so she spent the whole evening trying to sit with her feet hidden.

Anyway, Diana arrived and made her entrance from above, long heels long before the short skirt. The gentlemen tried to be polite and not look upwards as she tottered down the stairs. As she was sitting down, she took one of the cushions from the sofa and held it on her lap, feigning coyness, pretending that she didn't want a Sharon Stone moment. But then, why oh why had she dressed like that in the first place?

That was her way: a kind of provocative false modesty, which I found rather unattractive because it was so choreographed, even the way she tilted her head and looked up through her eyelashes. I was disdainful of her and probably showed it: I barely spoke all night, which I think she found disagreeable, in the way that women who are almost invariably fawned over react badly when they find themselves not being fawned over. I couldn't make myself interested in her (to be frank) banal air-headedness – spending most of her time talking about herself and her clothes and things that had little relevance to any of us there (except Gordon, in his dream-state). I thought she looked like a horse with those legs, so I used to call her the clothes-horse. I'm afraid I was very, very cynical about her.

It may seem an odd comparison, but I find myself, at this point, thinking of Michael Caine – a good friend and a fabulous man – and such a *real* person. There's no self-importance with him. No vanity. No pretence. But intelligence and self-deprecation in spades. He's forever surprised that he has got to be successful, and still laughs about it: after well over a hundred feature films. That's what I like in people – when they don't take themselves too seriously – which is probably why he's able to play all the different parts he plays. He's just a very funny, jolly decent human being. And another interesting element – which I guess adds to the contrast with the story of Diana – is that he's achieved a very happy marriage with his wife Shakira.

Michael has never allowed himself to be put into a box: he's neither Hollywood nor Elstree Films, and he's never allowed himself to be imprisoned by the clichés that develop around such cultures. Instead, he's one of the most eclectic, worldly-wise people I've known. He would love to say (and you can imagine the accent), 'I've been rich and I've been poor, and rich is better.'

He had a restaurant called The Canteen in Chelsea Harbour. We were having dinner there with Val Kilmer, who was about to play the lead in *The Saint*, and his director (or maybe the producer – I can't remember which), along with Victoria – my wife – and Michael and Shakira. Now it just so happened that the Leslie Charteris books were always one of my interests, and over the years, I'd actually read and re-read many of the novels and short stories (there were well over a hundred of them). But there was a non-sequitur moment when the director said to me, 'Do you know anything about *The Saint*?' So I said, 'Yes I do. I've read *all* the books.' He looked back blankly at me and said, 'What books? I thought it was a television series with Roger Moore in it.' (He didn't seem to know that there had been numerous films made, as well.) At that point, I thought that the world had ended. How could you be that ignorant of the subject if you were making the film? So I just went off on one, babbling away about *Meet the Tiger* (the original story from 1928), *Enter the Saint, Knight Templar*, and all the characters like Simon Templar, Roger Conway, Norman Kent, Dicky Tremaine, and the hero's adventurer-girlfriend Patricia Holm. I was, of course, behaving like a nerdy madman, and they were all staring at me, wondering what on earth they had let themselves in for. I wouldn't stop. Michael was absolutely in stitches. It was exactly the sort of thing that made him laugh – at the very un-American absurdity of the scene. When they made the film, I thought that it was pretty much hopeless, so clearly, my ranting had done no good at all. Dealing with Hollywood – and with Americans – it rarely does. Michael knew that only too well.

I like people like Michael who've made their way through life without much help, who've done it themselves; paid their bills, paid their dues, and done their duty. They face up to their responsibilities and if they get it wrong they suffer the consequences; if they get it right, they get the rewards. Those are the kind of people with whom I identify. David Frost was another such person.

He was one of the most flamboyant characters I have ever known; a great friend and a great, great man – and it was a blow when he died in 2013, at the age of 74. David was obviously famous himself, but there can be few people who, in turn, have met, interviewed, and probably quite well understood so many – and such a broad spectrum – of the most famous figures on the planet. It's only mild hyperbole to say that David seemed to know *everybody* – and know something interesting and surprising about them. To his great credit, he was always less interested in winning a victory over an interviewee–adversary, and far more interested in making his interviewee seem a fascinating subject. That was the case when he battled with Thatcher or Nixon or Putin – in the case of the last, all the production team thought that the Russian had behaved like a powerful and dangerous bully, who might just let them leave the room alive, but Frosty thought that he was such an amazing *character*.

Bell Pottinger has Cunard as a client, and one Saturday evening (it was 31 August 2013), I got a phone call from the guy who handles that account, with the bad news that David Frost had died whilst on board the *Queen Elizabeth* liner, whilst giving a lecture about his life, during a Mediterranean cruise. No one knew how to get hold of his next-of-kin, so they called me to see if I had any of the telephone numbers. I said, 'I've got his wife Carina's mobile but she never answers it, so that's pointless; and she doesn't look at her texts. I know his Chelsea number but she's never there at the weekends.' Then, around 10.30 p.m., another official person rang me up, unable to find his wife or children, and trying instead to locate his father-in-law, the Duke of Norfolk. I said, 'Well, good luck with that, because he died about ten years ago.' Then they thought about calling the current Duke of Norfolk, who happens to be his brother-in-law Eddie, but I told them that by far the most sensible thing would be to try his agent.

I rang Peter Chadlington, who was David's oldest friend, who collapsed in tears, saying that we'd lost the most important person there'd ever been, that he couldn't cope with it, and that it was the end of the world.

He said, 'What I am supposed to do?'

I said, 'You're not supposed to do anything. Just give me a telephone number for their country house.' He managed to get that, but there was no reply there. Then, at 3.30 a.m., a policeman rang me up.

'Are you the person who has *the number*? Are you sure it's *the right number*?'

I said, 'I haven't the faintest idea – it's just the number I was given.'

'Well, who gave it to you?'

'Lord Chadlington', I said.

'Can we ring him?'

'Well it is 3.30 in the morning. I don't think I can really make decisions like that.'

'Can you just give us the number?'

So I gave the number to the policeman. Then, after a pause, he said, 'Well, we don't seem to have any address listed against that number.'

At which I said, 'Why don't you ring one of those private detectives you use? They can usually find anything for you.'

He replied, 'Steady on, Sir. No need to be abusive.'

Three hours and God knows what number of bureaucratic incompetences later, they had finally found Carina's location and I got a text saying that she had been told and there was someone with her. But it had been typical Frosty, to make his exit with a great drama. Later, after I'd had time to think about his death free of a practical crisis, it made me feel, yet again, that you've got to nurture your friendships – because you never know when they're going to vanish.

When he got his knighthood, it meant a huge amount to him. But he rang me up one Friday, a week or so before, saying that it presented him with a problem. He said, 'Do you know what's going to happen, Tim? I know, Carina knows, my agent knows, and I've had to tell Barney the producer. But nobody else knows, of course. So this conversation is completely off the record.' I said, 'Fine. So what's the problem, David?' He said, 'Well, I don't know whether to call my show *Sir David Frost on Sunday*, *Sir David on Sunday*, or just leave it as *Frost on Sunday*.' That was his dilemma. There's nothing like thinking ahead. So I told him that if you've got it, you should flaunt it, and therefore suggested *Sir David Frost on Sunday*. He said, 'Mmmm. Wery good, wery good argument. I favour that. Yes, I will use that argument. Thank you. But do you mind if I just check with Peter Chadlington whether he agrees?' So I said, 'No please do. Let's get him in on the secret too.' Once David had rung off, I rang Peter immediately and said, 'Whatever you do, say to him it has to be *Sir David Frost on Sunday*'. I was in the middle of telling him that, when he said, 'Hold on, Tim. David's on the other line.'

I first met him at the Revolution Club in Bruton Place. It was in the 1960s, and all the people from *That Was The Week That Was* used to be there: Lance Percival, playing the guitar, and with various sketches being done. David Frost must have been in his late 20s, and we remained friends from that point. He did so many things in his life, interviewed so many people – Nixon, Ali, Putin, Gaddafi, Oswald Mosley, Ian Smith, the Shah of Iran, the Beatles, and eight British prime ministers – to name a tiny selection. It's harder to think of people that he hadn't interviewed. Osama bin Laden, Barack Obama, J. Edgar Hoover (who thought that he was a Communist) – that's about it. Rupert Murdoch, incidentally, once called him an 'arrogant bastard'. There's probably a bit of truth in that: his wife was once asked if he was religious, and she replied, 'Yes. He believes he's God.' But the greater truth was that, once you got to know him, Frosty was almost impossible not to like.

He never had a bad word to say for anybody at all. He'd laugh about his interviewees – at their foibles and their eccentricities and even their nefariousnesses

– but he never said anything nasty about anybody. Stephen Sherbourne (one-time Margaret's political secretary) is exactly the same. And the interesting thing is that, in return, nobody's got anything nasty to say about them either. Now I know that's not true of me, so I'm rather jealous of them in that regard. But I think it proves how important it is to behave in the most proper and decent way you can.

David wasn't obsessed with his fame. He didn't expect to walk into restaurants and want people to spot him. Equally, if they did say something – which can be a nuisance if it's happening all the time – he would always say, 'Thank you very much.' He had the manners and courtesy to remember everybody's name, so that any restaurant we went into, he would remember the names of most of the staff.

I used to frequent L'Etoile in Charlotte Street for lunch. The place had a sort of main restaurant but there was a little corner in the window that had only two tables in it. John Pearce (of CDP) liked that spot and David did as well, but I had an agreement with the guy that ran L'Etoile that if three of us were after two seats David would always get the first choice, whatever I had booked, and, whatever he had booked, Pearce would always be the one bumped off to somewhere else in the restaurant. Of course, Pearce didn't know we had that arrangement. He was usually so drunk he didn't know where the fuck he was in the restaurant anyway. Invariably, I would potter in there and Frosty would be there with somebody or with nobody and I'd just sit and have lunch with him. I used to go to his house a lot and we used to have drinks and smoke and chat about this, that and the other. He will be missed.

When he did the Nixon interviews, he told me the three things that struck him most – the first two, by virtue of their striking irony. (I think Frosty told these to a lot of people, so I don't pretend that this is an original story.) The first was that he said to Nixon, 'Would you rather be the President of the United States, or the General Secretary of the USSR?' to which Nixon replied, ' I'd much rather be the President of the United States, because if you're the General Secretary of the Soviet Union, you're recorded all the time.' Then, one time, Nixon said to him, 'You're foreign aren't you? Well, you're being paid here in America, so make sure you pay all the right taxes.' Then there was the moment that has been re-enacted in various films on Nixon, which showed how inept he was with small talk. There was a further context to this, in that they'd been telling Nixon that he had to stop saying 'Fuck' all the time. Anyway, whatever the reasons, the way I heard it from David was that, on the final Sunday, before the last episode, he arrived early at Nixon's giant bungalow in Sacramento, and was let in by the butler, and told to help himself to some coffee. In due course, Nixon came down the stairs from the bedroom in his classic silk dressing gown and slippers, and said, 'Did you have a good Saturday, David?' Frosty said that he had indeed had a good night, to which Nixon replied, 'Did you do any fornicating?'

David knew, possibly more than anyone – and especially during and because of those Nixon moments – the enormous responsibility carried by the interviewer on behalf of the viewing public. I think that is often forgotten by today's lot. He once said, 'Television is an invention that permits you to be entertained in your living room by people you wouldn't have in your home.' Frosty was great entertainment no matter where he was.

20

How Great Thou Art

It is hard to generalise about powerful people: how they are different – which they usually are – and why. Of those I've known and admired, Reagan, de Klerk, Thatcher and Murdoch stand out as the four real game-changers. Each had remarkable strengths – along with the flaws that are natural to the human condition. Each changed the world; and meeting them changed mine. No words can do them proper justice.

In three of those cases, their days are over – the eras have passed. I'm not nostalgic about that, but what saddens me is that it is increasingly difficult to be like that any more – for such people to emerge. Left or Right, we used to actively *want* giants as our leaders and business and political heroes. Now, however, society no longer accepts 'greatness' and instead longs for greyness – for the shallow goo of mediocrity for all. The exception is in the Kremlin, where there is a giant – albeit a nasty one. This is why you need nice giants, and why the first Cold War was won. Let us see about the second.

It's all part of a general trend to drag ambition down: ostensibly in the cause of equality or democracy, but in truth, simply as a free licence for envy. 'Greatness' – at least in business and politics – is now frowned upon, as though greed and nastiness have to come as a consequence. So you see politicians and business people not aspiring to greatness but, instead, trying to pass off a kind of cod-normality – pretending to walk to the local supermarket for a loaf of bread, or play bingo or watch TV soaps or listen to iPods. (The 'rewards', meanwhile, have to come surreptitiously – the convoluted expense claims or tax avoidance schemes or such like, that they fatuously and futilely hope will never be discovered.) You see these people disguising where they come from (when I lived in Brookmans Park, we pretended we were in Elstree; now, they do it the opposite way round); dropping their aitches; eating crap; hiding any wealth or success – fearing that, if they disclose any ambition or aspiration, the mob will come and bay at them, or a Unite leverage squad will appear on the doorstep.

'Greatness' has become a kind of sin. Except in football and entertainment, where a different phenomenon is at play, where 'greatness' has been entirely redefined. Here, apparently, any vapid or dim-witted individual has a chance of being the new 'great', fawned over and idolised, regardless of the cheating or greed or nastiness that seems to come, mitigated and condoned, with those territories. Shows like *The X Factor* purport to demonstrate that anyone can make it to the top (though the truth is that they can't). Even if people have the talent, I question how many people have the work ethic or wherewithal or commitment to achieve anything worthwhile. Unfortunately, the implication is that you can short-cut the system, and rise to fame and fortune with no effort and in no time at all. You too can win a talent show and spew your wealth and bad taste across the tabloid pages. Of course, when people realise that it's not going to happen, and that they have to go back to a normal wage on Monday morning, they get disgruntled. When the children return to school on Monday, the teachers have to lie that they're all beautiful and intelligent and all worth an A*. This new world is rich with fools who think that they have a right to 'greatness'.

It all goes hand-in-hand with the gradual loss of aspiration in people. Thatcher tapped into a spirit of 'hard-working' people's aspiration that is no longer there. In fact, that phrase has been hijacked by the Left to mean something quite different. Nowadays, when politicians say 'hard-working people', they don't mean those with aspiration to earn more; they mean those with a desire to see others brought down nearer to their level. Look at taxation policy under Geoffrey Howe and Nigel Lawson – where the top rate fell from 83p in 1979 eventually to 40p, and got us associated, so successfully, with an age of entrepreneurship and renewed faith in Britain – upon which Blair duly seized. It's interesting that neither Thatcher nor Blair, who both had multiple election successes, seriously considered moving taxes upward (unlike, revealingly, John Major, and then Gordon Brown – who brought in the 50p rate). Thatcher and Blair both instinctively knew that taxing wealth is not only counterproductive, but it also gives the impression that you want to stifle the very aspiration that drives the less well-off to better themselves. Why should I want to earn more money if I know it will be taxed at an increasingly greater level if I do?

The financial crisis around 2008 was probably a turning point. That and the expenses scandal. After these defining moments, the culture of envy really took over in this country, and wealth per se came to be the bogey. That opened the door for the Socialists to start saying, 'It's not fair – they've got more than you; it's not fair.' So it was telling that, in the 2010 election, Labour and Gordon

Brown campaigned on a slogan of a 'future fair for all'. It was more like a free-for-all that they wanted.

Taxation is an evil, which takes away choice and incentive. In any case, the more you tax, the less revenue you pull in. Everyone knows that, but the Left uses taxation as a means of fuelling envy and then maintaining control. And the Tories have increasingly played such a stupid game that their reputation for being the party of lower taxation has been slowly but surely eroded. It's gone from the days of Thatcher when there was, broadly speaking, a positive mindset among the *Sun* readers – to which she had a strong appeal – to nowadays, when the mood is far more negatively oriented.

Thatcher appealed because she was an outsider, who demonstrated – in both word and deed – that aspiration could overcome stasis at both ends of the political spectrum. That is, not just the vested interests of the Left, but also the iniquities of the comfortable wealthy and privileged elites who disliked her radicalism as much as did the Left. In this way she laid the groundwork for Blair, who then came in and started pumping borrowed money into the creation of a vast Labour-leaning dependent client-state.

What we might call the Establishment – the people who really run the country – has changed, to the point where it is now predominantly Left-leaning, when once a significant proportion would have defaulted to the Right. (This is even before we consider the power of the EU over us.) So, for example, the judiciary is on the Left (they were on strike the other week), as are the majority of the heads of the quangos, as are the arts and much of the television media (especially the BBC); as are, obviously, the NHS and medical profession, education and police (given that both the teaching profession and police are now heavily unionised, which is a relatively new development); the clergy are there; and in Baroness Ashton, we have a Labour politician as head of EU foreign affairs and security.

The success of the Left, since Blair, has been its slow but impressive long march through the institutions, so that, as a country, our Establishment (at the highest level and in the form of the bureaucratic machinery that services it) has become default-Socialist – without most people even noticing. This Establishment was once the guardian of British culture; now, it continually questions it. If ever this Labour-dominated Establishment is challenged, the siren calls are shrill (as they are when comfortable power is threatened) with complaints about the elites. As for example, when Owen Jones screams about BBC Right-wing bias (as if), or when Michael Gove failed to reappoint Sally Morgan as Chair of Ofsted (when, had you listened to James Naughtie on the BBC, you could have been forgiven in thinking that a quango head *had* to be of the Left).

While the Left have been ruthless and devious about this, the moderates on the Right – that is, the non-extremists, not the Far Right – try too hard to play fair at making their case. Some of the time, they're greedy or they've got vested interests, and worry about being seen to be hypocritical. But at other times, they are at pains to acknowledge the right of the other person to hold a contrary opinion. This leads to the Right being more timid than the Left, who will happily shout down any opinion that does not chime with theirs. Look at the contrast in reactions to the deaths of Thatcher (who was, in death, vilified by the Left) and Tony Benn (even those on the Right, who believed his Socialism would have wrecked this country, still felt that they had to eulogise about the 'great man'); Bob Crow said that he wanted to dance on Thatcher's grave, yet when he died, everyone on the Right spent their time trying to be gracious. The Right try to be reasonable; the Left just scream and shout.

So nowadays, it is the Right that is the de facto outsider, while the Left is the real establishment wolf in progressive sheep's clothing. As for the Lords – there you really can see how this shift has occurred.

I was knighted in 1990, but it was not until eight years later that I became a life peer. All the time I was working with Thatcher I'd never expected it, and it was not one of my ambitions. But anybody who says they don't want a peerage is either a liar or a fool, especially when the time comes, and you become aware of its possibility. Major cut me off the list, because, he said, I'd already got the knighthood from Mrs Thatcher, and didn't warrant the next step. What upset me was that, of the three people who did the campaigns, Peter Gummer and Maurice Saatchi were given peerages by Major, but he pointedly left me out. Jeffrey Archer gave him a really bad time about that, and called him mean and vindictive.

Brian Mawhinney was Chairman of the Party when the Conservative government fell in 1997 and Blair took control with an enormous majority. Very quickly after that, Brian rang me up and said that he regarded it as 'unfinished business' that he said he'd sort out. So when William Hague took over as the Tory leader, Mawhinney told him that they owed me a peerage. One day, Seb Coe rang me up and said, 'William wants to give you a peerage: will you accept it?' That's how I got it.

It didn't make me think that I was more important than I had been the day before, but it brought me into a very exclusive club, the membership of which has pros and some cons. You do get very good tables in restaurants, and it allows me to wind up Martin Sorrell, by saying, 'Hello, Sir Martin – Lord Bell here.' The downside is that it makes some people act unnaturally towards me; and it can make people resentful; some call me '*Mr* Bell', with deliberate emphasis; and it encourages builders to put their prices up.

Devendra, my driver, who's a Gurkha, likes to call me 'My Lord'. And it's funny how some Americans think that it's my first name, and say, 'Hi Lord.' I've taken to being self-deprecatingly ironic about it, so that, when I start a speech, I sometimes say, 'Hello. My name's Tim Bell, but you can call me "My Lord".' However, if they don't get the irony, they think I'm a pompous fool.

I once had a rather surreal conversation about the Lords with Ahmed Mohammed Al-Sayed (who is now the Chief Executive of the Qatar Investment Authority). For a long time, he'd been introducing me as 'Lord Bell, a relative to the Queen', based on an assumption about why a Lord – *any* Lord – has his or her title. So the time came when I had to stop this carrying on, and explain to him that this was a mistake and that I was a *life* peer, which, unlike an hereditary title, has nothing to do with blood and is all about service and achievement. At this point, he looked at me very strangely and said, 'You mean you're a Lord who is not related to the Queen?' I replied, 'No, I'm afraid not. Not one bit of me.' At that, he paused, and said, 'Let me give you a word of advice. I think it will be better for you if you *never* tell anyone in Qatar that you're *not* related to the Queen.' So after that, I just stayed quiet and let people think what they liked.

I have to admit, however, that nowadays, people generally, and the Lords specifically, take themselves far too seriously. I really believe that Blair – and his period as leader – was in some way responsible for Britain losing some of its self-deprecating uniqueness. And maybe Princess Diana, who also took herself too seriously. It's an aspect of character that I find so depressing and, sitting there in the House of Lords, it is apparent in the way that so many of the peers talk. The popular view can be that the Lords are a patronising, self-important lot – and, do you know what? They are. They talk as though they know the answer to everything and nobody else does; they have a habit of saying, '*I* don't agree with this bill because *I* think ...' It's all 'I, I, I, I, I ...' – the heights of ego. They act like the whole nation is listening and is losing sleep over what they think. They can easily forget that it's the voting of the people that counts.

I remember being with Lord Thorneycroft and Lord Carrington when we were making a Party Political Broadcast. Lord Thorneycroft was a life peer, while Carrington was a 14th hereditary marquis. Carrington was the star of the PPB, and after the broadcast Thorneycroft asked me, 'How did you get on with

Carrington?' I told him that I'd found him to be a most charming person, and that we'd got on fabulously. Thorneycroft said, 'Yes, he is indeed very charming, but of course, he's like all these 14th hereditary marquises, constantly going on and on about the forming of the House of Lords. I always say to them that being an hereditary marquis could happen to anyone. It's no different from having a club foot.'

It's fairly self-evident, of course, because a life peerage is a meritocratic appointment that can't be passed on to anybody, whereas hereditary peers get it whether they're good, bad, indifferent, or insane. I'll let you judge what you think most of them are.

There are 26 bishops of the Church of England who sit in the House of Lords (as the 'Lords Spiritual'). There has to be at least one of them there each day, to say prayers. They are meant to be there as representatives of the people generally (rather than of their Christian congregation), but all this does, it seems to me, is encourage them to give free rein to any eccentric or random view they might have at any one moment.

In the main, Christianity – certainly in the UK – is losing its power and influence: its membership is diminishing; turning their premises into shops or nightclubs is much more profitable than fostering churchgoing. These institutions are in an existential struggle: with fundamentalist atheism on one side, and Islamofascism on the other. Yet, like great brands that fall into decline, they have not bothered to remember what actually is the essence of the brand. In this case, the belief in God. But that is something that they never talk about, or only with a kind of passive detachment. Instead, they get bogged down in process and administration; or in increasingly undisguised party politics, tacking increasingly to the Left and banging on about social liberalism, public welfare and climate change.

I've seen this in so many churchmen. But one notable exception is Richard Chartres, the Bishop of London: a fire-and-brimstone guy (who thinks the Church should 'speak in words of fire'), he is an old-fashioned kind of believer with a profound faith – and comes over as a thoroughly impassioned and honest character because of it. He does not try to appease anyone who disagrees with him (and when he was appointed, the BBC, predictably, majored on the gay and feminist reaction).

I've had some refreshing conversations with him about God, and how he regards heaven and a hell as manifestations of how we behave on earth, what we do right and what we do wrong. Most of us (who are not psychopaths or sociopaths or some other kind of path) understand the difference between right and wrong. We don't always practise right and avoid wrong; we make mistakes or choose the wrong course of action. I actually had a discussion with Richard about this, and he seemed to be saying, in his view, that, having made the mistake, you have to work your way through it. You have to suffer the consequences of it, and you have to come out the other side and start living properly again. That's the dilemma and the consequences that everybody faces throughout life in trying to choose between doing the right thing and the wrong thing.

The first Archbishop of Canterbury that I met was George Carey. Brian (Lord) Griffiths, who was the head of Margaret's policy unit from 1985 until 1990, was a very devout Christian and has written books about ethics and so forth, and he had for years sat as Chairman of the Archbishop of Canterbury's Lambeth Fund. He rang me up one day and said, 'Tim. The Archbishop is having a bit of trouble with *The Sunday Times*. They've written an article saying that he's very tired and emotional and his marriage is falling apart. Well, I wonder if you'd come in and talk to him and see if you can help with the media?' I have to say that I found the offer quite interesting, mainly because I'd never met an Archbishop before, let alone a tired and emotional one, so I thought it would be rather fun, and I agreed. On the day Brian and I went over to Lambeth Palace, Terry Waite was sitting in his office, just back from his internment, trying to become normal again.

We all gathered in Carey's study and straight away, he pointed to himself and said, 'Right! Do I look tired and emotional?' I said, 'Well, let me give you one immediate piece of advice, Your Grace. Don't ever say that again. Because the moment you say it, you put the thought into somebody's mind and they start imagining that you do indeed look tired and emotional.' Meanwhile, I was thinking that it was already turning into a very funny conversation. He kept on going on about how he was very happily married and how dare the journalists say such things. 'You're a PR man. Should we have a conversation about it?' So I said, 'Yes, Your Grace. But forgive me; I've never met an Archbishop before, so I wonder if you wouldn't mind us saying a prayer to make our consultation successful.' This completely nonplussed him. Obviously, nobody had ever asked him to say a prayer before. He said, 'Er, do you have any particular prayer in mind?' I said, 'No, you're the Archbishop. You know all the prayers. You decide what's best?' He said, 'Do you want us to kneel?' and I said, 'That's not a bad idea.' So we all knelt. Actually, I don't think Terry did, as he was still sitting on a chair in the corner, trying to figure out what had happened to him.

Anyway, I seem to remember that the three of us knelt at the desk and Carey started with his prayer, and at that precise moment, the door of his study opened and a lady with a tea tray walked in, and looked at us very strangely, and said, 'Where do you want me to put the tea?' and then sauntered back out shaking her head.

In the end, we had a perfectly good and constructive session. I told him to stop going on and on about homosexual priests and same-sex marriage and about women priests and about this and that and instead start talking about belief in God. These people never talk about faith. All they talk about is structure; they argue about whether they should have women priests or black priests or white priests or gay priests. And they're obsessed with sex of course. But after that, there's not much else, which is quite extraordinary actually. I said, 'Talk about faith' and he replied, 'No. That's the job of Evangelists.' To which I replied, 'No it's not. It's the job of all of you clergy. If you believe in something, spread the word. Isn't that how it works?' He looked at me as though I was very naïve. Then he took me over to a horizontal framed picture on the wall, like one of those school photos, but this one with all his bishops in a series of long rows. And he said, 'It's not easy, you know. This job. I mean I have to control this lot.' He started to point at individual bishops in the photograph, saying things like, 'This one's gay, this one has no belief in God, this one believes in black magic, this one is a suspected paedophile ...' It was extraordinary. I said, 'I feel very sorry for you. But surely there's one thing that you've got in common. You believe in God; you have faith. Well, most of you, anyway.' He looked back at me as though he was anything but sure. I got the impression that he was being overwhelmed by issues of management, rather than being able to concentrate on what he was supposed to be doing, which is spreading the word of God.

I find it increasingly disappointing how the Church gets itself embroiled in day-to-day politics, to the point where they all start behaving more like politicians, squabbling about policy, whilst trying to secure 50 per cent of the popular vote. The politicians that I admire are people who believe in something, and who are absolutely passionate about their belief – who'd prefer to lose their job for their belief, so strong are their principles. You would have thought that, when it comes to the Church, it would be more likely to be run by people who are like that. But I suspect that it's not. Passionate beliefs can seem a long way from modern sanitised politics nowadays, but God can seem even further away from the Church.

When people lack strong beliefs, they also find it hard to come up with great ideas: the latter being, in a sense, a function of the former. And I think we have a shortage of people having *real* ideas, and producing *real* solutions to problems. Nowadays, it's the entrepreneurial class that deliver most in this respect, but the politicians are very slow to understand this and to adopt the kind of agile practices that modern organisations demand and adopt. Look at how often public-sector procurement goes wrong and wastes millions, simply by ignoring all that the SME sector can offer. Our CEO at Bell Pottinger, James Henderson, has a friend who has started a taxi company in which all the drivers are war-wounded ex-servicemen – because even if you have a severe arm or leg injury, you can still drive a car. It's an absolutely brilliant idea, particularly because it is all about self-reliance, self-help and individual responsibility. No one there turned round to the NHS and asked for a grant. They just got on and did it. Why the government hasn't immediately hired them to supply all cars to the government, I don't know.

Thinking about ingenious schemes to help those in need, and the great people who make such things happen, it's worth mentioning one Jane Tewson, whose name may be relatively unfamiliar, but whose achievements are not. When she was only in her early 20s, Tewson was laying the groundwork for probably the most successful fund-raising idea of all time. (This extraordinary woman left school with few qualifications – she has battled with serious dyslexia – and then worked in Sudan, where, on one occasion, she contracted malaria and was even declared to be dead, before she pulled through.) Her entire philosophy is about getting people involved with charity rather than simply giving to it. In the 1980s, I was privileged to provide her with the money that started something called the Charity Projects addressing homelessness, which over time spawned Comic Relief. Although I'm no longer directly connected, I'm still the Life President. The determination and pragmatism of people like this really does put politics into an unfavourable perspective.

One problem is that people hear politicians and it sounds like white noise. The only ones who hear anything relevant are the political class themselves. So it's the political class speaking to the political class. Everyone else is excluded by lack of interest from the conversation. So party membership and, more importantly, the actual numbers of people who vote, seem to be in perpetual decline.

In any case – because of the real-time dissemination of material on the web – it feels that, in politics, everything's already been done and said. There have been various people, including Churchill, who have made the point that the only original remark is something that hasn't been said for a long time. And the only way that you achieve any stand-out is, also paradoxically, to add an apparent irrelevancy or absurdity to what you say or how you say it. So Boris Johnson becomes the enigma by making a fool of himself and looking dishevelled; but he gets away with his sartorial and presentational untidiness in a way that Michael Foot never could. The problem with that is when he needs to be serious, he can't be. If you watch him in Mayor's question time, it can quickly deteriorate into jokes and cheap political cracks and so on.

I think this is even more acute in the US than it is in the UK. They have the most sophisticated and complex campaigning in the world, to get the most powerful person in the world elected. But one has to wonder how one man or woman can do that job in today's political and media climates. How can anyone cope with what a President has to endure? Well clearly some couldn't.

In the course of five decades, I met Nixon, Carter, Ford (elegant and charming), Reagan, Clinton, and both Bushes, Senior and Junior. I rather liked the last, and especially the drinking part of him over the more sober bit – but he was far sharper and shrewder than some people give him credit for. His father was quite an old man when I met him and I found him rather tall and dull. I talked with Frosty about his interviewing Nixon, but only met that President once, and only in passing. He was staying at Claridge's on a lecture tour or something like that. I think I was talking with Charles Powell and Jonathan Aitken and he appeared walking down that big sweeping staircase in the hotel. His aides were carrying these huge rectangular boards. We all wondered what on earth they were – were they ads or bulletproof shields or what? – then some joker said, 'They're his idiot boards in case he has to talk to someone he meets and needs to know what to say.'

Clinton was one of those men who can make anyone he meets feel special. He looks you in the eye, has a fantastic memory for names, and seems only interested in you, which means that he is very good on those occasions when they let him near a few 'ordinary' folk – he knows just how to talk to them, which is a surprisingly rare skill among most politicians, let alone Presidents. He is also physically huge – more so than you imagine from photographs. Unfortunately, when I met him for the first time, his more outrageous behaviour had been under scrutiny, so I already had a view, and to be honest, was already somewhat ill-disposed to him. He didn't look good, because by that time, he was punch-drunk from all the Lewinsky impeachment hearings and humiliation.

One can never overestimate the sheer attritional effect of high office. No one can ever anticipate the sheer weight of the task, and the pressure it brings. Some of them wear it very well; some of them don't. Carter looked wrecked by it long before he finished. Whenever I saw him, Reagan, by contrast, always looked fantastic – at least until he'd retired and the Alzheimer's got him. Despite the stress, Thatcher usually looked completely on her game as well, until those last few weeks and days. Major always looked worn out by it all; Wilson never did, except towards the end – and he got dementia as well. There's a remarkable aura that some of these people have – which I guess is something that the public recognise and like in them and why people duly vote them to the very top. And why, when that aura diminishes, for whatever reason, the public sense it just as clearly. How the mighty fall, indeed.

Epilogue
In the Abbey

Thursday 13 March 2014. Eleven months after Margaret Thatcher's funeral, I was at Westminster Abbey for another commemoration service. This time, it was in honour of Sir David Frost. The early morning fog had gone and the sun was shining outside. The day was an agreeable one, but the service felt somewhat impersonal, which I suppose is inevitable when so many people are there. They kept describing him as a great broadcaster: that misses the point; he was a great human being.

It seemed that every living personality from British stage, screen, sport and palace was packed inside, some of whom had the haziest of connections with Frosty: Pippa Middleton? Tony Hall, doing a reading? And, as for Sienna Miller, wearing a cream dress – what on earth has happened to us?

Prince Charles was there with Camilla. Before he arrived, the Duke of York came in with Sarah Ferguson and one daughter and Sophie, Countess of Wessex. All the royals walked up in a kind of procession, and met with Lady Carina Frost, before sitting down in the royal seating – except for Sarah Ferguson, who had to split off to a different area because she's no longer Her Royal Highness. I watched this little dumb-show take place, and thought how life will always be throwing its tiny cruelties at us, whatever the social context.

In that same vein, I was sitting next to Jane Birt, and at one point she started peering straight through the crowd at John, her ex-husband, with his new wife. She said to me, 'You're going through this aren't you?' It took me a second or two to work out that she was meaning divorce. 'How do you cope? ... The way John and I deal with it is by doing time-sharing.' I asked her what she was talking about, and she said, 'Well, if we're both asked to a party, I go for the first half, and then I text him when I'm leaving, and that is his cue to arrive for the second half. But you can't do that at a memorial service like this can you?'

It was appropriate that they put a stone down in the south transept of the Abbey – where Carina and Prince Charles placed flowers – so there will be a permanent memorial, as there should be. Ronnie Corbett and Michael Parkinson gave their readings with great dignity. Greg Dyke did a very good eulogy, but I rue the day that his brand of estuary English – 'I tought abaat it, and I tawk'd abaat that' – replaced RP as the national public-speaking norm. That criticism cannot be levelled at Joanna Lumley, who read a Richard Stilgoe tribute with the elegance that you would expect; nor at Lady Carina and the boys – examples of the best of the British aristocracy when faced with pain and sadness. It was a day of astonishing contrasts in that respect – which would have thrilled Frosty on the grounds of human interest alone.

I think David was unusual for a person in his position and in the media industry in that he was loved by most people. It is safe to say that, these days, there is a cynicism about the media and journalism in particular. Sometimes this is deserved; other times, it is not. I was dismayed at all the fuss generated by the Hacked Off group, which was entirely motivated by a politically Left suppression agenda – which likes to create moral panics and ban things and create rules and bureaucracy (and thus jobs for the people who administer all those things); it has nothing to do with helping people.

Relationships in the media industry are complex and subtle. It is all about love and hate. When it comes to newspaper journalists in particular, you love them when they do something you want and you hate them when they do something you don't want. There is this unwritten understanding that, from our different sides, you're important to me and I'm important to you. That may vary in its weight and emphasis at different times – but it's always there at the heart of the relationship. It so happens that I like journalists in general, and many individual journalists in particular. (There are, of course, those that I don't like and who very much dislike me – but that comes with the territory.) Ultimately, I love the written word, and that means that I like the people who write it. These people, at different times, grossly overstate their importance and grossly underestimate their importance. But the world would be a much duller place without them. And excessive and interfering regulation would be a shame.

In Britain, we still have what I believe to be the finest newspaper industry in the world. It is one example of the many things that we can overlook when it comes to putting a value on the nation. As in so many things, it is in our nature to underrate ourselves.

Britain is a significant player in the cultural, political, military and sporting history of the world. That can be put down to (at least) three fortuitous elements of British development, which have given us our so-called 'soft power'. First, we do not do foreign languages, so everyone has to learn English, which is the language of international diplomacy, of the internet, of air traffic control, of the music industry, of America, and the rest of it. Most people – apart from the French, who are jealous – have grown accustomed to that. The second thing is that the British are quite nosy and interfering. We've got a point of view about most things that is often quite sensible, useful and valuable – which can't always be said of the American or European view of the world. And thirdly, we British are the world's great radical thinkers. We are creative and inventive, and have a pre-eminent ability to come up with solutions that are both smart and practical. Most of those ideas go abroad to get investment, but that's another story.

Moreover, in general terms, the British have a sense of decency and of right and wrong, good and bad, and effective and ineffective. In other words, we are good at seeing both sides of a coin, at expressing varying points of view and, thus, of acting as a mediator between warring factions – or, for that matter, bringing in a new thought that trumps all the other conflicting thoughts that are going on. Britain has argued with itself, it's argued within itself, and it's argued with other people. But at the end of the day, I think Britain is probably the best friend the world has had. That is because – in most cases – when there's an argument or crisis, Britain will be the first to know what to do and often the first to come running. And I think that Britain is at its best, and is best delineated, when it is the Right, not the Left, making the decisions.

With the Left, everything is engineered: financially, socially, organisationally – the bureaucracy is self-fulfilling. That's how they operate: building useless and stultifying bureaucracies that bring jobs that bring votes, all funded by state spending. That's why the Civil Service tends to lean towards the Left, dealing with everything through a cyclical process. They want to obliterate the concept of an individual's imagination and innovation and common sense. They don't want progress or change. (Never was the word 'progressive' so misused as when appropriated by the Left.) New ideas are not pioneered; old routines are enforced. Rules and regulations, health and safety, what we eat, what we drink – they're all controlled and pre-planned. You'll never find the Left supporting new ideas; they won't do that because they can't be individualistic. That's why I always thought that so many of the Left-wing creatives and copywriters and art directors with whom I worked in advertising were next to useless; unable to embrace a new idea. Their philosophical culture is against it and they misinterpret the individualism of the Right as egotism, selfishness, or elitism – which it does not have to be.

It's why most of the decent Foreign Secretaries have been Conservatives – because they are internationalists; they think about the world, and about the British influence on the world, and they believe in the free exchange of ideas. Whereas Labour Foreign Secretaries are still inward-looking at heart: the best example being Robin Cook, who came out with the cracking idea of an 'ethical foreign policy', which must have gone down well with most of the delegates at the UN when they were talking about their wars and famines.

It's why the EU is an intrinsically Left-wing entity. That's what it exists to be; to feed on itself and its own centralising bureaucracy and power to rule (without the encumbrance of messy national democracy). It acts *against* individuality – be it the interests of individual people or individual nations – by trying to implement ever more stultifying agreements and rules and regulations which serve to increase the power and status of its elites and reduce the power of ordinary citizenry and businesses. It has stupidly encouraged regions and separatists to look to the Centre for legitimacy over the heads of national governments, and when that leads to regional dissatisfaction, wonders why. These idiots in Brussels are currently engaged in the greatest irony of all time, in that the EU was set up to stop there ever being a war in Europe (through federalisation), yet it will probably eventually lead to one. And, of course, I cannot see anything but failure for the euro. The idea of a loose economic union was fine, but that was not what they were really after: they had to go and look for currency union and thus fiscal and then political union. The elites want it; no one else does.

A real Tory fundamentally believes in free trade. Yet the Americans are, at heart (Republican or Democrat) protectionist, the Russians are protectionist, and the European Union is protectionist. So you've got three protectionist blocks, and rather stupidly, we British have got ourselves stuck in one of the protectionist blocks. That original decision was partly born out of the subliminal British arrogance: when people voted in favour of joining, there was an automatic assumption that we'd be the leader of it, rather than what has happened, which is that we have allowed ourselves to be pushed around by it and be subordinate to its ever-expanding bureaucracy and control. The tragedy of the modern economic history of Europe is that EFTA was obliterated and the very different animal that was the EEC replaced it. And now the whole thing is bankrupt of money and ideas and democratic principle.

A much better alternative would be what might be called the 'chaordic' system (or 'chaord'), this portmanteau idea being first introduced by Dee Hock, the founder of VISA, in a speech in 1993, when he spoke of the synergies of versatility and equitability and the avoidance of anarchy and rigidity. At Bell Pottinger, we have been having some incredibly interesting discussions about this idea recently. Imagine a series of independent, uncentralised parties, none of which is more powerful than any other, working in mutual self-interest; imagine a state of being where there is no power imbalance between the parties because each party acts on its own incentive to equalise the power. Thatcher used to talk about wanting a world where everyone can aim to be strong but none do so at the expense of each other. This would be the way to go.

I think the UK is still capable of being the most relevant force for good in the world today. This is because we are probably the one and only nation with the mix of hard- and soft-diplomatic and military skills (and with a seat on the Security Council), allowing us the perfect role as intermediary and peacemaker. The British have the mentality, knowledge, understanding, skills and language that could allow them to take the world to a better place. We're empathetic and sympathetic when we need to be – our diplomats don't shout and scream and our soldiers don't shoot their guns into the air; but, so too, we can be quite cold-hearted and cold-blooded when we need to be. We're wise, yet pragmatic; innovative, yet realistic. We know how to get the Americans to calm down, we know how to get the Russians what they want without them being wiped out in the process. We are reasonably well respected by the Chinese, and we don't do a bad job with the Middle East either. In Europe, it's a good bet that most of its people (at least North of the Olive Line, where they have a reasonable work-ethic) have a view that is nearer to the non-Federalist, looser connectedness variety, than to that of José Manuel Barroso or Jean-Claude Juncker.

The problem that we face today is that the world has lost its political will: it no longer believes in any particular politics. Instead, it believes in anything: anything that will get you a vote; anything that will get you elected, and keep you there; anything that will get you some money and power.

I continually look at some of our political leaders – of the US, of the EU, of the UK – and it fills me with dismay. It's becoming a world of Pygmies. Labour governments have had to dilute their Socialism in order to be palatable, and the Conservatives got rid of Thatcher because they feared her radicalism – and put a wet in her place. She and Reagan were the last giants of the West, and I cannot see how their like may ever return.

Nowadays, when I talk to Lynton Crosby (running the Tories' 2015 election machine), I try to avoid politics. He's different from me. He doesn't have a desire to do things that can't be done. It sounds arrogant of me, but my starting position is that anything is possible. He starts from the point at which he considers only the things that feel achievable. He will say, 'Nah, they won't do that. No point in giving them that advice – they won't do it.' Of course, you'd expect him to say that because he's an Australian. And they're pragmatists, but only pragmatists.

As regards the forthcoming election in the UK, no one at the top of the Westminster government is really interested in what I think. Nonetheless, in the political and business spheres, people ask me to help them with all manner of things, from the sensible and flattering to the more convoluted and ludicrous: sometimes, things that I should have nothing to do with; other times, when I might be able to do something well and truly meaningful. Sometimes I ask myself, 'Why the fuck are they ringing me up about trying to resolve a situation in Ukraine? Or Iraq, or Libya, or Egypt or Syria?' Nothing is ever quite as it may seem. Sometimes I am asked for answers and solutions and I wonder where on earth am I going to find them. How will I even recognise them?

Given all this, it may surprise you to learn that I'm going through an optimistic phase right now, and long may it last. I feel that I'm fortunate; I don't owe anything; my house is paid for and my life is paid for. There's a new lady in my life called Jacqueline, who I call Jack. When she asks me how I am, it allows me to amuse myself with the response, 'I'm all right, Jack.' And indeed, I am.

With James Henderson, I help run a business of which I'm well and truly proud. We are extremely successful and – I'm not ashamed to say – very profitable. I have a very nice business relationship with James, and we have around us a wonderful community of people, many of whom have been with me for a very long time. Yet I try to treat somebody who's been with me a week exactly the same as I treat somebody who's been here 50 years. We do absolutely brilliant work, and we are obsessed with the quality of that work. It doesn't mean to say that we never make mistakes. But – forgive the sales pitch – we are very good at what we do.

I get up in the morning feeling good and go to bed feeling good. My daughter now also works in a PR agency; she has twice been promoted and has a successful and handsome Australian boyfriend. She looks like she might replicate the success part of my DNA. My son, meanwhile, is doing an internship at a headhunting firm, although his true love is Arsenal. People tell me that his inheritance is my charm genes. So with a bit of luck, they'll both be OK.

For myself, I haven't the faintest idea what is ahead, or how much of it there is left, but I'm still sufficiently fit and free of senescence that I want to go on living, not hiding. One's life should not be defined by the later years of deterioration, or giving in, or running away. And certainly not by a slow, dreary retirement – because retirement is not dissimilar to being dead. So I have limited ambitions for myself and I have broader views about how the world should function. As to the former, I'm very near fulfilling those ambitions, but there will be more in their wake. And anyway, who is to say that this feeling or my circumstances may not change tomorrow. But I will say this: whatever happens, I will accept it as my responsibility. And that is the essence of pure Conservative thinking, and the antithesis of Socialism.

I try, with mixed success, not to give a fuck about what people think of me – and there are quite a few people who don't think much. We're all more vulnerable nowadays – whether you're a media person, a world leader, or a child playing Xbox – because the internet has given a platform to every lunatic in the world to fling insults or threats or cyber-viruses at any target they can find anywhere at all in that world. (That's before we come on to Twitter, which I think represents the end of civilisation.) If I hear or read something unpleasant about me, it hurts me like it hurts anyone. But look at the business I'm in, and you see that if you don't have a very thick skin, you should not really be here. Go sell sheet-music or flowers. Words are not altogether different from sticks and stones, in that they have the potential to do terrible harm to you. But, as a self-respecting grown-up, it's up to you how far you let them, before you turn out the light and go to sleep.

Speaking of going to sleep, I think it's time to finish this story and let you close the book on me. Today, there are just as many uncertainties in the world as when we started 20-odd chapters ago. As we speak, there are new and terrifying problems in the Ukraine, and I have been asked to become involved at some modest level. In the UK, an election nears – heaven only knowing what the result will be. Whoever is elected will probably disappoint me, but I continue to harbour great hopes for this great country, nonetheless.

I know that I've been very, very lucky – and I continue to be so. Equally, there have been times when I've been very ill and experienced divorces and dramas in my private life and controversies in my public life. I am not a paragon of virtue, and I have fallen from grace more times than you can shake a stick at. But you can't go back; you have to go forwards.

How long I will have the luxury of moving forwards is anyone's guess. We all, eventually, must keep our appointment at a great metaphorical Abbey. Personally, I refuse to feel sorry or sad at the prospect of my own mortality. That said, whether I keel over tomorrow or in 20 years' time, I think there are other reasons for regret. We are a great nation with a great tradition of tolerance, open-mindedness and freedom. Year by year, however, I have seen this tradition eroded. We live in a world where restraint has gone, where we must all rush to judgement, where we must all be quick to condemn. Shrill, hysterical group-think has replaced reasoned debate, and with each day that passes the state seems to take more control of our lives. For interfering Left-wing people this may be desirable, but for me it is nothing short of catastrophic.

As happens in times of prolonged peace, the weak have driven out the strong. A great nation requires great leaders, and these are now in short supply. Especially in politics. Everyone acquiesces to the insidious tyranny of entitlement, faux compassion and faceless bureaucracy which, taken together, are mutilating our political inheritance. As things get ever more turbulent, great leadership is ever more imperative. I fear that when we look for someone to lead us, we now search in vain. I fear that most of those with any true conviction have already had their rendezvous at the Abbey.

And yet I said earlier that I am an optimist. So let me end on this note. There is a wonderful human attribute that is called hope. And there is a wonderful system of government that is called democracy. Neither is sufficient individually. But together they make life worth living. A very short 35 years ago, we were writing our first Party Political Broadcast as part of Margaret Thatcher's first election campaign. And we came up with a slogan that, we felt, summed up everything that we were standing for at that time, in those circumstances. Hope and democracy. It applies – and they apply – equally well today. Perhaps it will always be so.

Our line was this: 'Don't just hope for a better life – vote for it.'

And that has to be Right.

Editors' Note

In 2013, we published a book called *The Branded Gentry: How a New Era of Entrepreneurs Made Their Names*. It was the story of 13 eponymous business leaders, with their surnames used, in whole or part, as their brand names. One of our first interviewees was Lord Bell – Timothy (Tim) John Leigh Bell, Baron Bell of Belgravia – part-founder of Bell Pottinger, a multinational public relations and marketing organisation. His reflections formed the basis of the first chapter in our book. And indeed, many people told us that this particular chapter was their favourite – which set us thinking.

Despite a varied, colourful, and at times controversial career, Tim Bell's main claim to fame is his role as adviser to the UK's first female Prime Minister, Margaret Thatcher, working with her through an unprecedented three successive terms in office. But he has also provided communications and media advice to all manner of world figures – be they presidents, prime ministers, sultans, statespersons, CEOs, media moguls, stars of the music and motion picture industries, and the rest of it. Spend a few hours with this man and there are two certainties: one is that he will smoke rather a few cigarettes during that time; the other is that his old-fashioned Nokia telephone will be continually ringing with international calls from the world's politicians and plutocrats.

In the course of our original interview, it became only too apparent that a single chapter in our anthology was never going to do justice to his full and fascinating story. That warranted something much more substantial. Which is why, just over a year later, we went back to him and suggested a memoir.

In the past, Tim Bell has always wanted the focus of attention to be on his clients and companies, not on himself. He has more often than not turned down or discouraged requests for biographies and is discriminating when it comes to media interviews. And, when we first approached him with the idea for a memoir, he wasn't sure about the idea. Some of his ambivalence came from his concerns over how strong would be his recollection of events, and whether he was able to devote time to the task of writing what would be a substantial tome; some of it was whether the time was right for him to make his personal views public, and how far that should go.

However, no sooner had we mooted the idea than it was gaining momentum – driven in particular by our publishers, Bloomsbury, and Tim's personal adviser, Phoebe Vela. With their help, we were able to convince him that his story was too rich and interesting *not* to be told. We suggested a methodology (not dissimilar to the one used in our previous book) whereby we could share the workload, based on a programme of discussions and conversations, that we could then help craft into a written manuscript. Tim agreed, and, in the summer of 2013, we set about our joint task.

Over many months, between 2013 and 2014, we conducted almost 40 hours' worth of taped interviews – discursive and conversational, sometimes structured, sometimes not – which formed our raw material. This was followed by us checking as best we could the dates and names and other items of factual detail that – Tim was the first to concede – may well have suffered the inevitable attrition of time and memory.

After which, we set about turning hours of spoken word into a structured and readable narrative – one which, all of us, including Tim, hope will bring an interesting, enjoyable and uncompromising perspective on moments personal and historical.

In bringing this book to print, we cannot fail to acknowledge the extraordinary support and advice of Robin Baird-Smith, Joel Simons, Jamie Birkett, Maria Hammershoy, Amanda Shipp, Helen Flood, Laura Brooke and Nigel Newton at Bloomsbury, and the assistance of James Henderson, Wendy Ridley, Teresa Woodley and Victoria Blackshaw at Bell Pottinger. Plus Michael Lee, Simon Marquis, Emily Cooper, Henry Bilson and Caitlin Morley at VCCP, and the transcription team at Language Insight.

David Hopper
Charles Vallance
London 2014

Sources and Bibliography

Aitken, Jonathan, *Margaret Thatcher: Power and Personality* (London, Bloomsbury Continuum 2013)

Aitken, Robin, *Can We Trust the BBC?* (London, Continuum 2007)

Bootle, Roger, *The Trouble with Europe: Why the EU isn't Working; How It Can Be Reformed; What Could Take Its Place* (London, Nicholas Brealey Publishing 2014)

Caine, Michael, *The Elephant to Hollywood: The Autobiography* (London, Hodder & Stoughton 2010)

Campbell, Alastair and Stott, Richard, *The Blair Years: Extracts from the Alastair Campbell Diaries* (London, Hutchinson 2007)

Carr, Allen, *The Easy Way to Stop Smoking: Be a Happy Non-smoker for the Rest of your Life* (London, Penguin 2013)

Edmonds, Mark and Harnden, Toby, 'Westminster Abbey's Hello and Welcome to David Frost' (London, *The Sunday Times* Magazine, 23 February 2014)

Fallon, Ivan, *The Brothers: The Rise and Rise of Saatchi & Saatchi* (London, Hutchinson 1998)

Hegarty, John, *Hegarty on Advertising: Turning Intelligence into Magic* (London, Thames & Hudson 2011)

Hitchens, Christopher, *Mortality* (London, Atlantic 2012)

Hollingsworth, Mark, *Tim Bell: The Ultimate Spin Doctor* (London, Hodder & Stoughton 1997)

Low, Robbie, 'Interview with Richard Chartres', *New Directions* (January 1996)

MacGregor, Ian, *The Enemies Within: The Story of the Miners' Strike 1984–5* (London, Collins 1986)

Major, John, *John Major: The Autobiography* (London, HarperCollins 2010)

Moore, Charles, *Margaret Thatcher: The Authorised Biography, Volume 1, Not for Turning* (London, Allen Lane 2013)

Neil, Andrew, *Full Disclosure* (London, Macmillan 1996)

Rand, Ayn, *Atlas Shrugged* (New York, Penguin 1957)

—*For the New Intellectual: The Philosophy of Ayn Rand* (New York, Random House 1961)

Saatchi, Maurice, *Brutal Simplicity of Thought: How it Changed the World* (London, Ebury 2013)

Schlichter, Kurt, *I am a Conservative: Uncensored, Undiluted and Absolutely Un-PC* (Amazon Kindle 2012)

Sergeant, John, *Maggie: Her Fatal Legacy* (London, Macmillan 2005)

Shephard, Gillian, *The Real Iron Lady: Working with Margaret Thatcher* (London, Biteback 2013)

Swift, Jonathan, *Gulliver's Travels* (1726)

Thatcher, Margaret, *The Downing Street Years* (London, HarperCollins 1993)

—*The Path to Power* (London, HarperCollins 1995)

Vallance, Charles and Hopper, David, *The Branded Gentry: How a New Era of Entrepreneurs Made Their Names* (London, Elliott & Thompson 2013)

Index

Throughout the index Tim Bell is abbreviated to TB